'THE CHURCH AND ITS SPIRE'

To Mum, a lively Kerrywoman
who loves to tell funny stories

Eamon Maher

'The Church and its Spire':

JOHN MCGAHERN AND THE CATHOLIC QUESTION

the columba press

First published in 2011 by
the columba press
55A Spruce Avenue, Stillorgan Industrial Park,
Blackrock, Co Dublin

Cover by Bill Bolger
Origination by The Columba Press
Printed in Ireland by Brunswick Press Ltd, Dublin

ISBN 978 1 85607 728 6

Contents

Acknowledgements

There are so many people who have helped me in the composition of this study that it would be impossible to mention them all. So I beg the forbearance of anyone who has been omitted.

The Irish Research Council for the Humanities and the Social Sciences awarded me a small project grant in 2004 to help me carry out the research associated with this monograph. I am happy to be in a position now to acknowledge that invaluable assistance, albeit somewhat later than originally planned!

Fergus Fahey, from the John McGahern Archive in the James Hardiman Library at NUI Galway, has been most supportive in locating material and preparing documents for my study visits to Galway. Similarly, Dr John Kenny, the John McGahern Lecturer in Creative Writing in NUI Galway, was kind enough to invite me to speak at the inaugural McGahern International Seminar in 2007, where I developed some of the main ideas of this book.

The library staff in IT Tallaght, where I work, are most generous with their time and expert in their advice about where to locate relevant materials. I am most fortunate, in fact, to have so many colleagues in Tallaght who are encouraging of my research; this has created a wonderful work environment for the past 16 years.

The editor of *Studies: An Irish Quarterly*, Fr Fergus O'Donoghue SJ, kindly granted me permission to reproduce the interview that appears at the end of this book that was first published in *Studies* in 2001.

Dr Eugene O'Brien, Head of English in MIC Limerick, has provided indispensable assistance with compiling the Index and helping to iron out glitches with the manuscript.

Dr Peter Guy and Fr John Littleton have offered astute advice in terms of the content of the book and assisted hugely with proof reading.

Dr Victor Merriman of Liverpool Hope University was kind

enough to read chapter four and to give me the benefit of his considerable knowledge of Irish theatre, which was precious when it came to assessing McGahern's sole foray into theatre and TV drama.

Dr Dermot McCarthy of Huron University College in London, Ontario, Canada, author of the definitive study, *John McGahern and the Art of Memory* (2010), read the initial manuscript in minute detail and offered sound advice on how it might be improved.

Seán O Boyle and his staff at The Columba Press are a pleasure to work with because of their professionalism and amiable way of doing business.

Fintan O'Toole of *The Irish Times* is owed a huge debt of gratitude for supplying such an insightful Foreword.

My wife Liz and our three children, Liam, Marcella and Kevin, are the ones who create the structure and loving atmosphere that allow me to pursue my literary interests. Without them, none of this would mean anything.

List of Abbreviations

B	*The Barracks* (London: Faber & Faber, 1963).
D	*The Dark* (London: Faber & Faber, 1964).
L	*The Leavetaking* (London: Faber & Faber, 2nd edition, 1984).
P	*The Pornographer* (London: Faber & Faber, 1979).
AW	*Amongst Women* (London: Faber & Faber, 1990).
PD	*The Power of Darkness* (London: Faber & Faber, 1991).
CS	*The Collected Stories* (London: Faber & Faber, 1992).
RS	*That They May Face the Rising Sun* (London: Faber & Faber, 2002).
M	*Memoir* (London: Faber & Faber, 2005).
CE	*Creatures of the Earth: New and Selected Stories* (London: Faber & Faber, 2006).
LW	*Love of the World: Essays* (London: Faber & Faber, 2009).

Foreword

by Fintan O'Toole

If you were presented, without context, with quotes from an essay by an Irish writer about another Irish writer and asked to guess who was being written about, you would know at once that the subject was the work of Samuel Beckett:

> Places are seen in their essential outline, which is inseparable from their use and function ... Sometimes a place is seen as friendly to whatever action happens to be afoot, more often it is hostile ... These are all near and concrete realities, but so stripped down to their essentials because of the necessities of the action as to seem free of all local characteristics ... The strange sense of timelessness that the book has, of being out-side time, comes from the day, a single day, breaking continually over the scene and the action.

Yet, as readers of John McGahern will know, these words are not about Beckett but are from his brilliant essay on Thomas O'Crohan's *The Islandman*. That they could have been applied to a Beckett novel or, with a few small changes, to *Waiting for Godot*, just as easily as to O'Crohan, tells us something about both writers. But it also tells us something about McGahern himself, for the words could, of course, also apply to much of his own work – the plainness and austerity of his sense of place, the constant sense of 'the day, a single day' breaking over the action.

One way of seeing McGahern, indeed, would be as the link between O'Crohan and Beckett, between a specific, rooted Irish life and a metaphysical entropy that expresses a more abstract sense of the human condition. All three give us, albeit in very different forms, a stripped down humanity – reduced to the frame of a small island, to the bare bones of a godless existence, to life in a republic that has never come into being. All three deal in the same condition – exposure. And each has, again in very different forms, a deep connection to ideas of what is moribund and what survives. McGahern's words about death in the splendid interview with Eamon Maher at the end of this book express that connection perfectly: 'When you're in danger of losing a thing it becomes precious and when it's around us, it's in tedious abundance and we take it for granted as if we're going to live forever, which we're not.'

Those concerns are not in themselves religious, but they do connect to what religion is, or should be, about. McGahern beautifully expressed it as that which 'surrounds life'. When life is exposed, absence becomes tangible. And the thing about absence is that it is endless. Whatever is present is finite; all that is not present is infinite. It has no given form and thus remains unbounded and unlimited.

This is, of course, the way McGahern writes. His novels and stories are all about what is *not* happening – the emotions unexpressed, the connections not made, the society unformed, the retreats, the silences. And it is this which connects him (and Beckett) to a certain kind of religious impulse, the *via negativa* of the mystics. Thomas Aquinas suggested that, since God is unknowable, we must 'consider the ways in which God does not exist rather than the ways in which he does'.[1] This idea is equally accessible to non-believers like McGahern as to faithful Christians. It is the ground on which McGahern's aesthetics of absence encounter the mysteries of religious faith.

Think, for example, of the relevance of R .S. Thomas's poem, 'Via Negativa', to McGahern's dark fictions of what does not exist:

Why no! I never thought other than
That God is that great absence
In our lives, the empty silence
Within, the place where we go
Seeking, not in hope to
Arrive or find. He keeps the interstices
In our knowledge, the darkness
Between stars ...[2]

1. Brian Davies and Brian Leftow (eds), *Aquinas, Summa Theologiae, Questions on God* (Cambridge: Cambridge University Press, 2006), p 28.
2. R. S. Thomas, *Collected Poems* (London: Phoenix, 2000), p 220.

McGahern's sense of religion is also, oddly enough, that of Karl Marx, not in the famously dismissive and oft-quoted phrase about the 'opium of the people' but in the fuller and much richer context in which that phrase appears: 'Religion is at once an expression of and a protest against real wretchedness. Religion is the sigh of the oppressed creature, the heart of a heartless world, and the soul of soulless conditions. It is the opium of the people.'[3]

The heart of the heartless and the soul of the soulless are of course oxymorons, but for McGahern they are also tangible realities. Is there a more moving evocation of 'the heart of a heartless world' than McGahern's evocation of his mother's religious faith, her persistence in hope and meaning, in *Memoir*? And 'the soul of soulless conditions' is precisely the way McGahern regards the rituals and learning, the language and architecture of the Church in the otherwise bleak Ireland of his youth.

There is nothing remotely sentimental or nostalgic about this attachment. McGahern never left any room for doubt about his own status as a non-believer. He is, as Eamon Maher shows so convincingly here, a great enemy of the Church's abuse of power – from which, of course, he suffered directly. The intimations of violence and sexual abuse in his early fiction prefigure the revelation of the systemic nature of such horrors many decades later. He diagnosed more acutely than anyone the 'sexual sickness' of a repressive culture. The stultifying narrowness of the official culture of Church and State clings like a bad smell to the people whose lives he explores. The phrase he uses about the Church – 'an ancient, ruthless, autocratic organisation'— in his essay 'The Church and its Spire', could hardly be more damning. He saw official religious doctrine as having produced, not a race of saints, but a nation of hypocrites, outwardly serving a cause they inwardly believed to be just another form of authority to be managed.

In some respects, indeed, even the nice things McGahern has to say about the Church could be seen as back-handed compliments: without it, things would have been even worse. His generosity towards the Church that attacked him, the lack of bitter-

3. Karl Marx, *Critique of Hegel's Philosophy of Right* (Cambridge: Cambridge University Press, 1972), p 131.

ness on which Eamon Maher remarks, could also be seen as a form of aesthetic self-defence. McGahern knew that it was in his interests as a writer to approach his subjects without an agenda, to free himself from Irish hatreds and polemics. There may be a kindness in his forgiving attitude to the Church, but there is also a ruthless understanding of what he needed in order to be the writer he became. Like all great writers, McGahern knew how to shield his gift, even from the circumstances of his own life. He needed to be calm, measured, balanced. He simply had no use for an anti-Catholic animus and with the pitilessness of the true writer, he excised it. He knew that if he had become an anti-Catholic writer, the Church would still own him. Freedom lay on the path of forgiveness.

Yet it would be a mistake to divide McGahern's attitudes neatly into two: those of the Irishman for whom Catholicism is inescapably important, and those of the writer for whom intellectual freedom from the Church's authority is everything. The great strength of Eamon Maher's exploration of McGahern's relationship with Catholicism is that it goes beyond this neat distinction. It reminds us that Catholicism mattered to McGahern *as a writer*.

It mattered, firstly, as a force that shapes the mental world of his characters, an interaction that is deftly charted here. It mattered, secondly, as a signpost to the larger universe that surrounds those detailed, often enclosed lives. McGahern is a great realist but he is never a mere realist, and it is his sense of the amplitude of the unspoken and unseen that allows him to write about the seemingly inconsequential without ever approaching the banal.

Finally, Catholicism matters to McGahern as a writer because it shapes his notion of what being a writer means. As with other male Irish writers of his generation, writing, for McGahern, is an alternative to the priesthood. (Brian Friel, for example, explores this idea in *Faith Healer*.) This is not a mere biographical detail, though it is striking that in *Memoir* he seems to have felt some lasting guilt at breaking his promise to his mother that he would become a priest. It also shapes the nature of McGahern's literary career. Writing, for him, was not a luxuriant escape from the rigours of a priestly life. It was, rather, even more rigorous, more demanding, more insistent on a life of total dedication. The austerity of his style is moral and spiritual as well as literary.

Eamon Maher's book is important, not just for its astute and subtle account of the complexities of McGahern's relationship to Catholicism, but because that relationship has an importance even beyond its centrality to the work of a great writer. Ireland is struggling to define itself in the wake of its long boom and sudden bust. A large part of its identity crisis has to do with 'that great absence/In our lives, the empty silence' where the Church used to be. McGahern reminds us that nostalgia for a Catholic past is utterly misplaced. But he also warns us against simply ditching a whole framework of meaning in which we might be able to imagine what lies beyond ourselves. In bringing to the fore his unique combination of intellectual courage, moral toughness and ultimate wisdom, Eamon Maher has done a service to much more than the world of literary scholarship.

Introduction

The question of John McGahern's relationship with the Catholic Church is a far from simple one. Anyone with even a passing knowledge of his writing knows that he was very critical of the authoritarian manner in which the Church ruled Irish society during the period when he was growing up. For example, he regularly expressed the view that the Church's attitude towards sexuality was damaging:

> I would think that if there was one thing injurious about the Church, it would be its attitude to sexuality. I see sexuality as just a part of life. Either all of life is sacred or none of it is sacred ... And I think that it [the Church] made a difficult enough relationship – which is between people, between men and women – even more difficult by imparting an unhealthy attitude to sexuality.[1]

On the other hand, he repeated in numerous interviews and articles the debt of gratitude he owed to the Church for introducing him to a sense of the sacred, and instilling in him an appreciation of the mystery that lies at the heart of existence. Catholicism was the 'dominating force' in McGahern's upbringing and early working life. He could not avoid its influence at home, in school or in his subsequent work as a teacher. Nevertheless, he spoke at length of his indebtedness to Catholicism in his wonderful essay 'The Church and its Spire':

> I have nothing but gratitude for the spiritual remnants of that upbringing, the sense of our origins beyond the bounds of

1. 'Catholicism and National Identity in the Works of John McGahern.' Interview between Eamon Maher and John McGahern, in *Studies: An Irish Quarterly*, Vol 90, no 357, Spring 2001, pp 73-4.

sense, an awareness of mystery and wonderment, grace and sacrament, and the absolute equality of all women and men underneath the sun of heaven. That is all that now remains. Belief as such has long gone. (*LW*, 133)

The ceremonies of Christmas and Easter were recalled with particular fondness, the Stations of the Cross during Lent, the Corpus Christi processions. The smell of incense in the church, the beautiful flowers decorating the altar, the priest's vestments, the congregation all dressed in their best clothes, these were the things he missed when he ceased practising his religion. McGahern bemoaned how in Ireland, instead of espousing the Gothic form of Catholicism, with its church spires reaching towards the sky and raising Man's glance from the avaricious earth, we instead went for the Romanesque spirit – 'the low roof, the fortress, the fundamentalists' pulpit-pounding zeal, the darkly ominous and fearful warnings to transgressors' (*LW*, 145). Such an approach reminded him of his father's iron-fist rule in the home, a regime that ruthlessly crushed any challenge to its authority with psychological or physical violence, and gave the children a negative image of themselves by constantly complaining about their lack of gratitude, or the cost of feeding and clothing them.

In some ways, the Catholic Church of McGahern's youth worked hand-in-glove with the emerging State and together they controlled a generally docile population who were happy to do what they were told most of the time. The father's position in the family was sacrosanct, because it was sanctioned by the ruling elite: 'Authority's writ ran from God the Father down and could not be questioned. Violence reigned as often as not in the homes as well. One of the compounds at its base was sexual sickness and frustration, as sex was seen, officially, as unclean and sinful, allowable only when it too was licensed' (*M*, 18). We now know the dangers such a repressive and unhealthy regime can lead to, but at the time it was generally accepted without demur. Women were given an especially raw deal in that society. They were usually forced to give up work as soon as they got married and were deprived of access to artificial contraception, which would have allowed them to control the number of children they conceived. But there were even more sinister practices: 'The breaking of pelvic bones took place during difficult births in hospitals because it was thought to be more in conformity with Catholic teaching than Caesarian section, presumably be- cause it was considered more "natural"' (M, 210).

Women becoming pregnant outside of marriage were often committed to institutions like the Magdalene Laundries, where they were treated like slaves and separated from their babies and families. Then there were the children who, often for no rea- son other than that they came from destitute families or were illegitimate, were sent to Industrial Schools, which were run by male and female religious orders and where they experienced horrors like the following, described in the Ryan Report and quoted in various Irish newspapers on 21 May 2009, shortly after the findings of that report were published:

> In addition to being hit and beaten, witnesses described other forms of abuse such as being flogged, kicked and otherwise physically assaulted, scalded, burned and held under water. Witnesses reported being beaten publicly in front of other staff, residents, patients and pupils as well as in private. Many reports were heard of witnesses being beaten naked and partially clothed, both in private and in front of others. They reported being beaten and physically assaulted with implements that were for the specific purpose of inflict- ing pain and punishment, such as leather straps, bamboo canes and wooden sticks.[2]

I do not wish to equate legally proven horrors like those described above with what John McGahern maintained was en- dured by himself and his siblings. But neither would I want to downplay the callous way in which the McGahern children were apparently treated after the death of their mother. Being hit on the head with a shovel, or receiving a beating so severe that it provoked a cataleptic fit (M, 198, 199), this type of indis- criminate and unjustified punishment within the McGahern household is described graphically in Memoir. The children

---

2. *Report of the Commission to Inquire into Child Abuse* (Ryan Report), Volume 3 (Dublin: The Stationery Office, 2009), p 393.

banded together in order to survive the regime to which they were subjected: 'When there was a bad beating and the storm had died, we'd gather round whoever was beaten to comfort and affirm its unfairness, and it lessened our misery and gave strength to our anger' (M, 159). The saddest part of it all as far as the writer was concerned was the way in which people who knew what was going on did nothing to stop the abuse. The serving gardaí in the barracks were in an awkward position in that Francis McGahern was their commanding officer and this was 'a time when any authority went unquestioned' (M, 198). They came to him in a deputation to say that if the beatings didn't stop they would be forced to report him, but when that did not have the desired effect they never followed through on their threat. Complicit silence is what allowed the horror of the industrial schools to go undetected for such a long time, or that led to abusive priests being shunted from parish to parish instead of being removed permanently from their ministry and deprived of access to children. McGahern's writings underline the fact that the priests and male and female religious were not the only ones with responsibility for the many crimes perpetrated against children in the past. In this regard, the comments of Peter Guy are apposite. He cites the Joseph McColgan trial of 1995, the Kilkenny incest case and the death of Kelly Fitzgerald in 1993 as examples of where family abuse and/or neglect occurred and only came to light years afterwards. In Guy's view, the clergy formed an integral part of the prevailing authoritarian regime, but they did not operate within some sheltered space beyond the norms and foibles of society: 'My belief is that the Church offered status of sorts to the people and, in such a class-conscious society, pious supplications to the faith were the norm'.[3] In October 2010, the findings of yet another case of

3. Peter Guy, 'Reading John McGahern in the Light of the Murphy Report', in Studies: An Irish Quarterly, vol. 99, no 383, Spring 2010, pp 91-101, p 92. Guy offers the following information in relation to the cases cited: 'The McColgan case involved a Sligo farmer who had systematically raped and tortured his four children over a twenty year period. The Kilkenny incest case concerned a father who had raped and tortured his daughter for sixteen years and sired a child by her. Kelly Fitzgerald was systematically abused by her father from the age of five, deprived of food and adequate clothing, demonised by her parents,

unspeakable neglect in Roscommon became public. It recounted how a couple systematically neglected and abused their children over several years. The family was well-known to social services because of various complaints made by neighbours and relatives in relation to how the children were left alone in the house while the parents went drinking, or were sent to school without lunches and in an unkempt state. In the end, the mother was sentenced to seven years in prison for incest, sexual assault and the abuse of her children. The father was sentenced to 14 years in prison on 47 counts of rape and sexual assault. How such a glaringly obvious case of abuse could have gone undetected for such a long time, with disastrous effects on the children, calls into question the whole system of child protection in Ireland. Writing in *The Irish Times*, Carl O'Brien noted how familiar the findings of the Roscommon abuse report are: 'They are found in the reports of other cases such as the Kilkenny incest case, the Kelly Fitzgerald case in Mayo, the McColgan cases in Sligo …'[4] Similarly, many horrific descriptions of clerical child abuse are chronicled in the Ferns, Ryan and Murphy reports. All speak of how children's safety was put at risk because of systemic failures, cover-up and the failure of those who knew what was happening to intervene.

Balance and objectivity are vital, particularly when it comes to an emotive issue like child abuse. McGahern demonstrated a rigorous fairness in his reaction to such events: 'People do not live in decades or histories', he wrote. 'They live in moments, hours, days, and it is easy to fall into the trap of looking back in judgement in the light of our own day rather than the more difficult realisation of the natural process of living, which was the same then as it is now' (*LW*, 130). The Catholic Church in Ireland developed in the way it did largely because that was the way society at the time wanted or allowed it to behave. McGahern did not believe in applying standards of the present to past

isolated from her siblings, beaten daily and made to sleep outside the back door with the dogs, attired only in a nightie. At the age of eleven she weighed under three-and-a-half stone. She died three years later from malnutrition and neglect.'
4. Carl O'Brien, 'Report's findings are shocking – but all too familiar', in *The Irish Times*, 28 October 2010, p 9.

events and he regretted the way in which religion at a certain point came under constant attack from its critics: 'Today the climate has swung to an opposite extreme in that everything religious is now held in deep suspicion. A new injustice may be replacing the old' (*LW*, 131). He reminded his readers that many who entered the Church were victims themselves. During the 1940s and 50s brothers, nuns and priests were recruited at a very young age, often coming from poorer families who felt honoured to see their children become men and women of the cloth, people who were respected, looked up to, sought out for guidance: 'Many young men and women entered the convents and the priesthood for high and idealistic reasons, but with the stigma of leaving then so strong, what chance had they in an ancient, ruthless, autocratic organisation?' (*LW*, 131) This was a prescient observation to make in 1999 when the article was first published and the public mood was very hostile to the Catholic Church in the wake of the raft of revelations about clerical sex abuse and the horrors endured by young Irish people in the Magdalene Laundries and other religious-run organisations. Never one to get on a bandwagon, McGahern's preference was always to try and see the two sides of an argument.

This desire to be fair and objective did not prevent the writer from exposing many of the skeletons lurking in the cupboard of the hidden Ireland of his time. Throughout his writing career, McGahern was not afraid to tackle taboo issues like masturbation, homosexuality (including among members of the clergy), sexual and physical abuse, the residual damage done to people like Bill Evans (*That They May Face the Rising Sun*), who was sent from an orphanage or an Industrial School to work as a farm hand and be treated like a skivvy. Because of his experience of living with a tyrannical father, McGahern was more sensitive than most to the misery endured in many Irish homes, a misery made all the worse for being kept secret because of a blind eye being turned to what was happening. His novels and short stories are full of characters who suffer at the hands of powerful figures – be they parents, priests, teachers, Christian Brothers or politicians – who use their authority in an inequitable manner. Although he never laid all the blame for the ills of Irish society at the door of the Catholic Church, he believed that its alliance with the emerging State led to the establishment of an unhealthy theocracy in Ireland. But while there was external conformity and obsequiousness, there lingered nevertheless a fierce independence among the population: 'Most ordinary people went about their sensible pagan lives as they had done for centuries, seeing all this as just another veneer they had to pretend to wear like all the others they had worn since the time of the Druids' (LW, 130).

If his father was the incarnation of the authoritarian side of Catholicism, his mother represented the softer side which McGahern associated with beauty and mystery: 'Heaven was in the sky. My mother spoke to me of heaven as concretely and with as much love as she named the wild flowers. Above us the sun of heaven shone. Beyond the sun was the gate of heaven … It was her prayer and fervent hope that we would all live there together in happiness with God for all eternity' (M, 10). His mother's deep faith clearly left its mark, as did the broken promise he made to her that he would one day become a priest and say Mass for the repose of her soul. (We will deal with the death of his mother and the broken promise when we come to discuss the strongly autobiographical novel, The Leavetaking). Prayers were said in the McGahern household every morning, and at night the newspapers were spread out on the kitchen floor in preparation for the Rosary: 'Religion and religious imagery were part of the air we breathed' (M, 10). There was a strong sense of heaven and hell, which were viewed as real places. As a young child, Seán (the name assigned to him by his siblings) had tried to 'walk into the sun' (M, 11-12) where the gate to heaven was supposedly located: 'I had not understood that you have to pass through death to reach that gate' (M, 12). Memoir recounts several instances of how religion was interwoven into the everyday life of McGahern and his family; how they sought forgiveness for their sins through the sacrament of confession, the cleansing they felt afterwards, the regular attendance at Mass (Seán was an altar boy), the processions, the May altars they erected in honour of the Virgin Mary, the sermons of the priests during the parish missions. Certain priests were particularly adept at inspiring fear: 'The Redemptorists were brought in to purify through terror, and were appreciated like horror movies' (M, 202).

All these anecdotes strike a chord with anyone who was brought up a Catholic in rural Ireland a few decades ago. It was not the norm then to question the fundamental dogmas on which one's faith was based; being Catholic was something that was taken for granted, a type of identity badge as it were. The journalist Patsy McGarry, a perceptive reader of McGahern's work, describes a religious childhood that closely mirrors many of the sentiments evoked in *Memoir*: 'In those times I prayed as easily as I drew breath', he writes, 'sometimes using formal prayers, more frequently just talking directly to God.'[5] McGarry's description of his Catholic upbringing in Ballaghaderreen Co Roscommon is characteristic of the experiences of many of his generation. He writes of his belief that he was destined to become a priest, his disillusionment on discovering that the ideas of social justice so prominently outlined in the Second Vatican Council document *Gaudium et Spes* were not being adhered to, his subsequent difficulties with Church teaching on issues such as contraception, homosexuality, people in second relationships, the Resurrection, the Real Presence in the Eucharist. Finally, he came to the unhappy realisation that he no longer believed in God. The pain was intense for a time afterwards: 'I missed the closeness to God that I once had. I missed above all the extraordinary dimension and depth God had added to my life, the solid assurance, the shape to this existence he had given me, the direction, the stimulus, the happiness.'[6] McGarry endured much of the same nostalgia as that experienced by McGahern on discovering that he could no longer adhere to the religious structure that had framed his childhood and early adulthood.

With McGahern, there was no one moment or event that caused this disenchantment; it was more a slow but steady drifting away from Catholicism: 'So imperceptibly did it happen that it was not clear even to me whether I had left the Church or the Church had left me' (*M*, 222). In spite of this rupture or leavetaking, there is no evidence of rancour on the writer's part: 'I don't

---

5. Patsy McGarry, 'An Irish Catholic Agnostic', in John Littleton and Eamon Maher (eds), *What Being Catholic Means to Me* (Dublin: The Columba Press, 2009), pp 13-24, p 15.
6. McGarry, 'An Irish Catholic Agnostic', p 23.

think it's possible for a writer of my generation born in Ireland to avoid religion, even if it has to be by the path of opposition. It was the dominant force in that society and, in any sense of the spirit, it was mostly all that was there, even if some of it was unattractive'.[7]

McGahern belongs to a group of fiction writers who emerged in the years 1955-66 that includes Aidan Higgins, Brian Moore, Edna O'Brien and John Broderick. Their immediate predecessors, of whom Frank O'Connor and Seán Ó Faoláin were the most notable, had been involved in the struggle for Irish independence and felt a responsibility to assume a prominent role in public life through their writings. (Another predecessor, Liam O'Flaherty, is discussed later on in the Introduction). The earlier group, represented by James Joyce, Samuel Beckett and Flann O'Brien, employed daring literary devices designed to revolutionise form and belonged more to the international modernist movement than to any Irish literary movement *per se*. McGahern and his generation were likewise not unduly bothered with the question of defining their Irishness and so they moved away from the perceived need of O'Connor and Ó Faoláin to champion a political cause, in order to plunge the depths of personal experience. An important part of what Maurice Harmon referred to as their exploration of the 'private graph of feeling'[8] was the issue of faith. Brian Moore stated in an interview with Joe O'Connor in 1995: 'Belief is an obsession of mine. I think that everybody wants to believe in something – politics, religion, something that makes life worthwhile for them … So faith is my obsession'.[9] An unbeliever like McGahern, Moore persisted in portraying characters that are haunted by their Catholic formation, who struggle with its precepts and sometimes question its validity as a belief system. Try as they might, however, they can

7. 'Interview with John McGahern', in Eamon Maher, *John McGahern: From the Local to the Universal* (Dublin: The Liffey Press, 2003), pp 143-161, p 155.
8. Maurice Harmon, 'Generations Apart: 1925-1975', in Maurice Harmon Harmon and Patrick Rafroidi (eds), *The Irish Novel in Our Time* (Lille: Publications de l'Université de Lille3, 1975/76), pp 49-65, p 56.
9. Joe O'Connor, 'An Intervierw with Brian Moore', in *The Sunday Tribune*, 1 October 1995.

never ignore the religion into which they were born. It sticks to them like a birthmark; they contract it as they would a disease.

Joyce is someone whom no Irish writer can ignore. McGahern was acutely aware of the way in which Joyce forged a completely new approach to the issue of language and the elevation of art to the level of a worthwhile vocation, conceivably even the only worthwhile vocation. Perhaps it was the Joycean influence that caused McGahern to break the promise he made to his mother that he would one day become a priest, a betrayal he explains in the following manner in *Memoir*:

> Instead of being a priest of god, I would be the god of a small, vivid world. I must have had some sense of how outrageous and laughable this would appear to the world, because I told no one, but it did serve its first purpose – it set me free (*M*, 205).

Art replaced religion as McGahern's abiding preoccupation. In *A Portrait of the Artist as a Young Man*, we encounter the seminal stages of a type of secularisation of the transcendental where Stephen, in spite of his cry of *Non Serviam* and his refusal to accept the call to the priesthood, nonetheless describes his aesthetic purpose in terms that are suffused with Catholic imagery. This is evident in his image of the girl coming out of Jacob's biscuit factory and how it made him ponder the nature of women and of beauty:

> His anger against her found vent in coarse railing at her paramour, whose name and voice offended his baffled pride: a priested peasant, with a brother a policeman in Dublin and a brother a potboy in Moycullen. To him she would unveil his soul's shy nakedness, to one who was but schooled in the discharging of a formal rite rather than to him, a priest of the eternal imagination, transmuting the daily bread of experience into the radiant body of everliving life.
>
> The radiant image of the eucharist united again in an instant his bitter and despairing thoughts …[10]

---

10. James Joyce, *A Portrait of the Artist as a Young Man* (London: Penguin Classics, 1996), pp. 251-252.

For all that he is clearly at variance with the Catholic world-view and vows not to serve it, Stephen Dedalus' own signifiers are filled with references to Catholicism. The description quoted above culminates in a translation of the aesthetic in terms of the transubstantiation of the Eucharist, with the artist now a priest of a more secular movement towards transcendence, with Jacob's biscuits seen as a secular form of the Eucharistic wafer. This lingering fascination with Catholic vocabulary and concepts is remarked on by his interlocutor later on in the novel: 'It is a curious thing, do you know, Cranly said dispassionately, how your mind is supersaturated with the religion in which you say you disbelieve'.[11] In a manner that is similar to Joyce, whose *Portrait of the Artist as a Young Man* has strong autobiographical overtones, McGahern's mind was equally full of the religious imagery that pierced his consciousness as a child and remained there long after belief had dissipated. Although his writings form a type of secular poetics, they nevertheless retain much of the language and vision of Catholicism.

Catholicism became a central plank in post-Independence Ireland for a number of reasons. Louise Fuller's *Irish Catholicism Since 1950: The Undoing of a Culture* (2002) relates how the main political figure in the early years of the Irish Free State and Republic, Eamon De Valera, 'repeatedly expounded a vision of Irishness which upheld spiritual values and eschewed the materialistic and secularist attitudes which were developing on mainland Europe. His guiding principle had been to create an Ireland which would be culturally and economically insulated from such corrupting influences'.[12] The arrival of Seán Lemass as Taoiseach in 1959 would mark the beginning of a decade of prosperity during the 1960s and an opening up of Ireland to the outside world. Increased mobility due to air travel and the widespread availability of cars, the arrival of the television set in many Irish homes and the images it beamed in of people living lives that were very far removed from the model Christian ethos that was being preached in Catholic churches the length and breadth of Ireland, the blossoming dance hall phenomenon

11. Joyce, *A Portrait*, p 273.
12. Louise Fuller, *Irish Catholicism Since 1950: The Undoing of a Culture* (Dublin: Gill and Macmillan, 2002), p 79.

which provided a venue where young people could congregate
and form relationships more freely, greater disposable income,
all these developments would eventually lead to the 'undoing'
of a Catholic culture that had held sway for many years. Fintan
O'Toole emphasises the strong links between Catholicism and a
certain insular notion of Irish identity: 'The words "Irish
Catholic" did not denote merely a person of specific faith born
in a specific country. They also had come to stand for a country,
a culture, a politics. Catholicism in Ireland has been a matter of
public identity more than of private faith. For most of its history,
the Republic of Ireland was essentially a Catholic State, one in
which the limits of law and of behaviour were set by Church
orthodoxy and the beliefs of Catholic bishops'.[13] Clearly a type
of fortress mentality developed whereby in the early stages of
the new State, Church and politicians sought to preserve Ireland
from dangerous outside influences. McGahern noted in this regard:

> After independence, Church and State became inseparable,
> with unhealthy consequences for both. The Church grew
> even more powerful and authoritarian: it controlled all of
> education, and, through its control of hospitals, practically
> all of healthcare too … Faith and obedience were demanded,
> mostly taking the form of empty outward observances and a
> busy interest that other people do likewise, which cannot be
> described as anything other than coercive (*LW*, 146).

There was limited scope for freedom of expression in such an
environment, which is why so many Irish writers found the atmosphere stifling and oppressive. While someone like
McGahern, as we have seen, was attracted to the various rituals
of the Church, he would also resent the imposition of a belief
system that did not tolerate dissent and demanded blind adher-
ence to all its pronouncements. Such a system undoubtedly suited
a largely rural-based Irish society, poorly educated and thus
apparently prepared to accept without demur what their local
priests and bishops told them. But when change did come, it
came quickly and caught a complacent clergy by surprise.

---

13. Fintan O'Toole, *The Ex-Isle of Erin* (Dublin: New Island, 1997), p 15.

Vatican II, with its emphasis on the increased involvement of the laity in the running of the Church, which was to be now defined as 'the people of God', ushered in heightened expectations which did not always come to fruition. The pronouncement by the Archbishop of Dublin, John Charles McQuaid, on his return from Rome after the Council, that, 'No change will worry the tranquility of your Christian lives',[14] was far from prophetic as things transpired. McQuaid would soon be cognisant of the profound changes that were taking place in Catholicism, changes over which he would have little or no control. This was the same Archbishop who would ensure the sacking of McGahern from his position as a primary school teacher after the publication of his second novel, *The Dark*, in 1965. The book was banned and McQuaid intervened behind the scenes to ensure the writer was removed from his job in Scoil Eoin Baiste in Clontarf. In an interview with Julia Carlson, McGahern stated: 'The Archbishop was behind the whole thing, and he had an absolute obsession about what he called impure books.'[15]

So, McGahern fell foul of the Church hierarchy early in his career, an interlude that surprisingly would make him doubt the quality of his writing. He stated his belief on a number of occasions that perhaps if the novel had been better written it might have passed unnoticed by the censorship board. Happily, he would live to witness a more enlightened attitude towards the arts in the last few decades of his life, which saw his popularity soar and his work win prestigious literary prizes. He also began to appear more regularly on radio and television programmes, where he seemed to revel in his new-found popularity, something that must have been particularly welcome after the years when his novels inspired no small degree of hostility. Clearly, the Ireland of the 1960s and 70s was not ready to face up to the type of contentious issues McGahern explored in his fiction, a fiction that had very strong autobiographical nuances, as we now know. McGahern may have also suffered to some extent from what Augustine Martin describes as 'inherited dissent'.

14. Cited in Fuller, *Irish Catholicism Since 1950*, p 112.
15. Julia Carlson, *Banned in Ireland: Censorship and the Irish Writer* (Athens: University of Georgia Press, 1990), p 56. We will deal with the banning in more detail in our discussion of *The Dark*.

Ever since Joyce abandoned Catholicism to espouse a religion of art,[16] Martin argues, Irish writers have tended to replace their original faith with blends of the mystical and aesthetic: 'They seem to have been needled into apostasy by a Christianity which at that time, in both systems, appeared to be extremely philistine, anti-intellectual, disciplinarian and above all, anti-mystical. It was Christianity smug in the dry complacency of nineteenth century apologetics, suspicious of everything outside devotionalism and observance.'[17]

Many twentieth-century Irish writers fell prey to an ambient scepticism among the literati that made it difficult for them to pursue their writing while remaining members of the Church. Martin would contend, however, that this reality hardened into a cliché that viewed Ireland as 'a backward, insanitary, inert, despairing country; a people priest-ridden and superstitious, which despises its artists and intellectuals, treats its autocratic, avaricious and crafty clergy with a sanctimonious servility'.[18] One can find a good example of such a clichéd view in Liam O'Flaherty's novel *Skerrett* (1932). It relates the experiences of a national teacher, David Skerrett, who, following an incident where he used excessive violence on a student and then on the latter's father, is sent to the western island of 'Nara' (an obvious anagram for the Aran Islands). Initially resistant to the local language (Irish) and culture, Skerrett ends up becoming their great defender. By following this course, he comes into conflict with the domineering parish priest, Fr Moclair. Based on real events that were a cause célèbre in their day, *Skerrett* has strong political overtones. The omniscient narrator, the mouthpiece of O'Flaherty, does not hesitate to give his view of the Ireland of the time and of the island inhabitants: 'It must be remembered that this was the period when the whole of Ireland began to emerge from feudalism, as the result of the guerilla war waged by the peasants against the landowners'. After this short histori-

---

16. In spite of this espousal of art, we have already discussed the extent to which Joyce held onto a vocabulary that was shot through with Catholic imagery.
17. Augustine Martin, 'Inherited Dissent: The Dilemma of the Irish Writer', in *Studies: An Irish Quarterly* (Spring 1965), pp 1-20, p 6.
18. Martin, 'Inherited Dissent' p 10.

cal overview, we read: 'Even in Nara, that remote and poor island, which had experienced no change for hundreds of years and where people still used the tools and dwellings of prehistoric times, the will towards civilisation had been stirred into life. And the island had been fortunate in the possession of Father Moclair to direct that will.'[19] O'Flaherty is being ironic here, as Fr Moclair's interest in 'civilisation' is confined to ensuring that the islanders embrace economic developments that will lead primarily to the priest's enrichment at the expense of traditional island culture.

The tragic death of his son forges a strong bond between Skerrett and the English doctor, Melia, whom Moclair accuses of being a pagan. Skerrett pits himself against the most powerful figure on the island in the full knowledge that such a course of action could have disastrous consequences for him. But the tragedy of his lost son and his disillusionment with the antics of his alcoholic wife fuel his naturally rebellious temperament and he resolves to overcome this tyranny: 'He saw how Moclair stood alone and impregnable, with the powerful structure of the Church standing behind him like an army …' (78). There can be only one winner in this conflict and Skerrett ends up in a lunatic asylum, while the priest continues to compile a fortune on the backs of the hapless islanders. In one of their numerous stand-offs, Moclair accuses Skerrett of being a pagan, to which the teacher retorts: 'According to you, a pagan is any man who dares to question the authority of men like yourself. It's you and priests like you that are the pagans' (219). *Skerrett* is rich in colourful drama and presents a certain traditional view of the domineering priest always ready to scythe down anyone who challenges his authority. The islanders are shown to be bereft of any deep religious sentiment, closer to their pagan past than to any Catholic doctrine. I cite this novel as an example of a specific type of literary representation of Catholicism that McGahern was conscious of but that he would not follow. This is in no way to imply that O'Flaherty and the writers of his generation were viewed as inferior by McGahern. It is merely a question of their

19. Liam O'Flaherty, *Skerrett* (Dublin: Wolfhound Press, 1977), p 33. Subsequent references will be to this edition, with the page numbers in brackets.

preoccupations being different from his and less in keeping with the changed social context which moulded McGahern and his generation. Skerrett's loss of faith is a key moment in O'Flaherty's novel:

> And it was made manifest to him as he watched this glisten-
> ing crust of sun-baked rock, beneath its dome of sky, that
> there was no God to reward the just or to punish the wicked,
> nothing beyond this unconquerable earth but the phantasies
> born of man's fear and man's vanity (262).

Martin argues that no writer was 'more free from didactic-ism than McGahern',[20] a fact that meant that he would never have been comfortable following the example set by his pre-decessors O'Connor, O'Flaherty and O'Faoláin. David Pierce of-fers the view that McGahern 'is not given to excess, as he might have been if he were writing in the 1930s about the Western seaboard' – an obvious reference to O'Flaherty among others.[21] His objective was not to use literature as a rallying cry for a reli-gious or political cause. He repeatedly stated that the task of a writer was to get his style right and to steer clear of public pro-nouncements: 'What is permanent is the spirit or the personality in language, the style, and that's what lasts. A book that was written two hundred years ago can be as alive today as when it was first published, and last month's novel can be as dead as a laboratory mouse. I do think that if a person gets his words right that he will reflect many things; but if he sets out deliberately to do it, he'll be writing journalism.'[22] The image of the artist as a maverick, or a pariah, has a long tradition and with some it was viewed as a badge of honour. McGahern steered clear of polemics whenever possible, preferring to follow the advice of the French writer, Gustave Flaubert, whom he admired greatly: 'The writer should be like God in nature, present everywhere but nowhere visible.'[23]

---

20. Martin, 'Inherited Dissent', p 9.
21. David Pierce, *Light, Freedom and Song: A Cultural History of Modern Irish Writing* (New Haven/London: Yale University Press, 2005), p 286.
22. 'Interview with John McGahern', in Eamon Maher, *John McGahern: From the Local to the Universal* (Dublin: The Liffey Press, 2003), p 145.
23. This is a favourite quote of McGahern's, but he never supplies a ref-erence for it. He was probably right in assuming that, like Joyce's 'scrupulous meanness', it has entered into the literary lexicon.

The purpose of this book is to tease out the many ways
Catholicism permeated McGahern's worldview and made its
presence felt in his work. There will be no attempt to disguise
his agnosticism or perform some type of death-bed conversion
on the writer. He had huge respect for tradition and a genuine
appreciation of the important role religion played in the life of
someone like his mother. Many passages in *Memoir* underline
her deep religious belief. For example, when the cancer to which
she would finally succumb was diagnosed, she resigned herself
to the will of God: 'When life became too difficult, it was to this
source she turned, and she was unreachable there even to my
father' (*M*, 47). It may well have been out respect for local customs and the faith of his dead mother that inspired McGahern to
arrange such a conventional funeral Mass in Aughawillan
church, complete with a decade of the Rosary recited at the
graveside. His friend and cousin, Fr Liam Kelly, who was chief
celebrant at the Mass, let the congregation know that he and
John had discussed the funeral arrangements before the author's
death. The extent of McGahern's rehabilitation in the eyes of the
Catholic Church can be gauged from the presence of seven
priests on the altar. On the occasion of the first anniversary of
McGahern's death, Patsy McGarry noted: 'It was heartwarming
to witness the manner in which the Catholic Church responded
to this unbeliever's death. The breadth and generosity of its comforting embrace at his funeral contrasted so favourably with
those grim days when neither unbaptised child nor suicide victim was allowed a funeral or Christian burial.'[24] The point is
well made, but I am sure that both the Church and McGahern
would have acknowledged how far the Ireland of 2006 had
moved on from the really bad repressive, intolerant days. Also,
and this is an important point, the Church must have appreciated how little bitterness McGahern bore his erstwhile persecutors.
Over four decades had passed since the banning of *The Dark* and
the Ireland of 2006 was one in which a self-confessed unbeliever
(albeit one who greatly valued the Catholic legacy) could be
afforded a Christian burial beside his beloved mother.

It is probably better to state from the outset also that this

24. Patsy McGarry, 'Writer's funeral was a triumph of compassion', in
The Irish Times, 28 March 2007.

study does not seek to examine in a forensic manner the evolution of Irish Catholicism from the 1940s through to the year of McGahern's death in 2006. Such an ambitious project would surpass the scope of a book of this nature. There can be no doubting the value of McGahern's contribution to the mapping or chronicling of the evolution of rural Ireland from the establishment of the Free State through to the beginning of the third millennium, a fact that is recognised by many historians. It is significant that Diarmuid Ferriter closes his study of twentieth-century Ireland with the following acknowledgement: 'McGahern's work remains both an indictment of the failures of Irish independence and a celebration of Ireland's distinctiveness. It is difficult for the historian to disagree with his assessment.'[25] It would be difficult to suggest a more ringing endorsement than this from one of Ireland's foremost historians.

Equally, I do not propose to treat of McGahern as a 'Catholic Writer', in the sense that this term would apply to the likes of Graham Greene, G. K. Chesterton, François Mauriac, Georges Bernanos or Flannery O'Connor. Mary Reichardt defines a work of Catholic literature as one that 'employs the history, traditions, culture, theology and/or spirituality of Catholicism in a substantial and informed manner. Whether it involves Catholic subject matter or not, and whether its author is a Catholic or not, such literature is substantially in a deep and realistic understanding of at least some aspects of the Catholic faith, Catholic life, or the Catholic tradition'.[26] While it might be possible to define McGahern as a Catholic writer under such a broad definition, I do not think it would be in keeping with the author's stated artistic goals. Declan Kiberd sees him as 'a religious writer' in spite of the clichéd image of him as someone who was ostracised by the religious establishment and thus inamical to any form of Catholicism: 'But actually he is totally interested in ritual and in the religious mind'.[27] Gearóid Ó Tuathaigh detects in him

25. Diarmuid Ferriter, *The Transformation of Ireland 1900-2000* (London: Profile Books, 2004), p 759.
26. 'Introduction', in Mary Reichardt (ed), *Between Human and Divine: The Catholic Vision in Contemporary Literature* (Washington DC: The Catholic University of America Press, 2010), p 3.

a preoccupation 'with the struggle between the redemptive and the reductive forces in the human spirit and character, between the impulse to elevate and the compulsion to suppress'.[28] His main attribute as far as I am concerned was his ability to transform personal experience into something that has a universal resonance. His birthright owed much to chance, but it could never be cast aside or ignored:

> I was born into Catholicism as I might have been born into Buddhism or Protestantism or any of the other isms or sects, and brought up as a Roman Catholic in the infancy of this small state when the Church had almost total power: it was the dominating force of my whole upbringing, education and early working life (LW, 133).

In such circumstances, it was inevitable that Catholicism would play an important role in his oeuvre. It is somewhat surprising that this aspect has not to date been the subject matter of a monograph. Hopefully what follows will fill that lacuna. It will be substantially different from my previous study, *John McGahern: From the Local to the Universal* (The Liffey Press, 2003), which was published when the author was still alive and before the publication of *Memoir* (2005), *Creatures of the Earth* (2006) and the very useful collection of his non-fiction, *Love of the World* (2009). My earlier book followed the lead taken by Denis Sampson in his *Outstaring Nature's Eye: The Fiction of John McGahern* (1993) and James Whyte's *History, Myth and Ritual in the Fiction of John McGahern* (2002). Since then, there has been a special issue of the *Irish University Review* dedicated to the work of McGahern (2005); NUI Galway has initiated the McGahern International Seminar and Summer School and the annual *John McGahern Yearbook*; David Malcolm's *Understanding John McGahern* appeared in 2007 and 2010 saw the publication of Dermot McCarthy's hugely significant *John McGahern and the Art of Memory*.

It is my opinion that the bard of Leitrim and Roscommon

---

27. Eamon Maher and Declan Kiberd, 'John McGahern: Writer, Stylist, Seeker of a Lost World', in *Doctrine & Life* 52.2 (February 2002), pp 82-97, p 96.
28. Gearóid Ó Tuathaigh, 'McGahern's Irelands', in John Kenny (ed), *The John McGahern Yearbook*, vol 2 (NUI Galway, 2009), pp 14-27, p 19.

will continue to attract critical attention from social scientists, historians and literary critics as the importance of his unique contribution to Irish letters comes to be fully appreciated. David Pierce is yet another commentator whose important survey ends with an assessment of McGahern's role in achieving what major writers aspire to, the reconfiguration of the cultural landscape: 'His landscape is a watery one of meadows and lakes, and there is time to observe animal tracks and the movement of the seasons. This is rural Ireland at its best, about two to three hours from the gridlock of Dublin traffic and the fast world of Temple Bar and the remains of the Celtic Tiger'.[29] It is also the Ireland in which Catholicism continued to play a significant role, a role that we will now set about exploring in McGahern's fiction.

29. Pierce, *Light, Freedom and Song*, pp 286-7.

CHAPTER ONE

'The Shameful Rags of Intimacy': Straining Towards the Light

This chapter will deal with McGahern's first two published novels, *The Barracks* (1963) and *The Dark* (1965). I have decided to treat of them in the same chapter because they closely resemble each other in terms of their portrayal of the harshness of puritanical rural Ireland and the struggle of the two main characters to reconcile Catholic teaching with their perceived human failings.

Both novels are set in the Leitrim-Roscommon landscape that is so familiar to McGahern's readers, *The Barracks* in the unmistakable setting of Cootehall, where the family moved after the death of their mother. In an interview with Nicole Ollier, McGahern stated: 'I deliberately used the barracks [I lived in], in fact it is the only one of my novels that is actually set in a very recognisable place ... Naturally the barracks is a specific place. People go and take photographs of it now. It is exactly the same in the book.'[1] The autobiographical setting is counterbalanced by the decision to have as its main character a middle-aged heroine, Elizabeth Reegan, who from the beginning of the novel senses that she is unwell. As a former nurse, she is aware that the cysts in her breast may well be cancerous. She must bear the frightening prospect of this uncertain future on her own, as her husband, a sergeant in the Garda Síochána, and his children from a first marriage, are absorbed in their own lives. In the case of Reegan, the main problem is having to put up with a superior officer, Superintendent Quirke, for whom he has no respect and whom he seeks to undermine at every opportunity. Ultimately, Reegan's frustration stems from what he perceives to be the fail-

---

1. 'Step by Step Though *The Barracks* with John McGahern'. Interview with Nicole Ollier, in *La Licorne*, Numéro Spécial John McGahern (Poitiers: UFR Langues littératures, 1995), p 55.

ure of the Irish revolution to bring about a proper Republic, one
based on egalitarian ideals and markedly different from what
had been in place under British rule. The leader of a flying column during the War of Independence, Reegan must now endure
the indignity of taking orders from a man far younger than he
and who contributed nothing to the cause of Irish freedom for
which Reegan and his comrades risked life and limb. In the
opening pages of the novel, Elizabeth, brooding on her potential
health problems, only half-listens to her husband's predictable
diatribe against Quirke. She marvels at how quickly life passes
by – 'the starkness of individual minutes passing among accid-
ental doors and windows' (B, 59) – and knows that it is not possible to 'get any ordered vision on her life' (B, 50).

It is noteworthy that from the outset the interior of the house
is described in some detail: the religious pictures on the walls
and the Sacred Heart lamp burning in front of the crib of
Bethlehem on the mantelpiece (B, 7) being the key elements.
After his meal, Reegan makes the sign of the cross, more out of
habit than anything else: 'He'd never known mental prayer, so
his lips shaped the words of the Grace as he repeated them to
himself' (B, 18). Religious symbols, prayer, quotes from the
Bible, references to God punctuate life in the Reegan household.
The sergeant empties the Rosary beads into the palm of his
hands and kneels on the newspaper he has placed on the cement
floor, which is the signal for family prayer to commence. At the
very end come the words that encapsulate many of Elizabeth's
fears: *'O Jesus, I must die, I know not where nor when nor how, but if
I do die in mortal sin I go to hell for all eternity'* (B, 37. Italics in the
original). There is a constant awareness of death throughout *The
Barracks*, death as a time for reckoning, a time when the all-pow-
erful God in heaven will decide the fate of the person appearing
before him for judgement. Anthony Burgess, in his review of the
novel, opined that nobody 'has caught so well the peculiar
hopelessness of contemporary Ireland'.[2] I agree that there is a
fair degree of hopelessness in this novel, but there is also a smat-

---

2 Burgess' review appeared in the *Observer* on 9 March 1963 and is cited
by Sampson, *Outstaring Nature's Eye: The Fiction of John McGahern*
(Washington DC: Catholic University of America Press, 1993), p 34.

tering of joy, an appreciation of nature (albeit at a stage when Elizabeth is on the point of departing the material world) and, it has to be said, an acknowledgement of some of the positive aspects of religion.

Elizabeth is probably untypical of many of the women of her acquaintance in that she spent a period nursing in England, where she discovered a different approach to religion and to life. Her affair with Halliday, a depressed doctor with a very bleak outlook on existence, taught her that there are many different types of pain and that it is up to the individual to cope as best he or she can with the hand that is dealt to them. One could say with some degree of justification that Elizabeth's particular fate has little to recommend it. Yet, it is she who is by far the stronger personality in the relationship with Halliday. The question he addressed to her on one occasion – 'What the hell is all this living and dying about anyway, Elizabeth? That's what I'd like to be told' (B, 85) – comes back into her mind at the point when her cancer is diagnosed for the first time. In some ways, McGahern's whole oeuvre is an attempt to unravel the mystery of 'all this living and dying'. Unable to find any cure for his despair, Halliday dies in a car accident that is a suspected case of suicide. Elizabeth had realised that the relationship was one-sided and had taken the decision to end it: 'She'd not be there when a mad fit of sexual desire came, to blind it in the darkness of her womb before it grew to desperate sight enough to see his life moving in a hell of loneliness between a dark birth and as dark a death' (B, 93). The language in this passage is shot-through with emotion but it has not attained anything like the perfection of the future masterpiece, *Amongst Women*. By attempting to understand the short but intense life of Elizabeth Reegan, the young novelist had to immerse himself in her consciousness, something that would unavoidably force him to recall the huge trauma of the death of his own mother from cancer when he was ten years old. One feels a hidden admiration for the stoicism of this relatively young woman forced to come to terms with her mortality, with the twists and turns of life – 'the road away becomes the road back' (B, 158). Her life would appear not to amount to much were one to discount the power of memory: 'She had a rich life and she could remember' (B, 115).

The mind can be an antidote to pain and Elizabeth uses it to telling effect throughout the novel. She refuses to succumb completely to despair and comforts herself by thinking that there are many people far worse off than she is. On a trip home to Ireland to rest up after the strain of nursing during the London blitz, she was struck by how little her childhood environment had changed: 'The eternal medals and rosary beads were waiting on the spikes of the gate for whoever had lost them; the evergreens did not even sway in their sleep in the churchyard where bees droned between the graves from dandelion to white clover …' (*B*, 14). This was still a world where Catholicism played a powerful role. The stay at home provided Elizabeth with the opportunity to meet Michael Reegan, who struck her as being very handsome in his Garda uniform, and not without charm. She had come to a crossroads in her life and knew that should she return to the small family farm she would end up keeping house for her mother and brother, a prospect that did not hold much appeal. Her mother warned her against marrying the widower and facing into a life that would revolve around his needs and those of her step-children: 'Marryin' isn't something, believe me, that can be jumped into today and outa tomorrow. It's wan bed you have to sleep on whether it's hard or soft, wance you make it' (*B*, 15). On a superficial level, it might seem as though the bed Elizabeth has to sleep in is of the 'hard' variety, but she remains positive, knowing that life is never the rose-tinted adventure described in romantic novels. As she awaits a consultation with the local doctor, she reflects: 'Whether she had cancer or not wasn't her whole life a waiting, the end would arrive sooner or later, twenty extra years meant nothing to the dead' (*B*, 72). And yet, she desperately wants to hold on to life and all its mundane duties and futile hopes: 'Time was only for the living. She wanted time, as much time as she could get' (*B*, 72).

The visit to the doctor reminds her of going to confession: 'It was her body's sickness and not her soul's that she was confessing now but as always there was the irrational fear and shame' (*B*, 81). The priest and the doctor are the ones with the power to bring hope or damnation. She thinks back to the time when the local parish priest approached her about joining the local branch of the Legion of Mary, 'a kind of legalised gossiping school to the women and a convenient pool of labour that the priests could draw on for catering committees' (*B*, 163). Elizabeth had incurred the priest's wrath by declining the invitation, which was more an order than a request. When pressed for her reasons for declining, she stated that it was because of a dislike for organisations, to which the priest retorts: 'So, my dear woman, you dislike the Catholic Church: it happens to be an organisation, you know, that's founded on the Divine Truth ...' (*B*, 163). Her anger at his pushiness had caused her to leave herself open to this attack and earned her the reputation of being a renegade, an eccentric. From that point onwards, there would always be a certain tension between her and the priest. While she is not willing to yield to clerical control of every aspect of her life, Elizabeth, like McGahern himself, appreciates the beauty of religious ceremonies: 'She'd been brought up in the fear of God but what remained most powerful in the memory was the church services, always beautiful, especially in Holy Week; witnessed so often in the same unchanging pattern that they didn't come in broken recollections, but flowed before the mind with the calm and grace and reassurance of all ritual ...' (*B*, 123). It is not the strict, authoritarian brand of Catholicism that she held on to, but the 'smells and bells' version of her childhood memories.

A question that arises in relation to Elizabeth is whether or not she is a 'believer' at all in the strict sense of the word. I agree with Denis Sampson's reading, which states: 'Her examination of a religious sense of ultimate reality becomes a central part of her effort to understand suffering and death.'[3] From her initial diagnosis, through the mastectomy operation and her convalescence in hospital, to her death in the barracks, Elizabeth ponders on what eternity will entail and leans on her religious beliefs to help her to better understand significant aspects of the material world as she journeys towards death. For example, at Easter she reflects: 'And if the Resurrection and still more the Ascension seemed shadowy and unreal compared to the way to Calvary, it might be because she could not know them with her own life, on the cross of her life she had to achieve her goal, and what came after was shut away from her eyes' (*B*, 195). She also comes to

---

3. *Outstaring Nature's Eye*, p 36.

appreciate how the Rosary had grown into her life: 'she'd come to love its words, its rhythm, its repetitions, its confident chanting, its eternal mysteries' (*B*, 220). She acknowledges that her response is purely instinctive, that the meaning of the prayer is not really important, that it's more a question of giving 'her heart release, the need to praise and celebrate, in which everything rejoiced' (*B*, 220). Similarly, she enjoys visiting the church for some quiet moments of meditation. She doesn't go with a view to asking for her problems to disappear: 'There were no answers … she'd no business to be in the church except she loved it and it was quiet …' (*B*, 165).

The relationship between Reegan and Elizabeth, in spite of appearances, is not devoid of love. Having already lost one wife to cancer, Reegan finds it difficult to envisage losing a second one. He does not have the courage to visit her in hospital as she recuperates from her operation, but she does not expect such a gesture from him. David Malcolm notes that the relationship is marked 'by lack of communication and emotional inadequacy',[4] and it is difficult to refute this reading of McGahern's presentation of the relationship. Nevertheless, Elizabeth does observe 'how lucky she was to have found Reegan, to be married to him and not to Halliday' (*B*, 153-4) and she understands that he is not a demonstrative person, a trait he shares with the vast majority of Irish men of his generation. Acts of intimacy were for the dark of night, but they were not sordid or mean. The coupling that takes place on the last Christmas eve they spend together shows tenderness: 'They'd try to fall apart without noticing much wrench and lie in the animal warmth and loving kindness of each other against the silence of the room' (*B*, 181). Grace Tighe Ledwidge argues that the silence surrounding sexuality in *The Barracks* is imputable to the 'woman's role at the centre of the Irish Catholic family'. She continues: 'The female role-model is the Virgin Mary, a woman who conceived a child without recourse to the 'impurity' of sexual contact with a man. Further, according to Church teaching, every sexual act must be open to conception'.[5] I find this is more typical of the attitude to sex

---

4. David Malcolm, *Understanding John McGahern* (Columbia, South Carolina Press: University of South Carolina Press, 2007), p 18.
5. Grace Tighe Ledwidge, 'Death in Marriage: The Tragedy of Elizabeth

found in some of McGahern's other fiction than in *The Barracks*. Elizabeth Reegan does not receive too much physical affection from her husband, but that is not solely as a result of his being conditioned by the Church's attitude to women. They continue to have a sexual life after her operation and there are signs of Elizabeth being grateful to him for the limited intimacy of which he is capable. After all, this is the same man who fiercely desires to be 'separate and alone', after yielding to an impulse of being close to his wife: 'The pain and frustration that the shame of intimacy brings started to nag him to desperation' (*B*, 18). (We will explore how Mahoney Junior in *The Dark* suffers from a different type of intimacy in the form of her father's abuse, referred to as 'the dirty rags of intimacy' – *D*, 19). Sampson thinks that Reegan is similar to Elizabeth 'because both have an urgent need to feel the authenticity of their own existence in the here and now. While both want to be anesthetised from the anguish of time passing, both also realise that to succumb to habit is to experience meaninglessness and a diminution of self to the point of becoming a mere phenomenon.'[6]

The following day, the Christmas meal has echoes of the Eucharist, with the bright table-cloth being produced for the occasion and the family members demonstrating 'such marvellous courtesy and ceremony' (*B*, 183). Similarly, the meal 'began and ended with the highest form of all human celebration, prayer' (*B*, 183). With Elizabeth, religious faith, while not providing any definitive answers, offers the hope of something beyond the grave: 'It seemed as a person grew older that the unknowable reality, God, was the one thing you could believe or disbelieve in with safety, it met you with imponderable silence and could never be reduced to the nothingness of certain knowledge' (*B*, 177). As the

Reegan in *The Barracks*', in *Irish University Review*, John McGahern Special, Spring/Summer, 2005, pp 90-103, p 100.
6. Sampson, *Outstaring Nature's Eye*, p 39. It may be argued that to link Reegan and Elizabeth in the way that Sampson does is to misrepresent the extent to which McGahern strives to build up Elizabeth's complex inner life. Also, she does not want to be 'anesthetised' to time: rather, everything about her is an affirmation of a desire to feel life in its daily magnificence. It is not so much time passing as time ending that preoccupies her thoughts. But the temptation of succumbing to 'habit' is very much something both want to avoid at all costs.

novel moves from Christmas through the Easter ceremonies which bring her death into sharp focus, she has a heightened awareness of the beauty of the landscape, a beauty that had escaped her when she was healthy. 'Jesus Christ' is all she can summon up to express her amazement as she observes the mundane scene from the window of the barracks (*B*, 170). It is a well-known fact that when one is in danger of losing a thing it becomes all the more precious. Nature, like religion, occasionally provides a comforting presence, even though it pains Elizabeth to be leaving such unspeakable beauty behind her. She finds herself increasingly drawn to look out through the curtained windows: 'the light had slanted, making such violence on the water that she'd to shade her eyes to see the reeds along the shore, the red navigation barrels caught in a swaying blaze at the mouth of the lake and the soft rectangles of shadow behind' (*B*, 151-2). The poignant tone conveys the nostalgia of suddenly recognising the astonishing beauty of an everyday scene which had remained obscured because of the busy routine associated with getting through her daily chores. Now it strikes her with great force, all the more heartrending because she knows she has not long left to contemplate it: 'Pray that you might get well,' was her first thought, and then the quietness started to seep into her mind' (*B*, 164). Elizabeth's reaction to the material world at this critical moment closely resembles that of McGahern himself in similar circumstances. He wrote in *Memoir*: 'We come from darkness into light and grow in the light until at death we return to that original darkness … We grow into a love of the world, a love that is all the more precious and poignant because the great glory of which we are but a particle is lost almost as soon as it is gathered' (*M*, 36).

David Coad would doubtless take issue with some of my reading of McGahern's first novel. In his opinion, 'John McGahern is neither a religious writer, nor a believer, but since he sets the actions for his novels and short stories mostly in Ireland, there is a constant preoccupation with the religious terminology of Ireland's predominant faith, Roman Catholicism.'[7]

7. David Coad, 'Religious References in *The Barracks*', in *Études Irlandaises*, Numéro special sur *The Barracks* de John McGahern. Textes

The setting of the novels definitely plays a role in ensuring the presence of Catholic rituals, but I do not think that the issue at stake in *The Barracks* has anything to do with McGahern's faith or lack of same. Coad is strong in the opinions he expresses: 'The author is condemning an opiate version of Catholicism' (133) – but McGahern studiously avoided condemnation in all his writings. He goes on: 'McGahern is deriding habit-driven Catholics who do not believe with conviction or see the relevance of the basic tenets of their faith' (134). Now, anyone who has read *That They May Face the Rising Sun* will recognise the affection displayed by McGahern for the simple, unthinking faith of people like Jamesie. Habit is part of the fabric of traditional rural Ireland, a glue that cements communities together, and religious belief, whether it's instinctive or more intellectually grasped, is an indispensable element of that fabric. Finally, Coad considers that McGahern makes 'comic' or 'ironic' references to the Bible. He cites Elizabeth's misquote: 'Woman, take up thy bed and walk to the Shelbourne hotel' as an example of how 'McGahern shows characters who more or less easily bring well known passages from the New Testament into their thoughts and conversation. These extracts tend to be merely personal talismanic tokens, wrenched from a theological context, and thus spiritually inert' (135). I remain to be convinced of how extracts 'wrenched from a theological context' would of necessity indicate that they were 'spiritually inert'.

I do not take issue with the contention that much of what passed for religion in traditional rural Ireland was far from orthodox or theologically sound. But that is not really the issue. McGahern, an unbeliever, never stooped to the level of deriding or belittling those who possessed an unthinking faith. If anything, he emphasised on several occasions the degree to which he missed church ceremonies: 'In an impoverished time they were my first introduction to an indoor beauty, of luxury and ornament, ceremony and sacrament and mystery' (*M*, 201). In the case of *The Barracks*, I do not agree that McGahern was seek-

réunis et présentés par Claude Fierobe, Octobre 1994, pp 131-138, p 131. Page numbers for subsequent references to this article will be supplied in brackets.

ing to undermine religious belief, or to condemn or deride those customs and practices that might not stand up to close theological scrutiny. Towards the end of the novel, Elizabeth appears reconciled to her approaching death by a belief in a world beyond this earth:

> Her life was either under the unimaginable God or the equally unimaginable nothing (B, 59).
> Nothing in life is ever resolved once and for all but changes with the changing life (B, 204).
> All the apparent futility of her life in this barracks came at last to rest on this sense of mystery. It gave the hours idled away in boredom or remorse as much validity as a blaze of passion, all was under its eternal sway. She felt for a moment pure, without guilt. She'd no desire to clutch for the facts and figures of explanation, only it was there or wasn't there and if there was any relationship they would meet in the moment of her death (B, 211).

Note how she does not seek to possess 'the facts and figures of explanation', the theological or rational elucidation of her faith. All was mystery and she was prepared to yield to that mystery, which might reveal its secrets beyond death. It is perhaps this new-found peace that helps her to put aside the enmity she feels towards the parish priest, as he administers Extreme Unction, the sacrament of the sick, to her. Her revolt has not been totally quenched, however. As the holy oil touches her organs of sense, through which 'sin had entered the soul', 'she wanted to declare ... that sense of truth and justice and beauty and all things else had entered that way too' (B, 216). She acknowledges that the priest shows her kindness now that she's ill, but her dislike of him persists. She had never told him all in confession, reverting instead to meaningless formulae. When, at her bedside, he impresses on her in an aggressive manner the importance of having devotion to the Virgin Mary, resentment is her first reaction, but that is followed by a serene calm: 'He was simply a person to be avoided if she had a choice in the matter but she didn't care whether she chose or was chosen any more, it was all the same' (B, 219). Shortly afterwards, she yields to death: 'her fingers groped at the sheets, the perishing senses trying to find root in something physical' (*B*, 221). After she has breathed her last, the corpse is laid out for the wake, food and drink are bought in the shops and the people begin to trickle into the house to pay their respects. The relief of the living is tangible in the unspoken feelings of the guards, Mullins and Casey, who take their leave from the cemetery as the clay begins to thud on the coffin: 'It's Elizabeth that's being covered and not me ...' (*B*, 223).

Eileen Kennedy provides an insightful reading of *The Barracks* when she writes: 'Elizabeth may not have found a completely fulfilling answer to Halliday's question about the meaning of life; but the reader is aware – much more than she – that she has taken her existential situation and, within the limits of her freedom, has shaped her life into one of significance and meaning.'[8] I concur with such a reading. There are no neat, comfortable answers to her existential plight at the conclusion of *The Barracks* – 'the facts and figures of explanation' are not revealed to her – but it is clear that she has reached some accommodation with her plight and that her Catholic faith has helped her to make the passage to eternity: 'She had come to life out of mystery and would return, it surrounded her life, it safely held it as by hands; she'd return into that which she could not know; she'd be consumed at last in whatever meaning her life had' (*B*, 211). Granted, this quote does not make any mention of an eternity spent in the company of a Divine Presence. What awaits her beyond death is a 'mystery' whose secrets will only be revealed when she departs this life. Elizabeth is not the type of person to accept all the pronouncements of the Church without question. She is 'Catholic' only insofar as that is the religion in which she was brought up and whose prayers and ceremonies exude beauty in her view. She is careful to distinguish between her private faith and all that she associates with the powerful institution that seeks to bring her within its sphere of influence and which she resists right up to her dying breath.

---

8. Eileen Kennedy, 'The Novels of John McGahern: The Road Away becomes the Road Back', in James D. Brophy and Richard J. Porter (eds), *Contemporary Irish Writing* (Boston: Iona College Press/Tayne, 1983), pp 115-126, p 119.

A first novel is clearly a landmark in any writer's career. In the case of *The Barracks*, the critical reception was extremely positive and marked McGahern out as a young writer with a bright future. It was published in three different journals prior to its publication in book form and an abstract won for its author the prestigious AE Memorial Award in 1962. In 1964 McGahern was awarded the Macauley Fellowship for the novel, which allowed him to take a year out of teaching – a sabbatical that would end up lasting four odd decades for reasons we will discuss later. Denis Sampson quotes from a statement McGahern wrote to the Trustees of the Macauley Fellowship in which he stated:

> As it is not a novel, but an attempt to break that form down into a religious poem, I can only hope to indicate some of its tones as it moves to its end. The vision is all that matters in it, and the style, for a banality in it can assume as much importance as the beautiful. What happens matters very little, the real things that happen are inevitable, and the others should be inevitable in the laws of the work.[9]

Sampson considers that a conflation of fictional realism with a 'religious poem' allows for a fruitful way of approaching 'the inevitability of what happens and the inevitability of art', an essential ingredient of McGahern's aesthetic approach.[10] He was not a writer who was driven by plot. In many instances, there is little or no action in his novels. It is the close identification that the reader develops with the intimate secrets of his characters, their dashed hopes, broken bodies, despair and joy that makes banal happenings assume global significance. Elizabeth is not just a stranger facing the torment of death by cancer; she is also someone who comes to assume the persona of a wife, a sister, a mother, a close personal friend. The narrative revolves around her painful path to self-awareness and death, a path that induces a hypnotic effect on readers as they accompany her on her journey.

In light of the subject matter of *The Barracks*, I would like to dwell for a while on the comments of the novelist Kate O'Brien.

9. Denis Sampson, 'The Solitary Hero', in John Kenny (ed), *The John McGahern Yearbook*, Vol 3 (Galway, NUI Galway, 2010), pp 74-81, p 76.
10. Sampson, 'The Solitary Hero', p 76.

Her review of *The Barracks* was very positive: 'It is difficult to find words exact enough to express my admiration of this subtle, close-woven, tender, true, poetic work'. The one slight flaw she noted concerns the portrayal of the heroine: 'I was not sure that the deeply seasoned philosophic reflections of the lonely woman Elizabeth were within the reach of her simple kind of consciousness. Her nature indeed might well have known such wisdom, but would she have been able to think with the lucid gravity her author gives her?'[11] I single out these comments by O'Brien for a number of reasons. First, she was a writer whom McGahern admired greatly and then there is the fact that she was a woman of deep Catholic convictions. *The Ante-Room* (1934) is, in my view, the closest any Irish writer has ever come to producing a 'Catholic Novel'. Its main character, Agnes Mulqueen, has a strong intellectual grasp of the theology that underpins her religious faith, something that McGahern's characters lack for the most part. If O'Brien expressed doubts about the 'lucid gravity' McGahern gave Elizabeth, it is possibly because she herself always took great care to link the moral dilemmas encountered by her heroines with their religious scruples.

A brief discussion of *The Ante-Room* will prove an interesting analogy with *The Barracks*. Agnes Mulqueen is a young woman from a well-to-do middle-class background, with a good education and high intelligence. She is destined for an unhappy future because of her feelings towards her sister's husband, Vincent de Courcy O'Regan. Her mother is dying from an incurable cancer and a problem arises for Agnes when it is announced that Canon Considine, her uncle, is going to say a triduum of Masses around All Saints' and All Souls' Day for her recovery. In order to participate fully in the liturgy, Agnes knows that she must go to confession. A central scene in the novel is the examination of conscience she undergoes before making her confession to a Jesuit priest. Obviously, she is keenly aware of the tenets of her faith. She wonders how it could be a sin to fall in love; was it not merely a quirk of fate, something over which she had no control? She soon acknowledges that her main sin is against her

11. Kate O'Brien, review of *The Barracks*, in *University Review*, Vol III, no 4, 1963, p 59.

sister Marie-Rose, whom she loves deeply: 'The common sin against the ninth commandment, enhanced by all the pitiful complications of sister love'.[12] We note the grim determination to face up to the sinfulness of her feelings for Vincent, her refusal to accept any self-deception: 'Faith, a cold thing, a fact – that was what she must use to destroy fantasy' (84).

On hearing her confession, the Jesuit is impressed with her lucidity and notes with approval that she has not given in to her inclinations and has not spoken of her love to Vincent. Then he gives what he considers to be consoling advice: earthly love is transient, 'whereas in the search for God, in the idea of God, there is matter for eternity' (89). We can see already how far removed we are from the world inhabited by Elizabeth Reegan. First of all, the latter never received the necessary education that would have enabled her to map out her sinfulness in this manner. Had she done so, it is highly unlikely that her 'friend', the local parish priest, would have been capable of supplying the type of intellectual response provided by the Jesuit. O'Brien's characters reflect her own life and experiences much like McGahern's do his. Agnes benefits from a liberal, European-type education, whereas Elizabeth got a limited schooling and spent most of her life in a restricted area of the northwest midlands. Elizabeth refuses to reveal all her sins to the priest in the confessional, believing that a lot of what goes on in her heart does not need to be shared with him. It is interesting to reflect on the importance Irish people in the past attached to confession. Louise Fuller remarks: 'Sins had to be confessed in detail, as well as the number of times they had been committed. There was a very real fear of dying in a state of mortal sin and thus losing salvation'.[13]

Elizabeth approaches death with an equanimity that owes something to her feeling that she has not been a bad person, that she has in general led a good life. The issue of mortal sin does not cross her mind. Agnes, on the other hand, feels the need to 'wipe the slate clean' and start anew. However, the strength she derives from confession dissipates as soon as she returns to the

---

12. Kate O'Brien, *The Ante-Room* (London: Virago, 1989), p 80. All subsequent quotes from this edition, with the page numbers in brackets.
13. Fuller, *Irish Catholicism Since 1950*, p 21.

family home, Roseholm, where she finds herself once more in the presence of Vincent, to whom she remains very attracted. This causes her to remark ruefully: 'Yes, holy Jesuit, that's all very fine. But we aren't made in the most convenient form in which to pursue ideas, and we have no notion at all of how to front eternity' (200). The strange thing is that Elizabeth is far better prepared to 'front eternity' than O'Brien's character. This is in part due to her stoicism, which results from her rural upbringing and her experience of the changing seasons, the cycle of life and death that unfolds in front of her eyes on a daily basis. Agnes is intensely aware of her duty and knows that it would be impossible for her to cast aside her religious beliefs for the love of Vincent. The latter, weaker than she (in this he resembles Halliday), seeks in Agnes a replacement for his dead and much regretted mother. When she tells him they have no future together, he commits suicide, thus adding to the turmoil of the Mulqueen household. Throughout *The Ante-Room* one encounters people who attempt to live their lives in accordance with a belief in a transcendent being and a respect for the mystery that lies at the heart of Catholicism. Thus, as they recite the 'Holy, Holy, Holy' at Roseholm during the Mass, 'they reached the quietest moment of their faith, a moment so still that bells must ring and sometimes guns must sound to make it humanly bearable' (173).[14] The Rosary in *The Barracks* does not elicit a similar response; it is merely a mechanical ritual which forms part of the daily routine in the Reegan household. This short comparison of novels by McGahern and O'Brien seeks to underline the different Catholic worlds inhabited by their characters. It does not wish to claim one is more authentic than the other, because each comes at the issue of Catholicism from a particular perspective, O'Brien's being of the liberal, educated, middle-class variety and McGahern's being based on the rural, at times instinctive, attitude to religion that dominates his characters' lives. Elizabeth Reegan is a character in whom the residual structures

---

14. For a more in-depth discussion of the similarities between McGahern and O'Brien, see my article, 'Irish Catholicism as seen Through the Lens of Kate O'Brien and John McGahern', in Yann Bévant and Anne Goarzin (eds), *Bretagne et Irlande : Pérégrinations – Mélange à Jean Brihault* (Rennes: TIR, 2009), pp 95-112.

of institutional religion have been charged with an intuitive spirituality based primarily on her attention to nature and its wonders and mysteries, of which she and her own life are embodiments. If one were to follow the reading of Tom Inglis, McGahern's characters would be the more typical representations of Irish Catholicism in the middle decades of the last century: 'Innocence was regarded as a virtue. People were not encouraged to question their religion or their priests ... The dominance of "the simple faith" has meant that many Irish Catholics have not developed an intellectual interest in, or critical attitude towards, their religion'.[15] Many problems were lurking as a result of such an attitude, as we shall see later in this study.

With McGahern's second novel, *The Dark*, we are introduced to an even gloomier and more spiritually arid atmosphere than is the case with *The Barracks*. The novel plunged McGahern into the public limelight in a way that was unpleasant for him and his family when it was banned by the Irish Censorship Board in 1965. While it was not in any way unusual for Irish writers to be subjected to this treatment, in the case of McGahern the ramifications were quite severe, as they caused him to lose his job as a primary school teacher in Clontarf. There was also the unwanted publicity it brought it its wake, the stigma of having a book on the banned list. In an interview with Julia Carlson, he commented: 'The unpleasant thing about both the banning and the sacking was that – for the writer all that matters is whether the work is good or bad – it brought something prurient into it, which for me has nothing to do with whether a book is good or bad. It confused the issue, and one also found that one was a sort of public figure from just being a writer, and there's some people that enjoy that, and I don't'.[16]

He admitted that for three to four years after this episode he

---

15. Tom Inglis, *Moral Monopoly: The Catholic Church in Modern Irish Society* (Dublin: Gill and Macmillan, 1987), p 2. For anyone wishing to gain an insight into the close interaction between Church and State in Ireland and the symbolic capital gained from being perceived to be a 'good Catholic', this is an indispensable reference. In 1998, Inglis produced a bigger, updated version of the study.
16. In Julia Carlson (ed), *Banned in Ireland*, pp 61-62.

was unable to write, such was his upset at what had happened. Declan Kiberd, who knew McGahern as a primary school teacher in Belgrove, notes how as a boy he overheard his parents discussing the sacking, something that made a huge impression on his young mind. From that moment on, the teacher became something of a figure of romance and writing assumed the allure of a subversive, dangerous activity. There were obvious downsides for McGahern: 'But actually it was a horrible way to go at the time, and also I am sure he missed it because he was a good teacher. And there must have been shame attached to his removal. In the Ireland of the time when there was still great prestige, rightly, attached to the career of school teaching, to be put out of it was almost like losing your licence to practice law or something nowadays ... It was a bitter pill to swallow'.[17]

Whether McGahern wanted it or not, the banning of *The Dark* was a major news item for a time. The fact that the novelist was a schoolteacher and that Archbishop John Charles McQuaid had intervened directly in the case gave it all the ingredients for a sensational news story. Samuel Beckett offered to take part in a protest if McGahern wanted one;[18] he was very grateful for the offer, but did not see the point in protesting. It would not get him his job back and it would not change the minds of the people who were ultimately responsible for the banning. The pitting of writers against the power of the Catholic Church is something that became very embittered in the early stages of post-independence Ireland. Because writers' subject matter re-volves around the human passions, there is the obvious potential to stray into areas where a zealous Church tried to guard its con-trol jealously. The issue of censorship was a particularly thorny one, as writers felt that they had to have the liberty to deal with any issue – be it religious, moral, sexual, historical, cultural – and in exactly the manner they saw fit. It was not just the priests and hierarchy who were active in vetting books either. There were also legions of lay Catholic activists who were ready and

17. Declan Kiberd and Eamon Maher, 'John McGahern: Writer, Stylist, Seeker of a Lost World', pp 85-86.
18. Clíodhna Ní Anluain (ed), *Reading the Future: Irish Writers in Conversation with Mike Murphy* (Dublin: The Lilliput Press, 2000), pp 144-145.

willing to submit reports about passages they found unsavoury
or offensive to public morality. The seven writers interviewed
by Julia Carlson were 'deeply critical of the society that gave rise
to and perpetrated censorship, identifying it with the xeno-
phobia of Irish nationalism, the Puritanism and authoritarianism
of the Irish Catholic Church, and the striving for respectability
of the Irish middle classes'.[19] The Church was certainly not acting alone in this matter. Diarmuid Ferriter argues that censorship
was in some way the result of the 'moral crisis' that characterised early twentieth-century Ireland. He quotes the Irish film
censor James Montgomery's memorable phrase, 'the morals of
the poultry yard' to describe the attitudes that led to the setting
up of the censorship culture. According to Ferriter, sex was not
the only concern at the time: 'The censorship process was also
about the interaction between Church, State and the power
(often resented) of social reform movements and lobby
groups.'[20]

In the 1960s (and the situation has not changed much since)
the Catholic Church controlled the vast majority of primary and
secondary schools in Ireland. In the case of primary schools, the
influence was more stark, as was pointed out by Senator Owen
Sheehy Skeffington, a renowned social campaigner:

> In practice, then, it is the clerical school manager who hires
> and fires the teachers, and though the Minister pays the
> teachers' salaries, and has to approve their initial appoint-
> ment by the clerical manager, he does not have to approve
> their dismissal for other than professional reasons, and if he
> is ordered by the school manager to stop paying, or not to
> resume paying, as in the McGahern case after the end of his
> officially approved year's leave of absence, the Minister just
> has to do what the Parish Priest tells him without question.
> The State pays the piper, but the Church calls the tune.[21]

19. Carlson, *Banned in Ireland*, p 17.
20. Diarmuid Ferriter, *Occasions of Sin: Sex and Society in Modern Ireland*
(London: Profile Books, 2009), p 186.
21. Owen Sheehy Skeffington, 'McGahern Affair', in *Censorship: A
Quarterly Report on Censorship of Ideas and the Arts*, 2.2 (Spring 1966), pp
27-30, p 28.

In all the discussion of the rights and wrongs of McGahern's dismissal, an important point is rarely raised, namely the feasibility of someone who wrote a novel like *The Dark* continuing as a primary school teacher at the time. This is not meant in any way as a criticism of the novel or its author, more as an observation on the closed mindset that dominated the Ireland of that period.[22] McGahern wanders into very dangerous territory in the novel, as Sheehy Skeffington remarks: 'The book itself is a sensitive, well-written, rather sad and poignant book, dealing with aspects of Irish life which officialdom prefers to pretend do not exist. Masturbation, homosexual tendencies, the sexual frustrations of many Irish men and women including some priests, are dealt with in a courageous and frank manner, but with a sobriety and seriousness of concern which are undeniable.'[23] This was a heady cocktail for the time and could only have resulted in McGahern's sacking in my view. Any Irish primary school teacher in a Catholic school who wanted to hold onto his job while continuing to write at this time needed to avoid wandering into such taboo areas.[24] In addition to the novel, there was

---

22. Ferriter maintains that there were many who shared the view articulated by the Fianna Fáil politician, Seán Lemass, who stated that there was nothing intrinsically wrong with sexual passion: 'The original proposed definition of indecency [in the censorship legislation] as 'calculated to excite sexual passion or to suggest or to excite sexual immorality, or in any other way to corrupt or deprave' was widely criticised as being too vague and the amended wording that became law did not include the phrase 'calculated to excite sexual passion'.' Ferriter, *Occasions of Sin*, p 186.
23. 'McGahern Affair', p 27.
24. McGahern's first wife, Annikki Laaksi, who studiously avoided making any commentary on the time spent with her former husband-writer, briefly emerged from obscurity in May 2006 to give an interview to the *Sunday Independent*. In it, she alleged that McGahern was far from upset at the banning of *The Dark* and the notoriety its banning brought in its wake: 'The truth is John was very pleased after the book was banned because it got him a lot of attention internationally, adding to his success. Marrying me soon afterwards in a registry office abroad was deliberate, to make the conflict even sharper ...' (Isobel Conway, '"A calculating, control freak", claims the first wife of late author John McGahern', in the *Sunday Independent*, 28 May, 2006). While it could be argued that his first wife had an axe to grind about the way their rela-

also the added complication of McGahern's marriage in a registry office to Annikki Laaksi, as was pointed out to him by the
manager of Belgrove, Fr Carton: 'He asked me what did I want
to write books for and why did I want to bring trouble, that their
phone had been annoyed with journalists and that he also heard
that I was married and didn't get married in a church.'[25] A
member of the executive of the teachers' union, the INTO, made
reference also to the irregular marriage: 'If it was just the banned
book, then we might have been able to do something for you,
though it would have been difficult. But with marrying this
woman, you're an impossible case'.[26] While there are comic elements to this comment, there is also a fair degree of truth in
what the executive member had to say.

Michael McLaverty, a primary school teacher also, but in the
North of Ireland, was someone for whom McGahern demonstrated huge regard. Their correspondence surrounding *The
Dark* and its banning is revealing. McGahern knew McLaverty
to be a devout Catholic and so his reaction would be a type of
litmus test. McLaverty declared himself 'greatly impressed by its
painful sincerity and its pared-to-the-bone style' and continued:
'The book rings with truth at every turn and it must have been a
heart-breaking and exhausting book to write'.[27] He is absolutely
correct in his comment about how difficult a book *The Dark* must
have been to write. He goes on to note how he 'recoiled' from a
few pages which were devoted to what he describes as 'a
priest's thoughts' and says he 'wished they hadn't been there',
but was positive overall. Subsequent to the banning, McGahern
expressed dismay that the novel should have fallen foul of the
censorship board: 'What disturbs me very much is that the
book's a religious work if it's anything at all.'[28] This most cer-

---

tionship ended, it is noteworthy the extent to which her account of the
banning has been ignored by the media in Ireland: it is significantly different to the one repeated by McGahern on numerous occasions.
25. *Banned in Ireland*, p 57.
26. *Banned in Ireland*, p 59.
27. John Killen (ed), *Dear Mr McLaverty: The Literary Correspondence of
John McGahern and Michael McLaverty 1959-1980* (Belfast: The Linen hall
Library, 2006), p 39.
28. *Dear Mr McLaverty*, p 42.

tainly was not the view of the Church or the board and for that reason McGahern found himself deprived of the safety net of a permanent position, a fact that may have allowed his full talents as a writer to emerge. Archbishop McQuaid was delivered his head on a plate, but it may well be the case that the sacked teacher has ended up capturing the *Zeitgeist* of the nation better than any bishop has ever done. Also, his willingness to forgive and forget what happened to him in 1965 demonstrates the type of tolerance with which the Church hierarchy does not seem to be endowed. McGahern may have been a catalyst for change in relation to censorship, as Dermot Keogh observes:

> The climate of tolerance improved for the arts about two years after the McGahern case. It must have precipitated the sense of urgency for legislative change … the Minister for Justice, Brian Lenihan … brought in legislation in 1967 to provide for the unbanning of books after twelve years … the result was the release of 5,000 titles, and re-banning has since proved the exception.[29]

So we come to the novel itself and the image it portrays of the Catholic Ireland of the 1950s. This time the main protagonist is an adolescent, Mahoney, who lives with his sisters and widowed father on a farm in the northwest midlands. The opening scene describes a simulated beating which involves the boy being told to strip while the father brings the strap down on the leather of the chair over which his son is bending. The sexual overtones are obvious: 'He didn't lift a hand, as if the stripping compelled by his will alone gave him pleasure' (*D*, 8); he issues orders in an imperious manner: 'Move and I'll cut that arse off you. I'm only giving you a taste of what you're going to get'; finally, when it's all over, the leather strap resembles a limp penis after ejaculation: 'his face still red and heated, the leather hanging dead in his hand' (*D*, 10). We know that McGahern's father was prone to violent outbursts like this one and that in time his eldest son would rear up on him in the manner Mahoney junior will do later in the novel. McLaverty's com-

29. Dermot Keogh, *Twentieth Century Ireland: Nation and State* (Dublin: Gill and Macmillan, 1994), p 258.

ment about the 'sincerity' of *The Dark* is in no small way due to the amount of his personal experiences McGahern drew on for this book.

We need to be careful not to accept fictional accounts, no matter how closely they stick to the facts, as being exact representations of events that took place in real life. The publication of *Memoir* demonstrated the extent to which McGahern produced what Thomas Kilroy would describe as 'autobiographical fiction'.[30] For example, the constant refrain of Mahoney Senior in *The Dark* of 'God, O God' (*D,* 14) is one that Francis McGahern was heard to utter on numerous occasions. There are therefore certain obvious connections between various fictional characters and real-life models. Kilroy warns, however, of the necessity to create 'a fictional distance between author and subject while at the same time preserving the personal statement at the novel's core'.[31] He then quotes from a wonderful interview with Patrick Kavanagh that appeared in *The Bell* in 1948 in which he compared the respective truth of his novel *Tarry Flynn* and the autobiography *The Green Fool*. According to Kavanagh, the novel was in many ways 'nearer the truth' than the autobiographical record:

> I've been telling lies all my life. I invented so many stories about myself in *The Green Fool* to illustrate my own unique character that I don't know myself what's true about me and what isn't.[32]

I would not like to imply that McGahern was as prone to hyperbole as Kavanagh, but I do get the sense that his novels at times also come 'nearer the truth' than *Memoir* did. The 'ring of truth' in *The Dark* stems from the keen understanding of the claustrophobia engendered by living in a house where the patriarch is self-absorbed, embittered and frustrated and where the children often pay the price for his dissatisfaction. They wreak their revenge by banding together and making the father suffer: they learn 'to close their life against him and to leave him to

---

30. Thomas Kilroy, 'The Autobiographical Novel', in Augustine Martin (ed), *The Genius of Irish Prose* (Cork: Mercier, 1985), pp 67-75, p 67.
31. Kilroy, p 69.
32. Quoted by Kilroy, p. 75.

himself' (*D*, 11). At the heart of their dilemma is the fact that they want to love their father, for all his faults: 'the nag-nag-nag went like a hacksaw across the steel of their hatred' (*D*, 15). The beatings are commonplace and mostly unprovoked. Worse than the physical abuse, however, was what happened between father and son on the nights when 'he wanted love' (*D*, 17). The child feels 'shame and embarrassment and loathing' when he considers 'the dirty rags of intimacy' (*D*, 19). What occurs is very similar to how McGahern describes the abuse he endured at the hands of his own father. There is massaging of the thighs and genitalia on the pretext that it is good for easing problems with wind:

> The words drummed softly as the stroking hands moved on his belly, down and up, touched with the fingers the thighs again, and came again on the back ... 'You like that. It's good for you', the voice breathed jerkily now to the stroking hands.
> 'I like that.'
> There was nothing else to say, it was better not to think or care (*D*, 20).[33]

The child has aspirations to become a priest, but he cannot feel worthy of the calling. His self-esteem is low because of the abuse he endures and his regular bouts of masturbation reinforce this negative self-image. He aspires to be different from his father at all costs: 'He'd be a priest if he got the chance ... He'd walk that way through life towards the unnamable heaven of joy, not his father's path' (*D*, 25). His cousin, Fr Gerald, is the conduit through whom this ambition might be achieved. The

---

33. Compare this with the account given in *Memoir*: 'He never interfered with me in an obviously sexual way, but he frequently massaged my belly and thighs. As in all other things connected with the family, he asserted that he was doing this for my good: it relaxed taut muscles, eased wind and helped bring on sleep. In these years, despite my increasing doctrinal knowledge of what was sinful, I had only the vaguest knowledge of sex or sexual functions, and took him at his word ... Looking back, and remembering his tone of voice and the rhythmic movement of his hand, I suspect he was masturbating. During the beatings, there was sometimes the same sexual undertow, but louder, coarser' (*M*, 188).

priest visited the Mahoneys' house every year, which prompted
great preparations: a hen was killed, the front room swept, the
wedding china placed on the table. Mahoney Senior hated this
fuss, 'but because of his fear of a priest's power he made sure to
give the appearance of a welcome' (D, 24). Fr Gerald, aware of
the burgeoning vocation in his cousin, suggests that he come
and stay with him the summer before he does his Leaving
Certificate exam. But the boy's problems with masturbation persist, brought on by certain stimuli such as the thought of a girl's
thighs 'working against the saddle', 'silk and all sorts of lace.
Nylons from Cassidy's stretched on round thighs in the
Independent' (D, 31). The same newspaper also provides the al-
luring advertisement 'REMOVE SUPERFLUOUS HAIR', with
an accompanying image of a shapely woman, which young
Mahoney fantasises about regularly. The guilt builds steadily:
'Five sins already today, filthiness spilling five times ... five sins
a day made thirty-five in a week, they'd not be easy to confess'
(D, 31). Such descriptions were certainly not usual in 1960s
Ireland and they would quite naturally have attracted the attention of groups such as the Catholic Truth Society. The *Independent*
was largely regarded as quite a conservative publication at this
time – 'the most staid newspaper in Ireland', according to James
Cahalan[34] – and so I suppose it is no surprise that the anonymous editorial writer of the same newspaper did not shower *The
Dark* with bouquets: 'It seems to us that the novel is unreal ...
unreal in its concentration on problems within a tiny group, unreal especially in its picture of provincial Ireland today'.[35] 'Too
real' would be a better description in my view, the type of realism for which the Irish public was not prepared.

Confession is something of an ordeal for Mahoney. He
knows it is important not to omit any of his sins and yet he is
also frightened that his revelations will shock the priest. On entering the church, he observes the queues of people waiting for
'forgiveness in the listless performance of habit and duty or torturing' (D, 39). He gazes at the soft red glow of the sanctuary
lamp and feels the nervous tension of degenerates about to

---

34. James Cahalan, *Double Visions: Men and Women in Modern and
Contemporary Irish Fiction* (NY: Syracuse University Press, 1999), p 123.
35. Anon, 'Banned', editorial of the *Irish Independent*, 3 June, 1965.

unburden themselves of their sins: 'In fear and shame you are moving to the death of having to describe the real face of your life to your God in his priest and to beg forgiveness, and promise, for there is still time' (D, 40). When he finally enters the confessional and admits his 'orgies of self-abuse' (D, 40), he is subjected to the kind of interrogation his cousin will subsequently employ: Did he deliberately excite himself? Cause the seed to come? Afterwards, he feels overjoyed, 'washed clean as snow' (D, 43), but then he remembers that his father is waiting for him at the gate of the church and that he must love this man, like everybody else. Brian Liddy sees the unhealthy side of the Church's role in protecting those responsible for perpetrating abuse: 'The church, if not responsible for the molestation by Mahoney's father, is responsible for the young protagonist's inability to deal realistically with these molestations.' He notes that after confession, 'the molestations of the father cannot even be considered – because they are in direct conflict with his duty as a child of God'.[36] This is an astute reading of the type of negative religious conditioning the boy receives from an institution where patriarchal authority is affirmed at every turn. As a result, Mahoney finds it difficult to make decisions for himself and is constantly in a state of flux with regard to the state of his soul.

The preoccupation with death is omnipresent in Mahoney's mind: 'The moment of confessing would be a kind of death' (D, 40); 'The moment of death was the one real moment in life; everything took its proper position there' (D, 69); '… nothing but this drifting death from hole to hole' (D, 56) – a rather depressing but very graphic vision of existence; 'Everything is dead as dirt … I'd committed five sins since morning' (D, 31); 'The wreaths and the Mass cards and the words meant nothing, these were for the living, to obscure the starkness with images of death … images of life and love in black cloth' (D, 69). Such dark thoughts betray the disturbed psyche of a boy who is in dread of the fate that will await a sinner like him in the next life. The one great advantage of the priesthood in Mahoney's eyes is the greater chances of salvation it guaranteed: 'Death would come.

---

36. Brian Liddy, 'State and Church: Darkness in the Fiction of John McGahern', in *New Hibernia Review* 3.2 (Summer 1999), pp 106-121, p 113.

Everything riveted into that. Possession of neither a world nor a
woman mattered then, whether you could go to the Judgment
or not without flinching was all that would matter' (*D*, 83). So
when he finally goes to visit his cousin Fr Gerald, he is struck by
the proximity of the graveyard to the presbytery. He also finds it
somewhat improper that a boy of his own age, John, is keeping
house for his cousin – such a situation would certainly not arise
today. In the middle of the night, Fr Gerald comes to his room
under the pretext of discussing his vocation. He gets into bed
alongside him and starts questioning him as to why he harbours
doubts about the vocation. Through skillful manipulation, he
gets the boy to tell all in relation to his problems with masturbation. When asked if he had to face the same type of problem
when he was Mahoney's age, Fr Gerald ignores the question.
The silence fills the boy with resentment: 'he had broken down
your life to the dirt, he'd reduced you to that, and no flesh was
superior to other flesh … he was above that, you were impertin-
ent to ask' (*D*, 74). There is the added feeling of discomfort
about having a semi-naked man in bed alongside him: it reminds him of the dreaded nights with his father: 'was this to be
another of the midnight horrors with your father' (*D*, 70).
Although nothing untoward happens on this occasion, it is hard
not to feel that the priest is 'grooming' the child and that there is
at the very least a chance of subsequent abuse. Fintan O'Toole
wrote the following comments about the issues raised by *The
Dark* in the immediate aftermath of McGahern's death:

> By accurately describing the human interiors of Ireland,
> McGahern helped to alter Ireland's sense of reality. The stark-
> est example of this is the issue of child sex abuse. When it hit
> the headlines in the 1990s, it was spoken of as a stunning and
> awful revelation, a secret that hardly anyone knew. Yet it is
> there in black and white in *The Dark*, thirty years before.[37]

Broaching the topic of clerical sex child abuse was undoubtedly courageous on McGahern's part: it was also professional
suicide, however. Such issues were not up for public discussion
at the time. Throughout the novel, there is a sordid picture of

---

37. Fintan O'Toole, 'Picking the Lock of Family Secrets', in *The Irish Times*,
1 April 2006.

provincial Ireland. Mahoney's sister, Joan, is given a job in the drapery shop run by one of the most respectable families in Fr Gerald's parish, the Ryans. On his arrival to visit his sister, she tells him that 'it's worse than home' (D, 63). It transpires that Mr Ryan has been making lewd comments to her and putting his hand up her dress on occasions. On discovering this, Mahoney makes the decision that he will bring his sister home with him the following day. When he explains to his cousin what has been happening, Fr Gerald's first question is whether Mahoney confronted the Ryans with this. Mahoney says he did not, which causes the priest to say: 'For that relief much thanks at least' (D, 99). Avoidance of scandal, the maintenance of an unblemished exterior, these are what matter most to the priest. He is not going to confront Mr Ryan with his improper behaviour. When Mahoney went to visit his sister and observed the Ryan daughters playing tennis in the back garden, Mr Ryan asked him if he found them 'tempting' (D, 92). As an 'upstanding' member of the community, Ryan knows that no sanction will emanate from his treatment of Joan. When we reflect on the findings of the various reports into clerical sex abuse and the horrors inflicted on young men and women in correctional institutions a few short decades ago, we should not be overly surprised that society was complicit in the injustices visited on innocent children. Priests were far from being alone in perpetuating such abuse.

When Fr Gerald finally opens up to Mahoney about the acute need for priests and the sacredness of the calling, it is too late. The moving comments about how 'The Society influences the Word far more that the Word influences the Society' (D, 100) or the way in which the priest's life 'is a great mystery in Christ and that nothing but your state of mind can change' (D, 101), fall on deaf ears. Mahoney's mind is made up. He rescues his sister and heads home the following day. His father asks him what happened and, on being told that Ryan was interfering with Joan, he does not become enraged or announce his intention to sort the issue out once and for all. He knows the rules of the game and feels that what happened to his daughter is due to his allowing her to go to work in the shop in the first place. Escape from the constrictions of rural life seems as far away for the Mahoneys as it did for Elizabeth Reegan. Religion offers the young protagonist of *The Dark* little or no comfort and, having turned his back on a religious vocation, he works hard to secure a university scholarship. He becomes annoyed with his father for praying for success in his exam: 'Ask for Grace if you want, but don't ask him to pass the exam –'. His father calls this 'heathen rubbish!', but the son stands firm: 'No. No exam deserves the Grace of God, nobody does' (*D*, 130). When his exam results arrive and his scholarship is secured, one might expect this to be the prelude to a new and better life in university, where his adolescent fantasies and sexual liberation might be realised. But Mahoney has been greatly wounded by his father's abuse and by his subsequent paralysis when it comes to making key decisions. When news comes of a job in the ESB, he chooses it ahead of a university degree. The Civil Service provides security, but it is not exactly in keeping with Mahoney's abilities. Richard Burr Lloyd sees much pessimism in the early novels: 'Thus, McGahern's vision is still unrelieved; the darkness confronting his protagonist has not been lifted – Ireland is still a prison from which there seems little hope of escape.'[38]

There is a strong sense in which both Elizabeth Reegan and Mahoney seem to be inhabiting a 'prison', the prison of a provincial Ireland that is obsessed with a puritanical brand of Catholicism that colours people's relationships with others, their daily routine, their perception of themselves, their thoughts about the future, life after death, heaven and hell, the final judgement. Inglis traces what he describes as the 'Irish Civilising Process' and shows how a very negative attitude developed towards sexuality, one that became acute in the nineteenth century: 'The body was seen as a major source of evil', he writes, and as a result, 'Sex became problematical and privatised.'[39] *The Dark*, in particular, portrays sex in a very negative light, with its image of life as 'this drifting death from hole to hole' (*D*, 56) being typical of a tendency to associate sex with death in the early novels. Ordination to the priesthood would have the advantage of enhancing one's chances of salvation in

---

38. Richard Burr Lloyd, 'The Symbolic Mass: Thematic Resolution in the Irish Novels of John McGahern', in *The Emporia Sate Research Research Studies*, Vol XXXVI (Fall, 1987), pp 5-23, p 15.
39. Inglis, *Moral Monopoly*, p 149.

the next life: 'All your life would be death in readiness for the last moment when you'd part with your flesh and leave' (*D*, 56). Speaking of the early fiction, James Whyte notes:

> McGahern's protagonists are distinguished by their awareness of the inadequacy of the Church to give meaning to their lives. While this causes them considerable anguish, however, it does not stop them from searching for some other generalising form in which to give expression to their sense of the spiritual ...[40]

This is a useful reading, as it demonstrates that the quest undertaken by someone like Elizabeth Reegan does not depend to anything like an exclusive manner on the Church to act as an intermediary between her and God. There is also nature, the family, the strong sense of community that can bring comfort in times of need. Mahoney, perhaps because of his young age, does not possess the same insights as Elizabeth and his 'false' epiphany at the end of *The Dark* has not advanced him in any significant way on the road to self-knowledge and self-acceptance. Nor does it accord him a more acute vision of existence as something that can be determined by one's own actions or interactions with others. Walking side-by-side with his father in the Galway rain, Mahoney experiences 'a kind of happiness' that is qualified in the following manner: '... at its heart, the terror of an unclear recognition of the reality that set you free, touching you with as much foreboding as the sodden leaves falling in this day, or any cliché' (*D*, 188). One detects a fear of liberation, of assuming responsibility for his decisions, of grasping the opportunities that are presented to him, in the behaviour of Mahoney. The accommodation with his father does not strike this reader as being completely convincing, as evidenced by the following lines: 'It seemed that the whole world must turn over in the night and howl in its boredom, for the father and for the son and for the whole shoot, but it did not' (*D*, 191). There is an existential feel to this description, a desperation felt by young Mahoney at his inability to give meaning to life. This is the result of the damage inflicted upon him by the unhealthy male role-models he has encountered. Shaun O'Connell points out that 'the whole male, adult population of *The Dark* is composed of child-moles-

40. Whyte, *History, Myth and Ritual*, p 111.

ters' – the father, clerical cousin and Ryan all conform to this description. This prompts O'Connell to consider *The Dark* 'a stark
parable' in which 'All elders are killers of the dreams of youth.'[41]

Eugene McCabe admits that reading *The Dark* forty years
after first encountering its grim message reminded him of what
a seminal text it is: 'Page after page, long ago and now, I wanted
to disbelieve what I was reading, but the integrity, the painful
honesty, were inescapably believable.'[42] Considering the novel
in the light of all the revelations of sinister happenings in Ireland
committed under the cloak of religion, McCabe notes that
'Mahoney unmarried would have made an exemplary Christian
brother of the bullying, abusive type – cruel, hypocritical, proud
and monstrous, terrorising small, helpless children day after
night after day.'[43] The analogy holds water, but what is remarkable is McGahern's courage in dealing in such a forthright manner with issues that would shock, frighten, enrage and sadden a
large number of his readers. McCabe continues:

> How were we to know then that McGahern was writing
> prophetically for the thousands of children, male and female,
> locked into similar homes urban and rural, into camps and con-
> vents, for beatings, and buggery? … In fact, I think McGahern
> held back in the bed scenes with young Mahoney and his father,
> and his cousin the priest. These were scenes of sexual abuse he
> couldn't bring himself to write in graphic detail, though God
> knows a blind man could read between the lines.[44]

McCabe's reading is that of someone who lived in the Ireland
where such horrors were swept under the carpet. He is obviously
in awe of what McGahern achieved and the price he was willing
to pay for being true to his authentic, prophetic voice. It is true
that, forty years on, *The Dark* 'continues to be like a magnetic
touchstone, exposing the hidden secrets of our tribe, and our
high priests were/are more than troubled by the secrets they

41. Shaun O'Connell, 'Door into the Light: John McGahern's Ireland', in
The Massachusetts Review, no 25, Summer 1984, pp 255-68, p 260.
42. Eugene McCabe, 'The Prophesy of *The Dark*', in *The John McGahern
Yearbook*, Vol 3, pp 37-8, p 37.
43. 'The Prophesy of *The Dark*', p 37.
44. 'The Prophesy of *The Dark*', p 37.

knew and ignored'.[45] The 'high priests' were not just members of the Church – the State and laity were equally complicit in conspiring to keep these horrors under wraps. DBC Pierre reckons that McGahern 'opened a valve' when he wrote *The Dark*, 'made a puncture in certain taboos so grave that it took forty more years for them to come to full light'.[46] This is possibly why it took some time for the Irish public to warm to his message. Being unwilling, or unable, to face the reality of physical, psychological and sexual abuse in homes all over the country, people preferred to claim that McGahern was not telling things as they were. We now see that he was doing the exact opposite.

The opening period of McGahern's literary career is therefore not an uplifting one in terms of its depiction of Irish Catholicism. But neither is it as unrelentingly bleak as some commentators would have us believe. Brian Liddy makes the interesting point that the influence of the Church is 'not always one of direct repression' and he says that Elizabeth Reegan, and to a lesser extent, young Mahoney, are symptomatic of a tendency whereby 'the Irish perpetuate their own sense of religious conformity even in the face of their thorough refusal to cooperate with the institution'.[47] There is a certain ambivalence about many of McGahern's characters in that their outward conformity sometimes masks a grim determination to choose a religion that best suits their personal convictions. As his oeuvre develops, McGahern became more nuanced in his portrayal of Irish Catholicism, although the central elements remain unchanged. Even if James Whyte is correct in his assertion that *The Dark* 'depicts a society in a flux and this is the main reason for the frustration and despair of its characters' , it should be pointed out that the same 'flux' persists, though in a less obvious way, in the next two novels to which we now turn our attention, *The Leavetaking* (1974/1984) and *The Pornographer* (1979).

---

45. 'The Prophesy of *The Dark*', p 38.
46. DBC Pierre, 'Where Light Begins', in *The John McGahern Yearbook,* Vol 3, pp 40-1, p 41.
47. Liddy, 'State and Church', p 116.
48. Whyte, *History, Myth and Ritual*, p 38.

CHAPTER TWO

'From the Womb to the Grave':
Escaping from the Constraints of Religion

We have seen how in *The Barracks* and *The Dark*, McGahern presented a rather depressing picture of the negative reinforcement that religious conditioning imposed on people in the Ireland of the 1940s and 50s in particular. With *The Leavetaking* (1974 and 1984) and *The Pornographer* (1979), we reach a transitional phase in McGahern's work, one in which he tested the artistic boundaries and attempted to deal in a more positive manner with issues like sexuality and relationships. He emphasised the importance of these two novels in a revealing interview with Denis Sampson:

> To some extent, *The Leavetaking* is a flawed book, but it was actually a book I had to write, and I think that the book I have written now is my best book; that's *The Pornographer*. But I couldn't have written *The Pornographer* if I hadn't taken the risks I took with *The Leavetaking* and they were conscious risks. It was actually something I had to do, and I don't think it was altogether successful.[1]

The words used by McGahern in relation to *The Leavetaking* are important: he insists that it was a book he 'had to write', something he 'had to do' in order to progress to the next level of his writing career. Readers of his work will be aware of the fact that he rewrote significant parts of *The Leavetaking* after working on the first version with the French translator Alain Delahaye. In the Preface to the second edition, he expressed his belief that it had to be changed for the following reason: 'The crudity I was attempting to portray, the irredeemable imprisonment of the beloved in reportage, had itself become blatant. I had been too

---

1. 'A Conversation with John McGahern', in Denis Sampson (ed), *Canadian Journal of Irish Studies*, Vol 17, July 1991, pp 13-18, p 15.

close to the "Idea", and the work lacked that distance, that inner formality or calm, that all writing, no matter what it is attempting, must possess.' The subject matter of the novel, revolving around the death of the protagonist's 'beloved', his mother, in a manner that draws heavily on the circumstances and emotion surrounding the passing of Susan McGahern, was still heart-wrenching for the author as he attempted to re-enact an episode that had taken place a few decades earlier. Writing about this seminal event was a key element in his evolution as an artist, a type of catharsis or purging of the trauma it induced in the young boy and, subsequently, the man. Given his comments in the Preface, however, and his awareness of how he had become 'too close to the "Idea",' it is interesting that the first part of the novel, dealing with the death of the mother in a highly autobiographical manner, was not changed in any way. In the same interview with Sampson, McGahern said:

> I have found that the most serious mistakes I have made were when I … have drawn from life, when I have actually stuck too close to the way things happen. Very seldom have I done that, but I have found that that's where the prose is dead. The way I got sacked and the way that the sacking is described in The Leavetaking really have got nothing to do with one another.[2]

In a later interview with Rosa González, he claimed that 'all autobiographical writing is by definition bad writing unless it's strictly autobiographical'.[3] For Dermot McCarthy, such comments raise important issues:

> By this standard, assuming that the memoir is 'strictly auto-biographical', or at least not fiction, much of McGahern's fiction is 'bad writing' because, as a reading of Memoir makes clear, for much of it he 'actually [has] stuck close to the way things happen[ed]', and the description of the sacking in The

---

2. 'A Conversation with John McGahern', p 14.
3. Rosa González, 'John McGahern', [Interview] in Jacqueline Hurtley et al (eds), Ireland in Writing: Interviews with Writers and Academics (Amsterdam: Rodopi, 1998), pp 39-50, p 45.

Leavetaking, for example, is closer to the account he provides in his memoir than his remarks to Sampson suggest.[4]

Having had the opportunity to interview McGahern on three separate occasions, my own view is that one should not always take his comments literally. It is not that he tried to conceal things from his interviewers exactly; it was more a question of there being a subconscious process in train when he recounted events that were closely linked to his life, a process of which he may have been largely unaware. McCarthy acknowledges that: 'In the novel (*The Leavetaking*), McGahern appears to use only the bare details of his family history and experience, whereas thirty years later in the memoir he is more forthcoming about the emotions involved.'[5] For the purposes of this study, the main interest of *The Leavetaking* lies in its portrayal of the deep faith of the mother, the broken promise made to her by the son that he would become a priest, and the discovery of literature as a replacement vocation. The centrality of the mother is obvious from the manner in which McGahern deliberately adapts the famous quote from the Bible, 'In the beginning was the Word ... And the Word was made flesh' (John 1:1, 14), to highlight how for him Susan McGahern was the Alpha and the Omega: 'In the beginning was my mother' (*M,* 203). Therefore, the process of writing about the life and death of this woman, the 'beloved', was never going to be easy. But it was essential that it be done, because it led to the vital discovery that literature was his means of paying homage to his mother and of coming to terms with the psychological toll that this episode exacted on him. According to McCarthy, 'memory is the *pharmakon,* the 'mystery' at the heart of McGahern's narrative art'[6] and in this regard he reminds one of the French priest-writer Jean Sulivan (1913-1980) who described how he coped with the death of his own mother in his memoir, *Anticipate Every Goodbye*: 'Writing down these anecdotes, expressing ordinary feelings, which quite possibly millions of people secretly feel after seeing their own mother dying, reassures and comforts me a bit.'[7]

4. Dermot McCarthy, *John McGahern and the Art of Memory*, p 124.

5. McCarthy, *John McGahern and the Art of Memory*, p 123.

6. McCarthy, *John McGahern and the Art of Memory*, p 22.

7. Jean Sulivan, *Anticipate Every Goodbye*, trs Eamon Maher (Dublin:

The mother is the person who was responsible for imparting the gift of faith to McGahern and Sulivan; she is the person to whom they looked for comfort and guidance. The emergence of the literary vocation was a release valve for both, as it was a means of giving concrete expression to the deep feelings they had for their mothers after the two women had died. The universality of the sentiments their accounts bring to the fore serves to transcend the personal experiences they describe, to such a degree that they succeed in capturing what so many people experience in times of loss. The extent to which this testimony is completely true to the facts is of little consequence – the memory is often an unreliable mechanism for conjuring up events that happened years previously. What counts is the manner in which it resonates with the reader, how it succeeds in sharing with others an unbearable loss.

Sulivan used to visit his mother every Sunday in the little Breton village of Montauban. In his memory, all these visits merged into the one visit, every goodbye became the last goodbye. Years after his mother's death, in an attempt to relive events from the 'beloved's past, Sulivan used to walk on the path that she followed on her way to school. On seeing trees and bushes blocking his passage, he was struck by how quickly nature regains its supremacy. But, like McGahern on those Leitrim lanes that he and his mother walked when going to school, there was something about the physical surroundings that caused recollections to flood back – some sad, others blissfully happy. As a child he had been oblivious to all but his most immediate needs: 'Childhood is full of new experiences. I know that I would have difficulty giving more than a very brief sketch of my own. The adult always tries to invent what is beyond mere words. And if life doesn't allow us to hold onto or relive one day something of the fullness or emptiness of childhood ... then it is merely pretentious and sterile.'[8] McGahern would have been

Veritas, 2000), p 124. For more on the connection between Sulivan and McGahern, see my article, 'Death in the Country: An intertextual Analysis of Jean Sulivan's *Anticipate Every Goodbye* and John McGahern's *The Leavetaking*, in Eamon Maher and Grace Neville (eds), *France and Ireland: Anatomy of a Relationship* (Frankfurt: Peter Lang, 2007), pp 111-121.
8. *Anticipate Every Goodbye*, p 36.

sympathetic to such sentiments[9] and, like Sulivan, his literary quest involved gathering 'something of the fullness or empti-ness of childhood'. *The Leavetaking* was an important step in that process, as is clear from what McGahern stated in the interview with Denis Sampson:

> I would actually have stopped as a writer unless I had broken out of my own moulds in *The Leavetaking*. What is done in *The Pornographer* is basically the same thing that started in *The Leavetaking*. I think that it is more interesting now, that it is brought out of the brutal experiment and brought more into the world of manners. It couldn't have been brought into the world of manners except for *The Leavetaking*.[10]

The novel deals with the situation confronting a young male primary school teacher, Patrick Moran, who, due to an irregular marriage to an American divorcee in a registry office in London during a year's leave of absence, finds himself back in his school in Ireland where he faces certain dismissal. His wife, Isobel, can-not understand why he would lose his job for what she regards as a minor matter and finds it strange that the Catholic Church should have such an inordinate influence over the hiring and firing of teachers. Moran knows the position only too well: 'All education in Ireland was denominational. While the State paid teachers, it was the Church who hired and fired' (L, 142). As he carries out his supervisory duties in the schoolyard, he thinks back to the circumstances surrounding his decision to become a teacher, the same profession as his mother's. Teaching was viewed, at the time, as the 'second priesthood' and this compen-sated in some small way for his reneging on the promise made to his mother that he would become a priest: 'I'd never have been a teacher, I see clearly, but for my mother. Her dead world comes to life in my mind as I drift away from the classroom and out of this last day in it on a tide of memory' (L, 25). Leaving teaching was another betrayal of the conversations mother and

9. In a letter to me, McGahern expressed admiration for the memoir, but claimed that it failed to ignite fully until Sulivan began to describe the death of the mother on page 95 – the book ends on page 135.
10. 'A Conversation with John McGahern', p 16.

son had had about his future: 'The dream never changed. She would go in a black car to my ordination. It would have no white ribbons or virginal flowers but it would be fulfilment of her wedding day' (L, 27).

Reference to her wedding day provokes anger in the young man. His father, a Garda sergeant, had proposed to the teacher Kate McLaughlin and then let the engagement drag on for years. A letter containing the engagement ring he had given her announcing that she saw no point in prolonging their relationship had forced him to come immediately to her school and arrange a quick marriage in order to prevent her from pursuing her dream of becoming a nun. Patrick imagines how she must have felt the morning after the wedding when she woke up in the North Star Hotel, 'the mind already trying to change the sheets and blood and sexual suck of the night into a sacrificial marble on which a cross stood in the centre of tulips and white candles' (L, 42). Shock at the realisation of how her life has changed is palpable in this description. The son appreciates that his becoming a priest would have transformed the 'sexual suck' of her wedding night into something transcendent, the fulfilment of her dream: 'One day I would say Mass for her soul' (L, 44). The father brings about her death by his inability to control his lustful longing at what he knows is a 'dangerous time' (L, 65). They had been told after her mastectomy that another pregnancy would almost certainly have disastrous consequences for her health. Patrick imagines his mother's submissiveness: 'She turned to him: it was her duty' (L, 65). Her 'quiet fatalism' is reflected in her comment: 'One way or another it will be the will of God' (L, 65). In spite of his self-absorption, her husband knows that 'if he'd got her pregnant that neither the pleasure nor the darkness would pardon a birth and a death ...' (L, 65).

When one considers the attitude in Ireland towards sexual relations within marriage in the period before and after the Second Vatican Council, Kate's commitment to comply with her husband's sexual needs, even at such fatal cost to her own health, is not unrealistic. Doing 'her duty', conforming to the Church's teaching on sexuality which implemented a strict ban on all forms of artificial contraception, this was seen as part of the wife's remit. 'The will of God' was stronger than any terrestrial force and placing yourself in the safe hands of the Almighty was what one had to do to ensure eternal salvation. Tom Inglis argues that, 'It was through a devotion to Our Lady that women gave control of their bodies to the Holy Spirit. Sex itself became a penitential practice'.[11] Susan McGahern displayed an uncanny trust in God after it was discovered that she was pregnant with the 'cancer child' and wrote to her husband: 'I am feeling very well. Yes, I know where I stand now and so God knows best. I am sure with his help I will be quite alright … I place my trust in God knowing all will be well' (*M*, 77). Of course, as is the case with Kate in *The Leavetaking*, all was not well and the cancer returned soon after the birth, this time with lethal consequences. Patrick Moran had experienced huge relief when his mother returned from hospital after her first encounter with cancer. His joy was unbounded at the thought of having his mother all to himself for a few days: '… my beloved was home, and I was alone with my beloved' (*L*, 64). The closeness between the two is clear, which means that it would prove difficult for the son to detach himself from the religious beliefs that she held on to so firmly: 'To get her love I'd have to trot out the catechism answers that I hated' (*L*, 25). The most abhorrent to him was the placing of the father on an equal footing as the mother in terms of the love owed to him. She was the one he adored above all others, the one who introduced him to gentleness, an appreciation of nature, the fascinating world of books and learning. So we can imagine his pain as he approaches her sickbed to say a last goodbye: '"I came to say goodbye, mother", the priest had a hand on my shoulder as I bent to kiss her, and as lips touched everything was burned away except that I had to leave at once' (*L*, 71).

The pages devoted to the 'leavetaking' and subsequent death of Kate Moran are reproduced almost word for word in *Memoir*. What McGahern's exact intention was is not clear. Did he wish to say that the novel was pure autobiography or that *Memoir* contained elements of fiction? In many ways, such issues are of secondary importance. The emotion the last contact with the mother engenders in the reader is what makes this scene so

---

11. Tom Inglis, *Moral Monopoly*, p 208.

memorable. We feel the intense pain of the young boy as he drags himself away from the loving gaze of his mother; we identify with how he reproaches himself afterwards for not staying longer, for not being with the 'beloved' in her time of greatest need. As he and his siblings are transported off to the barracks where their father is stationed, along with all their possessions, the horrific prospect of being separated for eternity from his mother hits home: 'She was gone where I could not follow and I would never lay eyes again on that face I loved' (L, 76). The inequity of the situation is stark: 'She has waited for the Lord as sentinels wait for the dawn, and now she goes to the Lord; but the Lord has many servants, and I had but the one beloved' (L, 80).

The father had not even deigned to visit his wife during the final stages of her illness, saying that it would be too upsetting for him to see her in such a state, but yet he is the only one permitted to attend the funeral. The child is forced to imagine all the rituals associated with the wake and the burial. McGahern was always adept at capturing the atmosphere of Irish funerals and their importance in rural Ireland in particular. Everything follows time-honoured customs. Patrick evokes in his mind how his mother's coffin will rest on chairs beside the bed while his father and her close relations come to look on her a last time and asks: 'and why could I not kneel to look on her face a last time too' (L, 78). Then she is brought to the church: 'All night they'd leave her before the high altar, under the red sanctuary lamp, candles in tall black candlesticks about the coffin' (L, 79). Before the Mass, people would process to the coffin and leave silver coins on the table and Canon Glyn's sermon would praise the deceased in accordance with the amount of money donated. The mother is finally placed in the earth as the 'child of her cancer slept through it all by the window' (L, 81-2).

Thus ends the first part of The Leavetaking, the more satisfactory section from a literary perspective. In spite of keeping so close to the 'Idea', to the way things happened in real life, McGahern succeeded in freeing himself of a burden he had been carrying for a few decades and that was gnawing away at him. The only way to recover from what he perceived as his crass betrayal of his mother was to write about it. Dermot McCarthy makes the points that there is one significant difference between the account of the mother's death in *The Leavetaking* and *Memoir*, it being that in the novel the young boy says a final goodbye, whereas he fails to do so in the memoir: 'Perhaps this is because the novel does set out to tell a story of self-liberation, whereas the memoir sets out to construct a myth of self-recovery. Or perhaps it is further evidence that from the outset McGahern, consciously or unconsciously, used the writing of fiction to redress the incompleteness of life'.[12] I agree fully with McCarthy that there was a definite tendency on the writer's part to use fiction as a balm or therapy and that he was acutely aware of the dreadful void or 'incompleteness' at the heart of life.

The second half of *The Leavetaking* does offer a more optimistic vision of existence than anything one encounters in the earlier fiction. It opens with the line: 'One day I'd say Mass for her' (*L*, 85). The fact that Patrick Moran has got married to a divorcee in a registry office renders the chances of his ever saying Mass extremely remote. That said, there are signs that he has a different vocation, writing, which could also be a type of prayer. In addition, he appears to have found a loving partner with whom he has the chance of living a more fulfilling life. Whether or not Isobel is an adequate replacement for the departed 'beloved' is couched in doubt. She has been wounded, like Patrick, by an abusive father and yet seems free from the constraints of a strict religious upbringing. Her first marriage did not work out and she had an abortion after finding herself pregnant at a young age. When asked by Patrick if she felt guilty afterwards, she replies: 'No, I felt great' (*L*, 116). Such a carefree attitude could never be adopted by her second husband, a man who was brought up in a culture that inculcated a strong sense of sinfulness in people, especially in relation to sex: 'The true life was death in life. The sexual life was destruction; the sweet mouth, ruin. In my end was my beginning. One day I would say Mass for her' (*L*, 156).[13] The repetition of the commitment to say Mass

---

12. McCarthy, *John McGahern and the Art of Memory*, p 143.
13. Diarmuid Ferriter detects a change of attitude to such a formulaic version of religion from the start of the 1960s in Ireland: 'At the personal level, many people were also challenging their religion and rejecting teaching they regarded as conditioning them to equate flesh with sin.' *Occasions of Sin*, p 335.

for his mother serves to underline the extent to which Patrick is still controlled by the example she set, the values she imparted to him, the selfless love she bestowed on her family. James Whyte thinks that *The Leavetaking* represents a move away from McGahern's usual 'preoccupation with death and life after death', noting how 'Patrick accepts the here and now and ordinary sexual love as worthy of celebration.'[14] To illustrate this point, Whyte quotes the following observation from the novel: 'Could not the small acts of love performed with care, each normal, mysterious day, be a continual celebration, as much as the surrender of the dream of woman would allow the dubious power of the laying on of anointed hands?' (*L*, 156).

Throughout the second part of *The Leavetaking*, there is a struggle between the strong Church-dominated society which, as soon as it discovers Patrick's true marital status, will move swiftly to remove him from his post, and the possible liberation of the protagonist as a result of his dismissal and subsequent exile. The situation is far from resolved at the close of the novel, however. Patrick knows that he cannot hope to successfully fight the Church authorities. He explains to his friend Lightfoot why the trade union will not take up his case: 'If it was some sort of inefficiency they'd probably fight, but not on such a private matter as faith or morals. They'd not confront the Church in light years on such a delicate matter' (*L*, 164). His refusal to resign is based on the principle that he should not be fired just because he is 'living in sin'. He would be quite prepared to teach catechism even though he has abandoned the practice of his faith, as his personal beliefs or lack thereof would not impact on his teaching of a set syllabus. His exit interview with Fr Curry (which is another deviation from McGahern's own departure from Belgrove, when Fr Carton merely sent him a letter of dismissal) is quite amiable. The couple with whom Patrick and Isobel were staying, the Logans, had informed Patrick of the visit from the local curate the previous day to check that the returned teacher was in fact accompanied by a wife. Mr Logan turns out to be virulently anti-clerical: 'Their style's to act by stealth. Even for them it's getting dangerous to display their power too obviously' (*L*, 159). Fr Curry does not enjoy dismiss-

14. James Whyte, *History, Myth and Ritual*, p 117.

ing Patrick and in a way Patrick does not enjoy putting him in this position. Previously he had told the Headmaster, Maloney, that it was the Manager's job to sack him: 'They are having others do their dirty work for them for too long' (L, 163).

The 'old fat priest', sitting in a chair with, suggestively, a 'red electric bar between his legs' (L, 167), reminds Patrick of where his mother's dream for him could have led, and he shivers. Fr Curry cannot understand why the young man had to go and get married to a foreigner when there were 'thousands of Irish Catholic girls crying out for a husband' (L, 166), a comment that eases the tension somewhat. He tells Patrick he will pray for him and asks that the favour be returned. Throughout their interview, there is not the slightest hint of acrimony; it appears as if both men know and regret the inevitable outcome. Patrick feels emotion as he thinks once more of his mother and the way the iron beds in the family home had to be hammered apart as she lay dying in an upstairs bedroom. Now that he is abandoning the 'second priesthood' too, he thinks of her dream: 'Dressed in scarlet and white I pour wine and water into the chalice in the priest's hands on the altar' (L, 168). But then there is the thought of his new love – who, it has to be said, will never really attain the mythic status of his mother in Patrick's eyes – awaiting him in the room in Howth and he utters the following prayer: 'I would pray for the boat of our sleep to reach its morning, and see that morning lengthen to an evening of calm weather that comes through night and sleep again to morning after morning, until we meet the first death' (L, 171).

While hardly an unconditional expression of happiness, these lines do hold out some hope that love may yet win out, that Patrick may finally be able to lay to rest the ghost of his mother and live a more fulfilled life with Isobel. In 'The Image', which is McGahern's unofficial literary credo, he wrote: 'Art is an attempt to create a world in which we can live: if not long or forever, still a world of the imagination over which we can reign, and by reign I mean to purely reflect on our situation through this created world of ours, this Medusa's mirror, allowing us to see and to celebrate even the totally intolerable.'[15] In

---

15. 'The Image', in *Canadian Journal of Irish Studies*, Vol 17, July 1991, p 12.

The Leavetaking, McGahern certainly faced up to some of his demons and created a world in which he could live, a world where only through imagination could he be reunited with his 'beloved'. This may be the reason why Terence Killeen sees a hint in the final paragraph of the novel of a 'life being summed up, brought to a single moment of completion and self-realisation', in a type of cyclical process: '… the conclusion that has been reached may not, in fact, be final but may be part of a continual growth, of construction and liberation'.[16] The novel is indeed part of a continuum, of a process that will eventually lead to healing and rebirth. McGahern moved gradually away from formal religion to embrace an artistic quest which transcended any earthly concerns. As he stated in 'The Image': 'Religion, in return for the imitation of its formal pattern, promises us the Eternal Kingdom. The Muse, under whose whim we reign for a lifetime of availability, may grant us the absurd crown of Style …'[17]

There is the unavoidable feeling at the end of *The Leavetaking* that his expulsion from his teaching position has liberated Patrick. Dermot McCarthy sees *The Leavetaking* as 'an attempt to atone for a sense of wrong done, to admit guilt and receive forgiveness; on a deeper level, it is the need to recover the 'lost beloved', to shape grief into a symbol of the 'lost image'.'[18] It is hard not to think of McGahern's relationship with Catholicism in this context. When he decided to abandon the practice of the religion his mother had imparted to him, it was not a decision that he could have taken lightly. Without art, without the soothing balm of words, he would have found it extremely difficult to come to terms with a double loss, that of his mother and of the religion to which she was hugely attached. When reflecting on the impact the death of his mother exerted on him, the priest Jean Sulivan came to the conclusion that it is important to value things for what they are and not for how they are perceived:

> We are all blind, thinking that life consists of possessing material goods, holding onto this, then that, getting to know

---

16. Terence Killeen, 'Versions of Exile: A Reading of *The Leavetaking*', in *Canadian Journal of Irish Studies*, Vol 17, July 1991, pp 69-78, p 71.

17. 'The Image', p 12.

18. McCarthy, *John McGahern and the Art of Memory*, p 163.

one thing, then another, trying desperately to ignore the fact that the whole process inevitably amounts to absolutely nothing. Life isn't just a game where you have to possess and know as many things as possible. Rather, it is about reducing yourself to zero, living in a new and more authentic way.[19]

I find it illuminating to discover so many similarities between a French priest writer and his agnostic Irish counterpart. It convinces me that McGahern possessed a mind that was well-attuned to the nuances of religion. What he rejected was a certain image of an authoritarian Church that did not hesitate to intervene in the lives of people, even to the extent of trying to control their sexual activities. The following lines from Sulivan further echo McGahern's sentiments:

The priests of this time tended to talk about laws and obligations. In this way they had succeeded in transforming Christianity into something approaching a natural religion. In their eyes the rural order in which the Church still played a dominant role was an expression of the divine will. They had forgotten about freedom, without which there is no real faith.[20]

At the end of The Leavetaking, one has the feeling that the lovers may well be insulated from this religion of 'laws and obligations' and that they have attained some 'freedom'. Michael J. Toolan argues that all of McGahern's novels are about life/death struggles: 'In The Leavetaking, Patrick reaches a state in which death is diminished, kept in perspective.'[21] David Malcolm opines that 'the novel's open ending suggests that the past can be left behind and that a new departure, a leavetaking, is possible'.[22] Most commentators agree that there is a positive feel to the concluding lines of the novel and that this is imputable to Patrick Moran's facing up to the death of his mother and his move away from the religious beliefs of his past.

19. *Anticipate Every Goodbye*, p 114.
20. *Anticipate Every Goodbye*, p 52.
21. Michael J. Toolan, 'John McGahern: The Historian and the Pornographer', in *Canadian Journal of Irish Studies*, No 7, December 1981, pp 39-55, p 50.
22. David Malcolm, *Understanding John McGahern*, p 60.

However, Richard Burr Lloyd does not concur: 'Patrick flees from his responsibility to his mother, and thus, his country. And while his leavetaking may temporarily lift the shadows from his own life, McGahern's vision is still unrelieved: Ireland is still imagined as a world lost.'[23] When one considers McGahern's work in blocks, an approach I find useful, with *The Leavetaking* and *The Pornographer* as his experimental phase, the reading of the latter novel supports Burr Lloyd's assertion that Ireland is still presented 'as a world lost' in *The Leavetaking*, but one that is being exposed to the winds of change in a dramatic manner. Our treatment of his next novel will now attempt to show the extent to which Irish society was changing.

The Pornographer contains many passages of rich philosophical insight that achieve a universal application and resonance and it is the novel that is perhaps the most 'optimistic' of the two early periods of McGahern's oeuvre. This may not sit easily with the theory that has been developed by Raymond Mullen, who sees it as an 'existential' novel.[24] The two need not necessarily be mutually exclusive, however, even if existentialism tends to be associated with solitude, dissatisfaction with the human condition, and a failure to find any worthwhile replacement for God in the quest to give meaning to existence. In this regard, some comments by Jean-Paul Sartre are helpful. The French philosopher most strongly associated with developing the theory of existentialism argued in *L'Existentialisme est un humanisme* (1967) that it made things very awkward for the existentialist if God did not exist, because without God or a belief in a transcendent being, Man would find himself alone, abandoned, without any safety net. The only way out of this dilemma was to take responsibility for one's freedom and to give meaning to one's actions. Existentialism was not a simple form of atheism which had as its goal the desire to prove that God did not exist:

Rather, it (existentialism) maintains that even if God existed,

---

23. Richard Burr Lloyd, 'The Symbolic Mass', p 19.
24. "The Womb and the Grave': Living, Loving and Dying in John McGahern's *The Pornographer* and Albert Camus' *L'Étranger*', in Eamon Maher, Eugene O'Brien and Grace Neville (eds), *Reinventing Ireland Through a French Prism* (Frankfurt am Main: Peter Lang, 2007), pp 229-243.

nothing would change – such is our point of view. Not that we believe that God exists, but we think that the problem has really nothing to do with his existence. Man must find himself on his own and accept that no external force can save him from himself, even if someone were to come up with a valid proof of the existence of God. In this sense, existentialism is an optimistic philosophy, a doctrine which promotes action, and it is merely bad faith and a confusion of their own anguish with ours, that causes Christians to paint us as depressed and desperate human beings.[25]

You may think that we have strayed a long way from the preoccupations of John McGahern at this stage, but it is my contention that *The Pornographer* was in many ways his attempt at writing a European novel, one that would explore the solitary plight of a young man who struggles to give meaning to his existence. It is noticeable that the usual religious reference points are largely absent from this novel. Mention of the Mass, or family prayer, the sacraments, pictures of the Sacred Heart, are all remarkable for their absence for the most part. (There is a brief reference to the character's duties as an altar boy during his youth in the West of Ireland, but very few of the normal reflections on the important role Catholicism played in his life.) Instead, we have a young man, possibly a development of Mahoney from *The Dark*, who makes a living from writing pornography. His personal life consists of roaming around the dance halls of Dublin in search of women and sex. Because of a failed relationship which left him emotionally scarred, he describes himself as 'dead of heart' (P, 13).[26] In the indifference he displays to the

---

25. Jean-Paul Sartre, *L'Existentialisme est un humanisme* (Paris: Les Éditions Nagel, 1967), p 95. (My translation.)
26. This description comes as a result of the pornographer's shock at his dispassionate reaction to the visit he and his uncle make to the hospital to see his seriously ill aunt. It was she and her brother who raised the protagonist after the death of his parents and he is extremely attached to both of them. Nevertheless, he observes: 'Our last conscious moment was the moment when our passing non-existence and our final one would marry. It seemed felicitous that our going out of life should be as similarly arranged as our coming in' (P, 13). He feels shame at the violence of his reflections and notes that 'the dead of heart can afford to be violent' (P, 13).

consequences of his actions, he recalls Meursault, Camus's hero or anti-hero from *The Outsider*. McGahern admitted to me his admiration for this book, which he described as 'probably Camus's best novel'.[27] I think a brief comparison of Camus's masterpiece and *The Pornographer* may serve as a means of demonstrating the extent to which McGahern could be said to have produced an existential novel.

The Outsider is set in Camus's native Algiers and begins with the famous lines: 'Mother died today. Or maybe yesterday, I don't know.'[28] Meursault, who narrates the story in the first person, subsequently kills an Arab on a beach under a blazing sun and will be judged a monster because of his failure to demonstrate adequate remorse at his mother's funeral. His crime will be portrayed as being consistent with the character of a man who buries his mother with a heart of stone. What readers are made to realise is that Meursault is merely someone who cannot feign emotions he does not feel. During the vigil for his mother in the mortuary of the old folks home where she spent the final days of her life, a number of the inmates join him: 'For a moment I had the ridiculous impression that they were there to judge me' (*O*, 15). As it transpires, they were. After the murder, all his actions during the funeral are parsed and analysed. He is criticised for not knowing his mother's age, for smoking in the presence of her corpse, for falling asleep during the vigil, for meeting a young woman, Marie, with whom he attends a comic film before they return to his apartment where they have sex a mere twenty four hours after the burial.

In the Afterword he added to an updated edition of the book, Camus noted: 'In our society any man who doesn't cry at his mother's funeral is liable to be condemned to death' (*O*, 118). He contended that Meursault is condemned 'because he doesn't play the game. In this sense, he is an outsider to the society in which he lives, wandering on the fringe, on the outskirts of life, solitary and sensual' (*O*, 118). This description of Meursault

27. Maher, *From the Local to the Universal*, p 151.
28. Albert Camus, *The Outsider*, trs Joseph Laredo (London/New York: Penguin Modern Classics, 1983), p 9. All future references will be to this edition, denoted in brackets as O, followed by the page number.

bears strong resemblances to McGahern's nameless pornographer. They both seem incapable of playing the game by the rules of 'respectable' society. As a result, they are ostracised, marginalised, treated as pariahs. Non-compliance with the accepted norms, a refusal to act in a manner that is acceptable to the dominant ideology causes them untold problems.

The pornographer is shown to be a callous manipulator of women. After writing about the exploits of Mavis and the Colonel, the two sexual athletes of his pornographic writing, the young man goes out in search of a suitable partner to assuage his lust: 'Everywhere now there was the sense of the fair and the hunt and the racecourse, the heavy excitement of preying and vulnerable flesh, though who were the hunters and who the prey was never clear' (P, 31). He happens upon a thirty-eight year old bank official, Josephine, whom he describes as 'a wonderful healthy animal' (P, 34). They have sex and embark on a relationship which for him is purely sexual but which assumes more heightened significance for Josephine when she becomes pregnant as a result of her not allowing him to use a condom, which in her view 'turns the whole thing into a kind of farce' (P, 56). The pornographer tells her that her being pregnant changes nothing in their relationship, that she should consider having an abortion, that he will help her arrange one and pay for it if that is what she wants. (McGahern was straying into very dangerous territory here – he was writing openly not merely about contraception, but also about abortion in a novel which, strange to say, was never banned in Ireland.) Josephine is horrified by his cold indifference (a trait he shares with Meursault), his lack of feeling for the unborn child she is carrying, but she holds on to the hope that with time he will come round to the idea – a hope that is never fulfilled. Interspersed throughout the narrative are a number of philosophical musings such as the following:

> The womb and the grave ... The christening party becomes the funeral, the shudder that makes us flesh becomes the shudder that makes us meat. They say that it is the religious instinct that makes us seek the relationships and laws in things. And in between there is time and work, as passing time, and killing time, and lessening time that'd lessen anyhow ... (P, 30).

The seamless manner in which we move from the cycle of life to consideration of the religious instinct is a departure for McGahern. At times, it seems as though he is attempting to come to grips with a number of issues from his personal life in this novel. He compares an orgasm to death: 'Death must sometimes come in the same way, the tension leaving the body, in pain and not in this sweetness and pride, but a last time, the circle completed ...' (P, 57). Throughout the narrative, we are confronted with a host of metaphysical questions which are rarely answered. It appears as though we are being asked to supply our own answers to issues of supreme importance. Throughout, men and women seem incapable of communicating their feelings to one another: 'We had shared nothing but pleasure, and no two people's pleasure can be the same at the same time for long, the screw turned tighter till it had to be forced on the wrong threads' (P, 88). Love is linked to pain, loss and futility: 'Having drunk from the infernal glass we call love and knowing we have lived our death, we turn to love another way, in the ordered calm of each thing counted and loved for its impending loss' (P, 97). McGahern's pornographer is shown in a different light when he is in the company of his aunt and uncle who encircle him with the warm glow of their love. We will also see how he adopts a different attitude when he encounters and falls in love with Nurse Brady.

For the purposes of the comparison I want to make with Camus's Meursault, it is noticeable that the latter never indulges in long reflections of the type we have outlined above. Denis Sampson points to 'McGahern's continuing preoccupations with metaphysical doubt and the passage of time, and their undermining effects on conventional ways of describing reality'[29] in *The Pornographer*. In *The Outsider*, Camus explores similar issues through the experiences of a man who finds himself face to face with the prospect of eternity. Meursault is a child of nature, a man who is receptive to bodily pleasures, who likes the feel of the sun on his back, swimming in the ocean, observing passers-by from the balcony of his apartment in the city. He appreciates the smell of Marie's hair, the bright colours of the dresses she

---

29. Sampson, *Outstaring Nature's Eye*, p 138.

wears and he enjoys making love to her. Communicating his feelings is not his strong point, however. On being asked one evening by Marie if he would like to marry her, he replied that he didn't mind if that was what she wanted. She then asked him if he loved her: 'I replied as I had done once already, that it didn't mean anything but that I probably didn't' (*O*, 44). Marie's reaction to this far from ringing endorsement was to state that Meursault was 'peculiar, that that was probably why she loved me but that one day I might disgust her for the very same reason' (*O*, 45). The primary attraction Marie holds for Meursault is sexual, just as the pornographer feels little more than lust for Josephine, but both are remarkable for their lack of dissemblance as to their true feelings. Camus's Afterword underlines how Meursault, 'refuses to hide his feelings and society immediately feels threatened' (*O*, 118-9).

The discomfort Meursault's attitude evokes is brought into sharp focus in his dealings with the examining magistrate. The latter brandishes a crucifix and asks Meursault if he believes in God. On discovering that he doesn't, the magistrate sits down indignantly: 'He told me it was impossible, that all men believed in God, even those who wouldn't face up to him' (*O*, 68). Had he pretended to be moved by the image of Jesus on the cross, it is likely that Meursault could have avoided the death sentence. Under French law in Algeria, an Arab did not enjoy the same rights as a *pied-noir*, or person of French lineage such as Meursault. It is thus likely that a positive report from the examining magistrate would have gone a long way towards ensuring his acquittal. As it is, he alienates the one person whose favour he should have secured at all costs. The extent to which he has disappointed the magistrate is obvious from his comment: 'I have never seen a soul as hardened as yours. The criminals who have come to me before have always wept at the sight of this symbol of suffering' (*O*, 69). The fact that Meursault does not break down and cry at the sight of the crucifix, or that he will not declare a belief in God, singles him out as a monster who must pay the ultimate price for his wrongdoing.

In their reactions to their 'crimes' (in technical terms, the pornographer does not commit any crime), Camus's and McGahern's protagonists display analogous traits. Neither considers he has committed a sin, as this theological concept is viewed by them as merely an extension of society's control over people. The term has no real meaning for them, as they do not believe in the existence of God. If they did possess this religious faith, they might see in the acknowledgement of their wrongdoing the possibility of being granted grace and forgiveness. They find themselves alienated and despised because of their lack of religious scruples. The pornographer travels to London to join Josephine after the birth of their child, whom he refuses to see, and is beaten up by Michael Kavanagh, Josephine's friend and protector. The beating has a cathartic effect and he finds himself, significantly, on the steps of a church, from which point he observes:

> … I was extraordinarily happy, the whole night and its lights and sounds passing in an amazing clarity that was yet completely calm, as if a beautiful incision had been made that separated me from the world and still left me at pure ease in its still centre (P, 229).

Meursault has a similar experience, as he is being driven back to his cell after the court case:

> In the darkness of my mobile prison I rediscovered one by one, as if rising from the depths of my fatigue, all the familiar sounds of a town that I loved and of a certain time of day when I sometimes used to feel happy. The cries of the newspaper sellers in the languid evening air, the last few birds in the square, the shouts of the sandwich sellers, the moaning of the trams high in the winding streets of the town and the murmuring of the sky before darkness spills over onto the port, all these sounds marked out an invisible route which I knew so well before going into prison (O, 93).

In the case of both men, this heightened perception serves as a consolation at a time when their lives are in turmoil. Meursault will soon receive the news that he is to die by having his head severed by the guillotine, whereas the pornographer will return to Dublin to discover that his beloved aunt has passed away. The telegram that arrived before he travelled to London could have brought news of a death or a birth. Now both events have taken place and he finds himself back in his native village mourning the passing of a woman whose strength and fortitude in the face of illness had greatly impressed her nephew. The trip west for the funeral provides another moment of enlightenment as the pornographer recognises that he has been an active agent in his own problems: 'By not attending, by thinking any one thing was as worth doing as any other, by sleeping with any-body who'd agree, I had been the cause of as much pain and confusion and evil as if I had actively set out to do it. I had not attended properly' (P, 251). He resolves to change his ways and 'to follow the instinct for the true' (P, 252). In order to do this, he plans to return to live in this place with Nurse Brady, if she will agree to marry him. Driving back to Dublin with his disillus-ioned confidant, Maloney, the pornographer feels the urge to pray: 'The prayers could not be answered, but prayers that can-not be answered need to be the more completely said, being their own beginning as well as end' (P, 252). Writing, too, seems to be a cure, a form of prayer. Denis Sampson says of this scene: 'The need to pray, to believe in a vision that is its own "begin-ning as well as end" is as much a poetic as a religious instinct, both reflecting the need to find "the truth" beyond the isolated self'.[30]

Meursault's encounter with the chaplain before his execution also has a therapeutic effect. Once more, the criminal must en-dure talk of God and his love for all those who have sinned. The chaplain cannot accept how a condemned man might not see the prospect of divine forgiveness as a comfort: 'I know how the suffering oozes from these stones', he says. 'I've never looked at them without a feeling of anguish. But deep in my heart I know that even the most wretched among you have looked at them and seen a divine face emerging from the darkness' (O, 113). At this point, something snaps in Meursault and he unleashes all his frustrations on the chaplain, telling him that he knows noth-ing about life, that he has been living as a dead man, never having known what it is like to make love to a woman. Everyone was condemned to die at some stage, so what difference did it make that this eventuality should happen sooner rather than later? At

30. Sampson, *Outstaring Nature's Eye*, p 157.

this moment, he thinks of his mother and realises how, so close to death, she 'must have felt liberated and ready to live her life again' (O, 117). Similarly, Meursault now feels ready to live his life again: 'As if this great outburst of anger had purged all my ills, killed all my hopes, I looked up at the mass of signs and stars in the night sky and laid myself open for the first time to the benign indifference of the world' (P, 117). Patrick McCarthy attaches great significance to this passage:

> So the experience of oneness marks not merely that death is near and that some kind of truth or harmony has been attained. Meursault does not develop this theme and the lyrical vein is less strong than in the earlier passages. Moreover, he ends on a note of dualism, because he imagines himself going to the guillotine amidst the cries of hatred. However, the special insight into his condition which he expresses in these last pages is linked with the moment of oneness.[31]

Raymond Mullen correctly points out that both Meursault and the pornographer 'are open to metaphysical insights precisely because they are not convinced or practising Christians with a wealth of doctrine and dogma upon which they can comfortably rely'. He quotes Terry Keefe's French Existentialist Fiction: Changing Moral Perspectives (1984) which points out that Meursault's insights are interesting precisely for the manner in which they are presented in marked contrast to Christian dogma.[32] All this conforms to Sartre's already quoted theory whereby Man must find his own way in the world, aware of the fact that in the absence of an all-loving God one must give meaning to one's existence through one's actions. There are obviously massive differences between Camus's pagan Meursault and McGahern's protagonist. The latter, while solitary and prone to introspection, does at least have one friend, Maloney, and a loving aunt and uncle. He also has the possibility of living a fulfilled life with the nurse, for whom he has deep feelings. It is remarkable how differently he feels about sex with her than with Josephine:

---

31. Patrick McCarthy, Albert Camus: The Stranger (Cambridge: CUP, 1966), p 77.
32. Mullen, "The Womb and the Grave", p 235.

This body (the nurse's) was the shelter of the self. Like all walls and shelters it would age and break and let the enemy in. But holding it now was like holding glory, and having held it once was to hold it – no matter how broken and conquered – in glory still, and with the more terrible tenderness (*P*, 177).

There is a spiritual quality to what is described here, a feeling of awe at the beauty revealed when he is holding the nurse in his arms. Meursault never appears to have anything approaching this type of revelation, the unique discovery of the transcendent in the female body. The feeling is made all the more intense by the fact that shortly beforehand the pornographer and the nurse had passed beneath the window of the ward in which his sick aunt was lying: 'I thought how one day my wheel would turn into her section, and I would lie beneath that window while a man and woman as we were now went past into the young excitement of a life that might seem without end in this light of the moon' (*P*, 172). Death is a constant in McGahern's writing and his reflections on the human condition, its fragility and transience, the stoicism of many of his characters, mostly female, when faced with the prospect of eternity (or of extinction – it is never explicitly stated what fate awaits them after death), give his work an existential quality. In this regard, he shares some common ground with Camus. However, given their differing backgrounds and training, it was natural that they should approach certain issues in a contrasting manner. Yet there are enough shared preoccupations to allow one to draw a fruitful comparison, which I hope is what has been achieved.

Dermot McCarthy states that '*The Pornographer* explores the hollowness – emotional, moral and spiritual – that follows the loss of meaning brought on by despair'.[33] Towards the end of the novel, some easing of the desolation and despair is evident as the pornographer listens to a classic comment made by Cyril, his aunt's husband: 'Ah yes … when you think of it, life's a shaky venture' (*P*, 247). It is natural not to 'think' too much about the precarious nature of life: if we did, it could prevent us from getting on with the business of living. The pornographer

33. McCarthy, *John McGahern and the Art of Memory*, p 181.

sees how people hide behind ceremonies in order to mask their own unease: 'We master the darkness with ceremonies: of delight at being taken from the darkness into this light, of regret on the inevitable leaving of the light, hope as founded on the social and as firm as the theological rock' (*P*, 238).

When I questioned McGahern about the relatively calm reaction evoked by a novel like *The Pornographer* in the Ireland of 1979 and what that said about the evolution of Irish society in the intervening period, he replied that people had become more 'sophisticated', that the public had 'learned to ignore the novel rather than to ban it!'[34] The very title of the novel was provocative, almost an attempt to show the Censorship Board what a real 'dirty book' was like and how *The Dark* should never have been placed in that category in the first place. It contains several passages of crude pornography, complete with foul language, and it graphically describes the sexual acts engaged in by the insatiable Mavis Carmichael and Colonel Grimshaw. In McGahern's own words:

> *The Pornographer* was a deliberate attempt to see could sex be written about. The reason that the main character is so uninteresting is that this obsession with sexuality is enervating. He falls into that disease, which is a very Irish malaise, that since all things are meaningless it makes no difference what you do, and best of all is to do nothing.[35]

The pornographer is indeed a rather indifferent individual who allows things to develop without thought for the possible consequences. His relationship with his editor, Maloney, a disillusioned romantic, a poet who finds himself tricked into marriage when his girlfriend thinks she's pregnant, demonstrates perspicacity when it comes to writing. He offers the pornographer the following advice: 'Above all the imagination requires distance … It can't function close up' (*P*, 21). In this, he is McGahern's mouthpiece and the link is even more obvious in another comment he makes: 'And be careful not to let life in. Life for art is about as healthy as fresh air is for a deep-sea diver' (*P*, 129). How plausible it is for a peddler of pornographic maga-

---

34. Maher, *From the Local to the Universal*, p 148.
35. Maher, *From the Local to the Universal*, p 149.

zines to be coming up with such insights into the literary process is questionable, but Maloney's disillusionment with the way he was ridiculed for writing poetry as a young man has taught him the importance of separating the personal from art in so far as possible. Surprisingly, he tells his friend that he should take his medicine and marry Josephine when she gets pregnant, just as he himself did some years previously in similar circumstances. He seems to harbour a desire to bring Ireland into the twentieth century and reduce everything to its most basic level. As he says to his bemused friend: 'Ireland wanking is Ireland free. Not only wanking but free. Not only free but wanking as well' (P, 25). On their way back to Dublin from the aunt's funeral, he rails against the pious religiosity he sees all around him:

> 'Look at today – isn't the whole country going around in its coffin! But show them a man and a woman making love – and worst of all enjoying it – and the streets are full of "Fathers of eleven", "Disgusted" and the rest of them. Haven't I been fighting it for the past several years, and giving hacks like you employment into the bargain' (P, 249).

For all his foul-mouthed profanities, Maloney captures certain attitudes that were prevalent in relation to sex in 1960s and 1970s Ireland. The winds of change were blowing across the country and the voices of dissent would not be silenced for much longer. Tom Inglis sees a close connection between Irish attitudes to sex and Church teaching:

> The Church was the authority on sexuality. Sex was a viper which operated in society. Lust and passions led to occasions of sin during which people could become possessed with evil desires. Sex was the problematic side of love. Chastity, modesty and purity were the natural allies of love. Sex was something which could enhance married love, but could destroy it, like it could other relationships. Outside marriage it was best kept at bay through the diligent institution of forms of external control and internal self-restraint. Sex was seen as a potential threat not just to the health, welfare and sanity of the individual, but to social order as a whole.[36]

---

36. Tom Inglis, *Lessons In Irish Sexuality* (Dublin: UCD Press, 1998), pp 38-9.

Diarmuid Ferriter quotes the following portrait of the Irishman's view of his wife from Donald Connery's book, *The Irish* (1968):

> ... a kingsize hot water bottle who also cooks his food and pays his bills and produces his heirs. In the intimate side of marriage he behaves as if he were slightly ashamed of having deserted his male friends and bachelorhood. He takes what should be the happy, leisurely lovemaking of marriage like a silent connubial supper of cold rice pudding. A rapid sex routine is effected as if his wife is some stray creature with whom he is sinning and hopes he may never see again.[37]

Such attitudes are at a serious remove from those encountered in *The Pornographer*. Josephine, who to all outward appearances seems to be a good Catholic girl, declares repeatedly that she doesn't feel at all guilty after sex. On one occasion, when in the throes of passion, she declares: 'This is what I needed. This-is-what-I-need-ed' (*P*, 39). The recourse to condoms is frequent in the novel and there are several quite explicit descriptions of oral sex and intercourse. I therefore cannot understand how the novel could have been 'ignored', as McGahern playfully suggested in the interview already cited. As so often happened, the novelist was ahead of his time in bringing to the fore issues that were pertinent at the time. He highlights the emptiness of sex without love, the yearning of the human spirit for union with another. Throughout the novel also, we encounter those moments when the pornographer sees into the heart of things. Walking in the city after a visit to his aunt, one of these occurs:

> And without any desire for meaning, in the same way as I had been surprised at her bedside, I sometimes felt meaning in this crowded solitude. That all had a purpose, that it had to have, the people coming and going, the ships tied up along the North Wall, the changing delicate lights and ripples of the river, the cranes and building, lights of shops, and the sky through a blue haze of smoke and frost (*P*, 62-3).

While not in the same league as his evocations of the landscape of his native Leitrim, this evocation of the city as an agent

---

37. Cited in Ferriter, *Occasions of Sin*, p 336.

of revelation is quite successful. Some of the most intense emotions are experienced while in the company of his aunt or after
having visited her. He is kind to this woman, brings brandy to
her in the hospital, as she claims it is the only thing gives her relief from the pain. He remembers the love she bestowed on him,
the shared memories: 'On many frozen evenings such as this she
and I used to go to Lenten Devotions, down the hill and to the
left up Church Street, and stand at the back of the cold, near-
empty church' (P, 60). After she is discharged from hospital, he
sees from her 'racked flesh' that 'it was little more than pure
spirit she was living on' (P, 121). It is evident to her nephew that
she just wants to be back in her own house, surrounded by
familiar faces and objects: 'I gathered that the place in eternity
she most hungered for was a half-mile down the abandoned
railway among the growing things in the garden' (P, 121).

The role of place is central to McGahern's artistic quest. He
sees the extent to which landscape, both physical and moral,
leaves its imprint on people, sculpts their character, shapes their
outlook on, and approach to, life. The pornographer is drawn
back to his rural roots little by little, as it dawns on him that the
possibilities for self-fulfilment will not be realised through
mindless sex and meaningless writing. The pull of the area in
which he grew up was carefully cultivated by his uncle when he
went to stay for a few days with his aunt. The uncle had outlined the benefits he would acquire from leaving the city and
reverting to the life of a farmer. His home place has a charming
allure now that he has experienced life far from its beauty and
calm. His uncle, who understands his nephew better than one
might think, keeps the idea firmly in the young man's head:
'"After all, the city is more a young man's place", he must have
repeated several times' (P, 147).

His aunt's death also brings to light the transience of life. She
cannot bear the thought of leaving her garden, her ordinary life
and her good-for-nothing husband, Cyril: 'It doesn't seem much
to ask', she says. 'To let things stay as they are. To go on' (P, 143).
Comments such as these remain with her nephew, as he con-
templates how he has been wasting his time on inconsequential
things. In the country he would have access to the wisdom and
support of his uncle, as well as the opportunity to lead a more

meaningful life with a partner, if she will have him. His aunt's fierce struggle to hold on to life shows him that it must have something to recommend it: 'I don't know. It's only after years that you get some shape on things, and then after all that you have to leave. It's comical. You want to go on and you can't', she says (P, 144). The pornographer is the first of McGahern's characters to voluntarily return to their rural roots. After this, the novels never leave the country.

David Malcolm notes that the pornographer is 'marked by a lack of belief in any God', but that 'there are other aspects of the narrator's character besides those of an emotionally dead atheist who has little time for other human beings'.[38] In spite of its powerful evocation of anguish and despair, there are places in the novel where something spiritual is glimpsed. We have already noted the narrator's belief that it is 'the religious instinct that makes us seek the relationships and laws in things' (P, 30). Rüdiger Imhof sees in this statement an illustration of how, 'The superstitious, the poetic, the religious are all secure within the social context, given a tangible form. The darkness is pushed out. All things become interrelated.'[39] In the case of the pornographer, I would maintain that his creative and analytical traits provide him with the capacity to see hidden meanings in the morass that is human existence. While there is a marked absence of any traditional religious customs and practice in The Pornographer, there are also elements that point to a belief in the transformative power of art and the healing power of love. The spire is more hidden than completely occluded in this instance.

The experimental phase of McGahern's career brought some aspects of his inner life into sharper focus. He was obsessed with memory and with its capacity to nurture his artistic quest, a quest that assumes more and more the appearance of a spiritual need to share with readers thoughts and experiences that resonate with their own experiences of anger and despair. Confessional and existential, these two novels branch into areas previously not touched on by McGahern and they reveal a man

38. Malcolm, Understanding John McGahern, p 87.
39. Rüdiger Imhof, The Modern Irish Novel: Irish Novelists after 1945 (Dublin: Wolfhound Press, 2002), p 225.

whose scepticism in relation to organised religion did not prevent him from looking for something akin to religious comfort
through his art. It was his way of living out his unending quest
for the right word, the correct image, the authentic tone that
would make him the accomplished writer he became.

CHAPTER THREE

'Getting Through' the 'Night(lines)' to reach 'High Ground': Catholicism in the Short Stories

McGahern is rightly considered a supremely gifted short story writer. Because of the brevity of this genre, each word needs to be chosen carefully and woven into the fabric of the text. It is a form that lends itself to rewriting and reshaping, tasks to which McGahern always applied himself with zeal. Those familiar with the novels will recognise some of the themes favoured by McGahern in the stories: disillusionment with a seemingly meaningless existence, problematic relationships between fathers and sons, family and community tensions, failed love affairs, death and eternity, emigration, the contrast between city and country. The three original collections – *Nightlines* (1970), *Getting Through* (1978) and *High Ground* (1985) – were brought together in a slightly revised form, with the addition of the classic 'The Country Funeral', in *The Collected Stories* (1992). Then, shortly after the author's death in 2006, *Creatures of the Earth* was published with the inclusion of two previously unpublished stories, 'Creatures of the Earth' and 'Love of the World'. Significantly, this posthumous volume did not contain the highly regarded 'Peaches' and some other stories. An indication of the esteem in which McGahern was held as a short story writer can be gauged by a review of *Nightlines* that appeared in the *New York Times Book Review* which provided the following assessment: 'He is his own master, and his stories owe nothing to anybody.'[1]

While he certainly brought his own unique stamp to short story writing, McGahern was more than a little aware of the contribution of some notable predecessors such as Joyce, Chekhov and Tolstoy. In a detailed essay on *Dubliners*, for example, McGahern singled out attributes that could apply to his own work: 'In *Dubliners* there is no self-expression; its truth is in

---

1. Cited in Sampson, *Outstaring Nature's Eye*, p 85.

every phrase'; 'The prose never draws attention to itself except at the end of 'The Dead' and by then it has been earned'; 'Joyce does not judge. His characters live within the human constraints in space and time and within their own city. The quality of the language is more important than any system of ethics or aesthetics. Material and form are inseparable. So happy is the union of subject and object that they never become statements of any kind, but in their richness and truth are representations of particular lives – and all of life'.[2] These comments say as much about McGahern's own literary philosophy as they do about Joyce's. He was completely committed to developing a careful, chiseled style, a style that never 'draws attention to itself' and its simplicity can mask the craft that went into its composition. I have already commented on the antipathy McGahern displayed towards judging his characters and their behaviour, another trait he shared with Joyce, but his concentration on the 'particular' allowed him, like Joyce, to capture something of universal significance, 'all of life'.[3]

This chapter will examine the manner in which Catholicism is portrayed in the short stories, as well as exploring the important and sometimes hazardous intersection between Catholicism and Protestantism in provincial Ireland: McGahern's own encounter with a local Protestant family, the Moroneys, exerted a significant influence on his youth and literary vocation, as we shall see. I have decided to concentrate on three key themes which encapsulate the complexity of the writer's somewhat paradoxical stance on Catholicism, summarised in the following manner by Declan Kiberd: 'The Catholic Ireland of his youth offered little by way of aesthetic experience, except through the sights, sounds and smells of the Mass or benediction, May altars or Easter rituals ... Irish Catholicism had declined from its pre-Famine gaiety into a rule-bound set of practices, scruples and interdictions; and McGahern ... knew the full wrath of such a raw, overweening authority'.[4] He had especial reason to resent the 'overweening authority' of the Catholic Church, but he man-

---

2. John McGahern, 'Dubliners', in *The Canadian Journal of Irish Studies*, Vol 17, No 1, July 1991, pp 31, 36.
3. My book, *John McGahern: From the Local to the Universal*, explores this dimension of his work in some detail.
4. Declan Kiberd, 'Introduction' to *Love of the World*, p xv.

aged to transcend such shortsightedness and bigotry in his fair and balanced portrayal of the religion of his birth.

Unlearning the Lessons of Youth
In many of McGahern's stories, the characters are forced to confront the religious lessons they gathered as children with the sometimes cruel realities of the world. Occasionally this occurs during childhood itself, but irrespective of when it happens, it is always a rude awakening. The exchange between the two men, Gillespie and Boles, in 'Why We're Here' is symptomatic of the meanness and rivalry that can dominate relationships in rural Ireland. The false concern they display for one another does not mask their underlying malevolence, but they find common ground when they evoke the memory of their former Protestant neighbour, Sinclair, recently spotted in Amiens Street in a rather dilapidated state. Sinclair had converted to Catholicism in order to marry a local woman, a decision that did nothing to improve his view of the female character: *'As good to engage a pig in serious conversation as a woman. All candles were made to burn before the high altar of their cunts. It was no rush of faith, let me tell you good sir, that led to my conversion. I was dragged into your Holy Roman Catholic Apostolic Church by my male member'* (CE, 15-6. Italics in original). This vulgar – yet in some ways, comic – outburst sums up the resentment of a man whose lust led to his economic – and perhaps, moral – downfall. The conversion, because it was motivated by desire rather than any religious conviction, led to resentment of what he had lost. The image of the candles burning 'before the high altar of their cunts' is emblematic of Sinclair's jaundiced view of women. He was brought under the control of the Catholic Church as a result of the urges of his 'male member', and after that moment he was on a downward spiral.

Gillespie and Boles appreciate the colourful manner in which Sinclair describes his predicament. They are not sympathetic to his plight, however, believing him to have been misguided in his sacrifice of a comfortable way of life for the sake of a woman.

Throughout the various short story collections, sexuality is problematic. Characters either take their relationships with others for granted until it's too late and they lose their partners, or else the perverse nature of certain people's sexual preferences is revealed to them. The stories illustrate that the influence of the Catholic Church did not prevent people from thinking about, or engaging in sexual activity. Warnings encountered in the Penny Catechism are quickly forgotten when lust takes hold.

'Lavin' is a particularly disturbing tale about a man whose tranquil life changes drastically after he has sex with a gypsy girl. The one-time handsome, diligent young man, who had inherited his uncle's farm and showed no interest in girls or alcohol, suddenly starts drinking heavily and ends up in trouble after becoming embroiled with the gypsy. The latter's family, on discovering the affair, demand money from him and the cunning publican Billy Burns supplies the finance in return for Lavin's farm, Willowfield. Afterwards, he is left destitute and becomes a figure of fascination and repulsion in the local community. Young children are warned to stay away from him, but the 'attraction of what's forbidden' (CE, 52) propels the narrator to speak to him. Immediately, Lavin questions him about the sexual maturation of his sisters: 'Those sisters of yours are growing into fine sprigs. Have you looked to see if any of them have started a little thatch?' (CE, 52) He urges the boy to 'keep your eyes skinned' (CE, 52) and to report anything he has seen back to him. Repulsed, the boy resolves to avoid Lavin at all costs in the future.

After he develops a crush on a school friend, Charley Casey, an intellectually limited boy who is good at games, he finds himself back in Lavin's company when Charley suggests they go and see him. Charley is asked to take out his penis so that Lavin can measure it and then allows himself to be fondled by the pervert who announces that there has been 'an increase of a good inch since the last year'[5] (CE, 55). Prior to this, Lavin had shown them his own 'John Charles', an admirable 'weapon' in Casey's view. The narrator is then asked to show his penis so that Lavin can compare them, but he refuses. At the end of the story, the boys discuss their fantasy of travelling around Ireland in two caravans, one of which would house their female sex slaves: 'They'd strip the minute we said strip. If they didn't we'd whip them. We'd whip them with those whips that have bits of metal on the ends' (CE, 56). They would take the women from behind 'the way the bull does' (CE, 56). When it is suggested

5. McGahern named a few of his characters 'McQuaid' and here refers to the penis as 'John Charles', all of which begs the question if he was having a slightly ironic dig at the venerable Archbishop with whom he had such a tumultuous relationship.

that they could do this to one another, there is hesitation as to who will go first: 'The fear was unspoken: whoever took his pleasure first would have the other in his power and then might not surrender his own body' (CE, 56). In the end, they fail to follow through on their inclination.

The voyeuristic antics of Lavin and the sado-masochistic imaginings of Charley and the narrator give a bleak view of sexuality in this story. Stanley van der Ziel notes: 'Sexuality is usually seen in these stories (*Nightlines*) as something to be feared, and is imbued with connotations of violence, decay, and the disgust of the unnatural.' He continues by remarking that the theme of 'violent sexuality' is 'far removed from the sacred life-giving force it would become in McGahern's later fiction'.[6]

The interdictions surrounding sex do not seem to bother the protagonists in the short stories to the same degree as they do the characters in the novels. Young people are much more likely to act on their sexual urges in the short stories. Childhood innocence is often destroyed in such a way as to leave a residual distaste for sexuality. In 'Coming into his Kingdom', a young boy called Stevie cannot comprehend why his school friends find it so amusing when he falls on Nora on the way home from school. They start shouting 'They're in love! They're in love!' in a frenzied manner. Stevie feels compelled to ask a friend, Teresa, the reason for the commotion and is shocked when she reveals that it's just 'like the bull and the cow':

> The world was changed, a covering torn away; he'd never be able to see anything the same again. His father had slept with his mother and done that to her, the same father that slept with him now in the big bed with the broken brass bells and rubbed his tummy at night, saying, 'That's what's good for you, Stevie. Isn't that what you like, Stevie?' ever since it happened the first night, the slow labouring voice explaining how the rubbing eased wind and relaxed you and let you sleep (CS, 21).

This description of paternal abuse in the home has strong echoes with what one encounters in *The Dark* and *Memoir*. Stevie's mother has passed away and he feels that her memory

---

6. Stanley van der Ziel, 'John McGahern: *Nightlines*', in Cheryl Alexander and David Malcolm (eds), *A Companion to the British and Irish Short Story* (Oxford and Malden: Wiley-Blackwell, 2008), pp 488-497, p 492.

is sullied by the thought of her lying naked under his father in order for him to be conceived. He wonders if he could get Teresa to do this with him some day behind the covering of bushes: 'His body was tingling and hot as the night in convalescence he'd watched his mother undress and get into the bed she'd moved into his room at the height of his illness ... and he'd ached to creep into her bed and touch every part of her body with his lips and the tips of his fingers' (CS, 22). The feverish longing for the mother is one of the rare times that incestuous desire is described in such a graphic manner in McGahern's work. It adds a disconcerting dimension to the boy's sexual awakening.

Adulthood does not forge a smooth transition in the man-woman dynamic either. 'Like All Other Men' tells of a chance encounter between an ex-seminarian and a nurse, Susan Spillane, in a Dublin dance hall. After the dance they emerge into a rain-sodden city and, to the man's amazement, the woman suggests that they get a hotel room together. Her request that the light be left on while they have sex surprises him: 'It was not clear whether she wanted the light for the practical acts of undressing or if she wanted these preliminaries to what is called the act of darkness to be free of all furtiveness, that they should be noted with care like the names of places passed on an important journey' (CE, 204-205). His disbelief at what is happening is compounded by the beauty of her naked body and the realisation that he is finally about to realise his sexual fantasies:

> What he had wanted so much that it had become frightening she made easy, but it was almost impossible to believe that he now rested in the still centre of what had long been a dream. After long deprivation the plain pleasures of bed and table grow sadly mystical (CE, 205).

The excitement is tempered by the 'sadly mystical' feeling that takes hold of him, a sentiment that reminds him of the time spent as a seminarian in Maynooth. He tells the woman his reason for leaving was, 'Because I no longer believed. I could hardly lead others to a life that I didn't believe in myself' (CE, 206). The loss of faith is a widespread theme in McGahern's work. Faith in God, in material possessions, in sex, in power, in knowledge is often shown to be unreliable, even futile, in the quest for greater self-understanding and fulfilment. The thought of celibacy was not what prompted the man's spoilt vocation: 'If anything, the giving up of sex – renunciation was the word we used – gave the vocation far more force' (CE, 206). The revelation the following day that Susan is joining a religious order later that week leaves him angry and bemused: 'Wasn't last night a strange preparation for your new life?' (CS, 208), he asks pointedly. Susan does not see anything wrong in what they have done. If it had happened after she had taken her final vows, then that would have been different. As both of them were free, where was the harm in it? she asks. As happens so often when confronted with the prospect of losing a lover in McGahern's stories, the man suggests that perhaps they could get married. Susan's mind is made up, however: she is going to join the Medical Missionaries and attempt to bring healing to people in the Third World.

Unrequited love is a strong motif running through McGahern's short stories. After the acrimonious ending of his relationship, the man in 'Parachutes' finds himself in the company of the heavy-drinking Mulveys, a husband and wife who scarcely find time from their socialising to feed their daughter. He wakes up in his companions' residence on a Sunday morning after a serious night's drinking and goes out for a walk among the throngs of people heading to Mass: 'I drifted with them as far as the church door, turning back into the empty streets once Mass had started, walking fast until I came to a quiet side street where I sat on the steps of one of the houses' (CE, 158). He thinks back to his days in school, where they were taught to pay attention to the world, and observes ruefully: 'I'd have to learn the world all over again' (CE, 158). He knows that spending time with the likes of the Mulveys will not bring him happiness. Their Beckettian wait for the return of Halloran, a man with a predilection for young boys, leaves him listless and disillusioned: 'I felt leaden with tiredness, the actual bar close to the enamelled memories of the morning' (CE, 163). He knows that Halloran's arrival will not change anything in his life, that the anguish will continue regardless. However, when Halloran does finally appear in the pub, the sight of a single thistledown floating in the doorway like a 'pale parachute' reminds him of the night he met his former girlfriend and how happy he had been at that time:

> As we kept turning to the music, we moved through the circle where the glass dome was still letting in daylight, and kept

on after we'd passed the last of the pillars hung with the wire baskets of flowers, out beyond the draped curtains, until we seemed to be turning in nothing but air beneath the sky, a sky that was neither agate nor blue, just the anonymous sky of any and every day above our lives as we set out (*CE*, 165).

This moment of spiritual revelation was made possible by thistles being able to install themselves in the very centre of the city, Grafton Street, attracted by the backyards and dumps found there. The 'uplift' that is experienced is associated with the 'anonymous sky', which implies that it may well be inspired more by a terrestrial force than a divine one. McGahern's later works portray the therapeutic aspects of nature and 'Parachutes' is a type of precursor to a theme that becomes more and more pronounced as his writing evolves. There is not much sign of it in the London building site that supplies the setting for 'Hearts of Oak and Bellies of Brass'. Its array of Irish emigrant workers is doggedly overseen by the site foreman Murphy, who regularly exhorts them with the refrain: 'Shovel or shite, shite or bust.' The same man defines the essential ingredients of life in the following manner: 'pork chops, pints of bitter, and a good old ride before you sleep, that's fukken ambition' (*CE*, 30). These men have long since given up hope of ever returning to live in Ireland, a country which did nothing to keep them there: '"They never did much for us except to starve us out to England. You have to have the pull there or you're dirt", Keegan advanced' (*CE*, 31).

Tipperary, a man who had trained to be a Christian Brother but decided to leave when he couldn't pass the exams for his teacher's qualification and was sent to work in the kitchens, constantly questions the narrator about the relative merits of Shakespeare. Tipperary is disapproving of the behaviour of his co-workers, their naked violence, drunken antics and visits to the local prostitutes. The narrator remembers his own sexual initiation with a prostitute whom he visited after several pints of bitter: 'Only for her practiced old hands it would have been impossible to raise desire, and if it was evil when it happened, the pumping of the tension of the instinct into her glycerined hole, then nothing was so extraordinarily ordinary as this evil' (*CE*, 35). Seeing sex as natural, 'ordinary', as being far removed from the 'evil' connotations associated with it during childhood and early adulthood, is a common thread running through the short stories. But this attitude tends to be most prevalent among single people.

In 'Love of the World', the self-obsessed former football star husband freely engages in extramarital sexual relationships while the wife remains steadfastly loyal to her marriage vows, even when she feels a strong attraction for a local businessman, Callaghan. Shortly after her marriage to Guard Harkin, Kate's father had been a little dubious about his future son-in-law's character: 'When God made us, he didn't allow for us all to be first all the time' (CE, 342). Harkin has difficulty coming to terms with the end of his dazzling Gaelic football career and with the fact that his professional advancement fails to materialise as a result of his arrogance and failure to curry favour with his superior officers. Nevertheless, after suffering a heart attack he is stationed back in his local village where he capitalises on the booming tourist industry in the area, acting as a property dealer and general advisor. When Kate takes up the offer of a job in the local mart, her enraged husband changes the locks in the house and retains custody of the children. When she had initially refused to cease working, Harkin had taken pleasure in telling her about a recent escapade in Germany: 'The woman who came to my room said when she opened the door, "I won the prize. I got the Irishman." We did everything man or beast can do and were the last couple to come down. Everyone clapped as soon as we came into the bar …' (CE, 351). This brazen admission makes it impossible for his wife to envisage any future with Harkin and tragedy strikes when, after her refusal to return to live in the house, he shoots and kills her.

Following the tragic murder and Harkin's subsequent suicide in prison, Kate's mother rears the children and, years later, on her way home from accepting the Senior Citizen of the Year Award, observes as she and her friend of many years turn round the lake: 'Even where I am now, it's still all very interesting. Sometimes even far, far too interesting' (CE, 368). Once more, this is a trait commonly found in the characters of the later period of McGahern's work: in spite of their advancing years and fate conspiring against them, notwithstanding the fact that the world reveals itself in a manner that is far removed from childhood expectations, it retains an attraction, a wholesome quality, an 'interest' that holds one's attention to the very end.

Stories like 'The Recruiting Officer', 'Crossing the Line' and

'High Ground' depict the disillusionment of primary school teachers at the end or beginning of their careers. In 'The Recruiting Officer', a former Christian Brother trainee finds himself in Arigna 'growing old in the school where I began' (*CE*, 69). It is rumoured that he drinks a lot and the school manger, Canon Reilly, resents the fact that he lives outside the parish, which prevents him from taking religious instruction after second Mass, as his predecessor had done. The Canon administers a brutal beating to a boy named Walshe who has confessed to stealing money from an offertory box in the church. The priest reminds the students present that Walshe has committed three sins – theft, lying and sacrilege – and offers the boy a choice between being sent to the reformatory and a beating. He naturally chooses the latter and has to endure an electric wire being violently administered to his legs. From the 'heavy breathing' of the priest, it is clear that he is deriving a type of sexual pleasure from the beating. The other students look on 'in frightened fascination' (*CE*, 72). No one dares to intervene, not even the teacher. This is part of the moral code passively accepted by the community: they silently accept a regime that dictates that an example has to be made of transgressors in order to warn off others thinking of following a similar path. Later that afternoon, the visit of a Christian Brother seeking vocations brings back memories of the teacher's own time with this Order: 'I wonder who'll rise to the gleaming spoon and find the sharpened hooks as I did once' (*CE*, 78).

His mother had been thrilled when the Brother came to visit their house and spoke of the training and education he would receive. Anxious that his brother should inherit the fields, she fell in with the idea and ended up regretting it when the installation of her son's wife deprived her of all influence in the house. Now, every summer she and her teacher son travel to a hotel by the sea: 'I want to ask her why she wanted the acres for my brother, why she pushed me away, but I don't ask. I walk by her side on the sand and echo her life with 'Yes and yes and yes,' for it is all a wheel' (*CE*, 80). Because of all that has happened to him in the course of his life, the teacher experiences a 'total paralysis of the will' and goes around with the 'feeling that any one thing in this life is almost as worthwhile doing as any other' (*CE*, 69). When he decided he wanted to leave the Christian Brothers, he took to his bed and refused to get up until the Order dismissed him: 'I was to get a suit of clothes, underwear, railway ticket and one pound' (*CE*, 81). This news revived him and he left without a moment's regret. Now he whiles away his time watching the clock slowly turn until his liberation at the end of the day: 'I feel born again as I start to pedal towards the town. How, how, though, can a man be born again when he is old? Can he enter a second time his mother's bag of tricks?' (*CE*, 82)

'Crossing the Line' and 'High Ground' examine the 'changing of the guard', the differing approaches of men embarking on a teaching career and those who are coming to the end of theirs. 'Crossing the Line' begins with a meeting between a young man and the headmaster of the school in which he wants to teach, a Master Kennedy. The ultimate decision in relation to who is offered the position rests with a ninety-eight year old Archdeacon, the manager of the school. Several years previously, Kennedy has incurred the wrath of the members of the INTO (Teachers' Union) by crossing the picket line during an industrial dispute. The secretary of the local branch, Owen Beirne, tells the young man that Kennedy refused to strike: 'For several months he crossed that picket line, while the Church and de Valera tried to starve us to our knees' (*CE*, 183). From that moment onwards, he was shunned by INTO members, an ostracism that he seems to take in his stride. He has financial security, having sent his children to good schools and university, and he looks forward to a carefree retirement in the near future. He recalls his pleasure, as a newly married man, at being able to go home at lunchtime and have sex with his wife: 'It was a great feeling afterwards, walking about with the Brothers, knowing that they'd never have it in the whole of their lives' (*CE*, 182). At the end of the story, the young teacher is somewhat appalled at how Kennedy is totally fixated on putting away money for his retirement: 'I was beginning to think that people grow less spiritual the older they become, contrary to what is thought. It was as if some desire to plunge their arms up to the elbow into the steaming entrails of the world grew more fierce the closer they got to leaving' (*CE*, 188).

In 'High Ground', the shift of power from the Church to the political elite is clear from the way in which a local politician, Senator Reegan, tells the young teacher who is home on a visit that he can have the job of Principal of the local primary school if he wants it. The person holding down that position, Master

Leddy, who had taught most of the children in the area, including the young teacher himself, has been found wanting in his duties. The young man makes the point to Reegan that a decision like this would rest with Canon Gallagher, only to be told: 'Listen. There are many people who feel the same way as I do. If I go to the Canon in the name of all those people and say that you're willing to take the job, the job is yours. Even if he didn't want to, he'd have no choice but to appoint you ...' (CE, 193-4). A definite swing in the balance of power is evident here. Master Leddy is a kindly man, but his days are numbered once Reegan has made up his mind that he must be removed. The negative impact his inadequate teaching could have on the local children is reason enough for his removal. It is also known that he spends every night drinking in the local bar, telling his past students how unique they are: 'Ye had the brains. There are people in this part of the country digging ditches who could have been engineers or doctors or judges or philosophers had they been given the opportunity. But the opportunity was lacking' (CE, 199). The man who may well be installed as his successor hears this after-hours banter as he goes to fetch water from the well and reflects with some remorse that he may well become a party to Reegan's plans.

At various stages in McGahern's short stories characters must unlearn the lessons of their youth, face up to unpalatable realities in relation to their professional future, their relationships, their faith, and start anew without the safety net of long-held beliefs. Their situation is well summed up in Murphy's blasphemous exhortation to his workers in 'Hearts of Oak and Bellies of Brass': 'Our fukker who art in heaven bought his boots for nine-and-eleven ... Come on: shovel or shite, shite or bust' (CE, 35).

A View from the Other Side

The three main stories in which McGahern deals in a sympathetic and insightful way with the Protestant minority in southern rural Ireland – 'Oldfashioned', 'Eddie Mac' and 'The Conversion of William Kirkwood' – are significant, in the opinion of David Malcolm, 'both because of the milieu that they depict, that of the descendants of the pre-1922 Protestant ruling class in southern Ireland, and because of the broad sweep of history that they encompass'.[7] Undoubtedly influenced by his own positive interaction with the Protestant Moroney family, who gave him

7. David Malcolm, *Understanding John McGahern*, p 97.

the run of their library when he was a young boy, McGahern imbued characters like Colonel Sinclair and his wife, along with the Kirkwood family, with a gentleness and sophistication totally lacking in the neighbouring Catholics whose philistine attitudes are well-summed up in his essay, 'The Solitary Reader':

> There were few books in our house, and reading for pleasure was not approved of. It was thought to be dangerous, like pure laughter. In the emerging class in the Ireland of the 1940s, when an insecure sectarian state was being guided by a philistine Church, the stolidity of a long empty grave face was thought to be the height of decorum and profundity. 'The devil always finds work for idle hands' was one of the warning catchphrases (LW, 87).

Enmity between Protestants and Catholics is a recurring theme in Irish history and it left a legacy of distrust and incomprehension long after the initial causes of the discord had dissipated. McGahern describes the dominant atmosphere in the following manner: 'At the time [the 1940s], Protestants were pitied because they were bound for hell in the next world, and they were considered to be abstemious, honest, and morally more correct than the general run of our fellow Catholics' (CE, 89). In the nineteenth and early twentieth centuries, there was a marked shift in power from the Anglo-Irish gentry to the Catholic middle class and its Church. McGahern regretted how this shift led to a move away from a system of manners which valued activities that served no obvious practical purpose. The act of staying 'still' long enough to appreciate the beauty and ornament that are in plentiful supply for those who have eyes to see is something that was held in deep suspicion by characters like the Sergeant in 'Oldfashioned'. After discovering that his son has been invited to work in the garden of Colonel Sinclair and his wife, who spend a few months each year in the renovated parsonage, the sergeant comments: 'All that work they do isn't work at all. They imagine it is. It's just fooling about' (CE, 245). This frivolous 'fooling about' does not appeal to the Sergeant whose best years were spent during the War of Independence when he was the commander of a flying squadron. This has resulted in an understandable antipathy towards the British, especially their military forces, of which Colonel Sinclair is an obvious representative. The disdain he has for the orchard and garden of the Sinclairs, where they produce goods for pleasure more than out of need, contrasts with his own cultivation of potatoes and vegetables for consumption at home. Belinda McKeon notes in relation to this:

> The difference between the worlds inhabited by the Sergeant and the Colonel is pointed up even more starkly by their attitude to the activity which bears a weight of meaning throughout McGahern's fiction: the saving of the harvest. In this instance, that harvest is the potato crop, indelibly associated with famine ... The Sinclairs have the playgrounds of Ascendancy, the orchard and the flower garden, and in these they find pleasure. The growing of fruit and vegetables is, for them, not about survival, but about sociability.[8]

The boy in the story, Johnny, eventually becomes the academic producer who returns with a film crew to do a documentary on the area in which he grew up. He notes the demise of the Protestant class in the locality and thinks back to a time when the Catholic church 'was so crowded for both Masses on Sundays that often children and old people would faint in the bad air and have to be carried outside'. Equally, the presbytery saw heavy traffic as people 'came for references, for birth certificates, to arrange for calls to the sick and dying, for baptism, marriages, churchings, to report their neighbours: they brought offerings and payments of dues' (CE, 237). Both the Catholic and Protestant institutions have undergone serious upheaval in the space of a few decades, with the Protestant presence almost completely obliterated and the Catholic priest a comical figure in the local community: 'He is a young priest and tells them that God is on their side and wants them to want children, bungalow bliss, a car and colour television ... [H]e plays the guitar and sings at local hotels where he is a hit with tourists' (CE, 260).

This is a very different scenario to the one that prevailed when Johnny was a child. People like the Sinclairs, with their gentile, suave manners, elegant clothes and car, their strange habits – the Colonel used to go to the local bar most evenings for a few drinks but his wife would never go in with him, preferring instead to have her gin and tonics brought out to her in the car –

8. Belinda McKeon, '"Robins Feeding with the Sparrows": The Protestant "Big House" in the Fiction of John McGahern', in *Irish University Review*, vol 35, no 1, Spring/Summer 2005, pp 72-89, p 77.

were viewed as something of an oddity. Charlie, the barman, tries to explain the differences to his customers: 'They're strange. They're different. They're not brought up the like of us. Those hot climates they get sent to does things to people' (CE, 240).

The tact is evident in the Colonel's refusal to broach topics that have the potential to bring discord and he notes, in an echo of David Hume: 'I never discuss religion because its base is faith – not reason' (CE, 241). He and his wife make the fatal mistake of taking a kindly interest in Johnny. They recognise the boy's intelligence and see that he could make a good life for himself in the British army. A visit to the local secondary school Principal, Brother Benedict, to discuss the plan, proves pleasant, largely as a result of the good whiskey that is produced to mark the occasion, and confirms their belief in Johnny's academic ability. The Brother does warn them about the father, however: 'He's a survivor and far from being without guile. Like the rest of the country he has a great store of negative capability' (CE, 249). Still suffering grief at the loss of their own son in the War, the couple persevere with their plans, with disastrous results. When the Colonel visits the Sergeant and reveals the idea they have been hatching, the Sergeant is incandescent with rage. At the first opportunity he confronts his son with what he knows: 'I hear we're about to have a young Sassenach on our hands, an officer and a gentleman to boot, not just the usual fool of an Irishman who rushes to the railway station at the first news of a war …' (CE, 250). The boy knows immediately that this outburst marks the end of his connection with the Sinclairs, a fact that is confirmed by Guard Casey: 'Your father would never have been able to live with that. You really have to be born into that class of people. You don't ever find robins feeding with the sparrows' (CE, 252). Deep differences do not disappear overnight: centuries of oppression under English rule weigh heavily on the mind of someone like Johnny's father.

Another prominent trope in 'Oldfashioned' is the manner in which the Church's dominance has been replaced by that of the politicians. We are told that a local politician now attracts the crowds that used to flock to the presbytery but who now attend his 'clinics': 'They come to look for grants, to try to get drunken driving convictions squashed, to get free medical cards, sickness benefit, to have planning application decisions that have gone against them reversed, to get children into jobs' (CE, 261). All of which merely confirms the point made by the sociologist Tom Inglis that many Irish people were committed to Catholicism only to the extent that it was of practical benefit to them. Inglis asserts that during the second half of the twentieth century a predominantly Catholic culture was replaced by one of consumer capitalism: 'Instead of realising ourselves as different through the language of the Church and its teachings and practices, we gradually switched to realising ourselves as different through the language of the market and its teachings and practices.'[9] This ultimately led, in Inglis's view, to a move from the Irish 'being quiet Catholic Church mice embodying a discourse and practice of piety and humility, to becoming busy, productive, self-indulgent rats searching for the next stimulation.'[10] Part of this process involved the switch of allegiance from the local parish priest to the politician.

When the crew came to film the episode of My Own Place devoted to the Sergeant's son's memories of the area, they invited the parish priest to dinner in the local hotel in an attempt to ensure that possible local hostility be avoided, whereas they should have invited the politician. Just as the Protestant influence waned with the establishment of the Irish Free State and Republic, that of the Catholic Church went the same way once people realised that greater symbolic capital and material benefit could be secured elsewhere.

'Eddie Mac' shows how the trust invested by the Kirkwood family in their employee, the local football star, is abused in a most cynical manner. For long the envy of the local male community, Eddie Mac finds, as his prowess as a footballer fades, that the steady stream of available girls diminishes with it. In the end, he resignedly turns to Annie May, the young housekeeper at the Kirkwood residence, who has long openly idolised him. Eddie's frustration with the bee-keeping of Kirkwood senior and the astronomy of the son is vented in the following outburst: 'Useless to themselves or anybody else. They'll be on the road before long, mark my words, and we'll be with them if we are not careful' (CE, 269). Eddie's treatment of Annie May, whom he abandons after she becomes pregnant, is in stark con-

---

9. Tom Inglis, Global Ireland: Same Difference (London/NY: Routledge, 2008), p 30.
10. Global Ireland, p 190.

trast to the Kirkwoods, who demonstrate great sympathy to the plight of the young woman and provide her and the baby with a home in spite of the fact that her former lover absconded with the proceeds of the sale of their prize livestock. This was not the first time Eddie Mac found himself in the position of making a girl pregnant. On previous occasions, however, it was the woman who had left for England. Denis Sampson argues that the story 'implies that the departure of pregnant women and now of Eddie Mac is due to the failure of Irish society to find social forms for sexual behaviour that might alleviate violence and fear'.[11] Sampson thinks it is remarkable that there is no mention of the Catholic Church's role as moral custodian in the story. I do not find it all that surprising, in that both Eddie and Annie May live at something of a remove from the local community due to their working environment. Annie May's exposure to the Kirkwoods' kindness seems to have rubbed off on the young woman, who is herself of a mild and kindly disposition.

When it comes to displaying Christian charity to a young woman in distress, the Protestants provide a much better example than their Catholic counterparts, as can be seen from the keen interest William Kirkwood, the son, takes in Annie May's daughter, Lucy. It is while helping her with her homework that he begins to think seriously about the Catholic religion, which is the first step in his conversion from Protestantism. Whereas nearly all the other Protestant landowners had emigrated after Independence to other colonial outposts such as Canada and Australia, or had simply moved up North, William Kirkwood stayed put, 'blessedly unaware that he had become a mild figure of fun, out watching the stars at night as a young man when he should have been partying with the Protestant blades …' (CE, 282). During World War II, or the 'Emergency' as it was referred to in neutral Ireland, a local defence force was formed and this paved the way for William's integration within the local community. He was a crack shot and could read maps with ease, so was soon promoted Commanding Officer for the north of the county. His changed status was manifest when a group of men from his unit arrived unexpectedly one day to help him with saving the hay before the rain came, as concrete a manifestation of solidarity as could be provided in rural Ireland.

On Sundays, William marched his men through the local vil-

11. Sampson, *Outstaring Nature's Eye*, p 200.

lage as far as the church and remained outside until Mass had ended: 'Now that he had become such a part of the people it was felt that such a pointed difference was a little sad' (CE, 287). So it came to pass that Garda Sergeant Moran made the following comment: 'Before the war, William, you were there on your own in that big house, helping nobody, getting no help. Now you're in with everybody. Only for your being a Protestant, there'd not be the slightest difference now between you and the rest of us.' Both Moran and the local schoolteacher McLoughlin are amazed when Kirkwood retorts: 'I'm seriously considering becoming a Catholic, but not, I'm afraid, in the interests of conformity' (CE, 287). The idea of 'robins feeding with the sparrows' is not what the two men had in mind: 'It broke the law that everybody stayed within the crowd they were born into …' (CE, 287).

William's religious instruction begins with Canon Glynn, an old priest who was of the view that 'the affairs of the earth ran more happily the less God was brought into them' (CE, 289). He soon finds the convert's zeal overpowering and tries to reassure him that all that is needed is for William to convince him of his belief in Catholic doctrine. The situation is rendered more acceptable when it is discovered, after his conversion, that William harbours a romantic attachment to a nurse from the district, Mary Kennedy. Moran and McLoughlin set about establishing whether or not the young woman might be prepared to accept the suitor. When he was considering this option, Kirkwood had visited McLoughlin's home: 'Not in all the years of Protestantism had he ever felt his difference so keenly. What struck him most was the absence of books in a schoolmaster's house' (CE, 294). It surprises Kirkwood that an educated man should show no obvious interest in literature – his own house had hundreds of books. The meeting with Miss Kennedy proves less of an ordeal and she is impressed with 'the worn but well-cut blue pinstripe, the thick, lank grey hair, the jutting Anglo-Irish jaw, the military appearance of alertness'. She also admires 'how soft and long his hands were from years of gentle living' (CE, 297). The match is agreed, but the negative impact the marriage will have on Annie May and Lucy, who, Mary Kennedy insists, will have to be given notice, is a source of disquiet for Kirkwood who wishes that his happiness 'could take place without bringing suffering on two people who had been a great part of his life …' (CE, 300).

At the end of 'The Conversion of William Kirkwood' one is left with the uneasy feeling that taking on the religious affiliation of the majority comes at a heavy price. Belinda McKeon suggests that the conversion 'leads not so much to an accommodation between the two communities as to a surrender on his [Kirkwood's] part'.[12] She notes that the way in which his father's beehives are left to rot in the orchard and the suffering of Annie May and Lucy, are signs of how much that was good in the Protestant tradition is being lost. In a very interesting essay, 'Life as It Is and Life as It Ought to Be', McGahern wrote about a funeral he attended in the Protestant church of Fenagh. The deceased's name was William Booth and McGahern was interested to hear comments like the following from mourners: 'There's no difference here any more between Protestants and Catholics ... They go to the same bars, play cards, drink together. They all pull and work together. No one passes the least heed. You'd wonder what's wrong with that crowd in the North that they can't be the same' (LW, 161). For McGahern, this was a rather idealised and naïve view of the situation. He described how the championing of the Irish language by Church and State in the South was a means of ensuring that Catholics could enjoy dominance in the civil service and the professions: 'The sectarian state here has largely disintegrated, probably because of a lack of a serious opposition, and it has been seen, increasingly, as the narrow, bigoted artifact it always was, and lest there be any self-congratulation, in many ways, still is' (LW, 162-3). Always the realist, McGahern's sympathetic portrayal of Protestants stems from an appreciation of their tolerant, easy-going and cultured disposition, traits which marked them out as distinctly different from the Catholic population that surrounded them.

Search for Knowledge and the Transcendent

Many of McGahern's best stories have little or no connection with Catholicism and hence do not feature in this book. For example, in 'Wheels' there is the comic incident of a man travelling home for a funeral being asked by a stranger if he works in London: 'I do and fukken all, for the last twenty-eight years, on the buildings' (CE, 4), he replies. He fails to see the clerical collar his interlocutor is wearing until the priest gets up to leave and then he is horrified to have used language like that to a man of

---

12. McKeon, 'Robins Feeding with the Sparrows', p 85.

the cloth. When told that the priest didn't appear to mind too much, he retorts: 'Still, he's a priest, isn't he? You have to draw the line fukken somewhere. I'll go and tell him I'm sorry' (*CE*, 5). The respect for the priestly function is strongly engrained even in someone like this man who has been so many years working outside of Ireland.

In 'All Sorts of Impossible Things' the refusal of the primary school teacher to remove his hat in church for Mass poses problems for the parish priest. The man's embarrassment over his premature balding has to be balanced against the absolute necessity of the teacher being seen to attend to his religious duties. Sharkey, as the teacher is called, claims that he has no desire to show disrespect: 'If the church can't include my old own brown hat, it can't include very much, can it, Father?' The priest replies: 'You know that and I know that, but we both know that the outward shows may least belie themselves. It'd not be tolerated' (*CE*, 96). In the end, good sense prevails and Sharkey is put in charge of collections, for which purpose the table is placed in the church porch, where wearing a hat is not an affront. Such a sensible accommodation reveals the flexibility that is occasionally displayed by the Church when it is obvious that to pursue the hard line will result in losing a valued member of the congregation. Later in the story, when cutting the hair of his friend Tom Lennon, who must pass a medical in order to secure a permanent position as an agricultural instructor, Sharkey has a moment of deep insight: 'he felt for the first time ever a mad desire to remove his hat and stand bareheaded in the room, as if for the first time in years he felt himself in the presence of something sacred' (*CE*, 101). Lennon falls dead at the wheel of the car the next morning, which leaves his widow without the security of a pension. Sharkey is given charge of the greyhound the two men trained. While petting the animal down, he experiences the same feeling he had when cutting his friend's hair, 'but instead of prayer he now felt a wild longing to throw his hat away and walk round the world bareheaded …' (*CE*, 103). In the past, the teacher missed out on the chance of love when, as his hair began to fall out, he latched on to the woman he was courting: 'Anxiety exasperated desire to a passion, the passion to secure his life as he felt it slip away, to moor it to the woman he loved' (*CE*, 95). The pressure he put on her to make a decision led to their break-up. Afterwards, he was left with the prospect of a lonely existence, which was exacerbated when he lost his best friend, Lennon. The glimpses of the transcendent therefore do little to alleviate Sharkey's existential suffering. Having said that, Sharkey is finally left with something of his own. The feeling he has when walking the dog with its soft, sleek coat, the bond that develops between them, gives him a whole new perspective on life. Maybe, just maybe, all sorts of impossible things are not impossible after all.

'The Wine Breath' describes a Proustian regaining of lost time by an elderly priest who, during a visit to a parishioner called Gillespie, associates the saw dust in the yard with the snow that covered the countryside at the time of the funeral of Michael Bruen thirty years previously. He stands at Gillespie's gate for an unknown length of time before he is roused from his reverie: 'He did not know how long he had stood in that lost day, in that white light, probably for no more than a moment. He could not have stood the intensity for any longer' (CS, 179).[13] The priest's heightened perception is largely due to a premonition of death. The story begins with the lines: 'If I were to die, I'd miss most the mornings and the evenings, he thought as he walked the narrow dirt-track by the lake in the late evening ...' (CS, 178). The 'intensity' he describes in relation to his experience of lost time has a mystical quality: 'Everything in that remembered day was so pure and perfect that he felt purged of all tiredness, was, for a moment, eager to begin life again' (CS, 180). When he emerges from the past into the present, he feels a wrench that is due to his unwillingness to leave behind this moment of heightened perception, characterized by calm and tranquillity. As a priest, he feels a duty to respect the 'actual day, the only day that mattered, the day from which our salvation had to be won or lost'. Yet, Michael Bruen's funeral, that took place on a day when the snow made the countryside appear to be 'bathed in the eternal' seemed consonant with 'everything we had been taught and told of the world of God' (CS, 180).

His vocation to the priesthood had been 'a way of vanquishing death and avoiding birth' (CS, 183). In the view of many

---

13. In *Memoir* McGahern described a similar experience when walking along the lanes of Leitrim: 'I have come into an extraordinary sense of security, a deep peace, in which I feel that I can live for ever. I suspect it is no more than the actual lane and the lost lane becoming one for a moment in an intensity of feeling, but without the usual attendants of pain and loss' (M, 4).

observers, his mother was the one with the real vocation and he
now realises that 'it was out of fear of death he became a priest,
which became in time the fear of life' (CS, 183). His life passes
before his eyes and does not appear to amount to much. His
mother lived with him for many years and she had been afraid
of ghosts. One of her great preoccupations was that the priests
who lived before them in the presbytery had neglected to say a
Mass for the dead, which in turn had prolonged the time spent
by souls in purgatory. He also recalls the angry exchanges he
had with another priest, Peter Joyce, about how much had been
lost by the replacement of the Latin Mass with the vernacular
form. With the onset of old age, he comes to see the limits of his
knowledge. Looking around the empty room of the presbytery,
he is afforded another moment of illumination: 'Then, quietly,
he saw that he had a ghost all right, one that he had been walking around with for a long time, a ghost he had not wanted to
recognise – his own death' (CS, 187). Relief more than fear ac-
companies this insight: afterwards, he seems ready to die.

The title of the story is revealed in the concluding paragraph
which describes the excitement of a young man – 'not unlike he
had once been' – visiting a woman with a bottle of wine in his
hands and looking forward to a pleasant evening in which he
will be 'immersed in time without end' (CS, 187). David
Malcolm sees the priest's memories as representing the wine
breath in that they are 'more intense than anything in the present and, thus, carrying all the transfigured and transfiguring
associations of the wine in the Eucharist'.[14] For the priest, the
Eucharist was a timeless 'mystery' which he enacted on a daily
basis and which memorialised the sacrifice of one life, that of
Jesus Christ, to ensure the salvation of many. 'The Wine Breath'
is a significant statement in relation to how unsolicited memories have the capacity to bring people into a closer relationship
with the transcendent and reveal a harmony between things
that in the past appeared to have nothing in common.

'The Country Funeral' is more a novella than a short story
and it provides an excellent insight into the support provided by
rural Irish communities to people in times of bereavement. It is
not as though the death of their uncle Peter is a source of great
loss to the brothers Fonsie, Philly and John Ryan. As children,
they were forced by their mother to travel to Peter's farm from

14. Malcolm, *Understanding John McGahern*, p 75.

Dublin during the summer holidays as a cost-saving measure. The invalided Fonsie has particularly bad memories of his uncle: 'He made us feel we were stealing bread out of his mouth' (CS, 389), he says. Also: 'The man wasn't civilised. I always felt if he got a chance he'd have put me in a bag with a stone and thrown me in a bog hole' (CS, 381-2). Fonsie is close to Philly, who works on the oil rigs and wastes the good money he earns buying drinks in their local Dublin pub. John, a mild-mannered married teacher, is the quietest of the three – it is implied that his ambitious wife is none too pleased with his lack of ambition – he makes little or no effort to gain promotion in his job. As they prepare to travel west to the funeral, their mother warns: 'Everything you do down there will be watched and gone over. I'll be following poor Peter in my mind until you rest him with Father and Mother in Killeelan [cemetery]' (CS, 378). She herself decides it is better not to travel given the fragile nature of her health, although one has the impression that her place of birth does not hold much attraction for the elderly woman.

What is noticeable about the journey is the extent to which Philly gets sucked into the life of his uncle, with whom he had a distant relationship at best, and how he falls under the spell of the community to which Peter belonged. As they are the only relatives present, the Ryans are expected to look after the funeral arrangements and meet the people from the surrounding area. McGahern's keen appreciation of the importance of funerals in rural Ireland can be seen in the attention to detail in his descriptions. It is not merely a question of putting Peter's corpse in a coffin and burying it. No, certain rituals must be followed: food and drink bought for the wake, a full discussion and appraisal of the man's life and character, the funeral Mass arranged and the laying to rest of the body. These are the rituals that have been observed for centuries and it is important for the local community that they be preserved. As the story progresses, it is clear that the atmosphere of the area around Gloria Bog, where their uncle lived, is exerting an influence on the brothers, almost without their realising it. The idea of journeying towards self-knowledge is prevalent in McGahern's writing, which was itself a type of never-ending quest. Thus, it is only after they leave Dublin that the men are free to get down to any meaningful discussion:

Not until they got past Leixlip, and fields and tress and

hedges started to be scattered between the new raw estates, did they begin to talk, and all their talk circled about the man they were going to bury, their mother's brother, their uncle Peter McDermott (CS, 379).

They are now getting prepared for the task ahead while at the same time memories of past journeys down these roads come flooding back. Thus, beyond Carrick-on-Shannon, there is a heightened sense of anticipation: 'They were coming into country that they knew. They had suffered here' (CS, 381). Soon they arrive at Peter's house where they are greeted by his neighbour Jim Cullen and a few other people who stand up and offer their condolences. Peter is laid out on his bed and already Mrs Cullen has prepared tea and sandwiches. The testimonies to the dead man's life begin: the pride he took in his garden is mentioned, along with the comment as to how selfless he was: 'If he saw you coming looking for help he'd drop whatever he was doing and swear black and blue he was doing nothing at all', an old man said' (CS, 383). Jim Cullen discreetly shows them the bill for the food and drink he has bought and hands over Peter's wallet filled with wads of notes. John offers to stay behind to meet the mourners while the two other brothers go to the village. As Philly drives, Fonsie's resentment boils over: 'The whole thing was barbaric, uncivilised, obscene: they should never have come'. His brother is not of that view at all: 'Isn't it as good anyhow as having the whole thing swept under the carpet as it is in the city?' he argues (CS, 385). The lack of change is striking as they enter the village. Fonsie refuses to accompany his brother into Luke Henry's bar where he acquires a generous amount of food and drink for the wake. On their way back to the house, Philly stops to look at Gloria Bog. Already the idea is taking shape in his mind that this could be the place for him to live after he has finished on the rigs. After they left the coffin in the church that evening, Philly bought everyone a round of drinks but was stopped when he went to get another: 'Custom allowed one round but no more' (CS, 394). He then returns to stay in his uncle's house where he is fascinated as he goes through the dead man's wallet containing thousands of pounds, along with dollars and receipts of all kinds – the remnants of a solitary life on a small farm. Most poignant of all are the little animals Peter made out of matchsticks, the contemplation of which causes Philly to reflect on his own life:

Tomorrow he'd lie in the earth on the top of Killeelan Hill. A man is born. He dies. Where he himself stood now on the path between those two points could not be known. He felt as much like the child that came each summer years ago to this bog from the city as the rough unfinished man he knew himself to be in the eyes of others, but feelings had nothing to do with it. He must be already well out past halfway (CS, 396).

There is evidence of heightened self-awareness here, as Philly seeks to put some order on his life, a life that is more than half over at this stage. The transformation in his character owes much to the esteem in which he holds the inhabitants and culture of this small outpost; he has the impression that he could very easily live out his final years around Gloria Bog, taking comfort from the beautiful landscape and the calm which it exudes.

The following day, Fonsie observes from the car the torturous ascent of the winding path by the cortege as they bring the corpse up to the cemetery: 'he found the coffin and the small band of toiling mourners unbearably moving as it made its low stumbling climb up the hill, and this deepened further his irritation and the sense of complete uselessness' (CS, 400). Fonsie resents his helplessness, his dependence on others, especially Philly, to get him around. He knows that the funeral has changed Philly in some way and he fears losing him to this place where he could never settle himself. He remonstrates with his brother that it is not respect for the dead that inspires Peter's neighbours: 'Oh, it's easy to honour the dead. It doesn't cost anything and gives them the chance to get out of their bloody houses before they start to eat one another within' (CS, 404-5). In spite of Fonsie's protestations, Philly's comments on the way home to Dublin indicate that he intends buying Peter's house from his mother and living there when he has earned enough money on the rigs to retire. He has undergone a major transformation:

'I felt something I never felt when we left the coffin on the edge of the grave. A rabbit hopped out of the briars a few yards off. He sat there and looked at us as if he didn't know what was going on before he bolted off. You could see the bog and all the shut houses next to Peter's below us. There wasn't even a wisp of smoke coming from any of the houses.

Everyone gathered around, and the priest started to speak of the dead and the Mystery and the Resurrection' (CS, 405).

One suspects that concepts like death and the Resurrection would not have meant too much to Philly up to this point. The 'rough unfinished man' has now assumed a spiritual dimension; he seems to have had an intuition of the transcendent, an experience that renders him more tranquil and serene. As one reads through 'The Country Funeral' one can see this transformation slowly taking shape. The religious significance of the funeral has its roots in the customs and beliefs of the inhabitants of the area. Philly is aware that his own roots lie in this soil, passed on to him by his mother and nurtured during their summer visits. The tact and concern displayed by the people of the area before, during and after Peter's funeral makes Philly's decision to settle here a logical one: 'I can't be going out to the oil fields for ever. It'll be a place to come home to. You saw how the little iron cross in the circle over the grave was eaten with rust. I'm going to have marble put up' (CS, 407). His days of heavy drinking will cease now that his life has assumed a new sense of purpose. Back in Dublin, he feels elated at the plan he has put in place, as he now has a direction he never before possessed. The gentle evocation of Irish rural community life gives a foretaste of McGahern's last novel, *That They May Face the Rising Sun*, but 'The Country Funeral' is an outstanding story in its own right and its unique representation of spiritual awakening and the irruption of the transcendent makes it a fitting concluding story for this section of my study.

Catholicism can be seen to play a subtle role in the lives of many of the characters portrayed in McGahern's short stories. One gets the strong sense when reading through them that there were changes afoot in Irish society and that attitudes to sex, in particular, were developing in a way that did not conform to Catholic teaching. The power base of the Church, the parish, was also being challenged by the politicians' clinics, where matters of economic importance could be resolved more successfully than by having the ear of the parish priest. A very interesting patchwork of adolescent desire, the difficult lives of Irish emigrants, the coming to terms with the transience of life, is sketched in a manner that brings into sharp relief that formal religious observance is but one means among many of making sense of life and surviving the trials that inevitably punctuate our existence.

CHAPTER FOUR

'You should only be afraid of God'[1]: Coping with Religious Change in The Rockingham Shoot and The Power of Darkness

In this chapter, I propose to deal with two lesser known works by John McGahern: *The Rockingham Shoot* and *The Power of Darkness*. A BBC Northern Ireland television drama and a play respectively, they are the only examples of McGahern experimenting with these particular genres. My treatment focuses on the light such works cast on McGahern's preoccupations as a writer and will not concern itself unduly with their success or otherwise in an artistic sense. Whereas *The Rockingham Shoot* enjoyed widespread critical acclaim, *The Power of Darkness* was far from well-received when it was first staged at the Abbey during the Dublin Theatre Festival of November 1991. Christopher Murray points out that '*The Power of Darkness* stands outside the oeuvre and tends to be ignored by the commentators, most of whom are purely literary rather than theatre critics.'[2] This chapter will attempt to fill that void, but will not concentrate so much on the broadcast or performative impact of the works as on the insights they offer with respect to McGahern's treatment of the Catholic question. It is important to state that both projects boasted highly regarded actors and directors, practitioners who were formidable interpreters of the type of socio-cultural material that McGahern explored in these works.

The Rockingham Shoot, directed by Kieran Hickey and featuring Bosco Hogan as the intensely nationalistic school teacher and keen Irish speaker, Reilly, and Niall Tóibín as the canny school manager who is referred to simply as 'Canon', was first screened in 1987. The screenplay is available in the McGahern

1. These words are uttered by Oliver towards the end of the play (*PD*, 51).
2. Christopher Murray, 'The "fallen world" of *The Power of Darkness*', in John Kenny (ed), *The John McGahern Yearbook* 2 (Galway: NUI Galway, 2009), pp 78-90, p 78. The publication of this defining study of the reception of the play has been of inestimable value to me.

Archive in NUI Galway under P71/765[3] and it is a good illustration of the writer's reservations with regard to the dangers associated with fanaticism. Reilly is a person who becomes greatly exercised every year when some of his students go absent from school in order to work on the shoot organised by the Rockingham estate and attended by the British Ambassador to Ireland. The teacher is a figure of fun in the local community for what are considered his outlandish political views. His lack of success in conveying his message of nationalistic fervour can be gauged by his ventures into the electoral domain, all of which end in abysmal failure. The Garda sergeant says of him: 'For Master Reilly the war is still going on. (Mimics) Not only Gaelic but free. Not only free but Gaelic as well. All unfinished business' (TRS, 5). As a teacher, however, Reilly is talented and he has a reputation for being successful in securing scholarships for his students. But his professional skills can do little to protect the school from what he considers the perfidious influence of the Rockingham estate. The noise of the shoot irritates him, prompting this remark to his female colleagues: 'You've heard the martial noises from our own little England all morning' (TRS, 38). He angrily warns his students not to miss school the following day under any circumstances:

> REILLY: I have something I want you to listen to carefully. (*pauses*) I'm informed that the British Ambassador is coming. As in other years, the peasants will beat the pheasants out of the bushes for the milords to go bang-bang. I know some of you here can earn half a crown for the day as a beater. This year I want you to show that we live in a free country and are proud of it. Tomorrow I want you to turn that half-crown down. Tomorrow I want to see every single one of you in school. Do you understand that? (TRS, 20)

Naturally, given the money that is on offer for working on the estate, the call for the children to 'strike a small blow for liberty' is ignored, and with painful consequences. Reilly sets his class a test the day after a number of them miss school on a topic

---

3. All my references will be to this manuscript and denoted by TRS, with the page number in brackets. My sincere thanks to Fergus Fahey and the library staff in NUI Galway for allowing me access to this document.

covered during their absence. They do poorly in the test and are beaten in a vicious manner. The following lines reveal the actions of a man who is out of control:

> The boys are struck savagely.
> The beating is ritualistic.
> For the final blow he has to physically hold the children.
> At its end he is dishevelled, out of breath, and probably sexually aroused (*TRS*, 66).

The sexual undertow in such beatings is commonplace in McGahern's writings. It stems from Reilly's frustration at what he perceives to be the betrayal of Ireland's fight for independence, but it almost certainly owes something also to the teacher's single status and lack of any healthy sexual outlets. There is no sign of his ever having had a girlfriend and there equally seems little prospect of such an eventuality arising in the future. He lives at home with his mother and brother – the latter is on the verge of getting married to his girlfriend Mary – and spends his time obsessing about the crimes committed against the Irish by the British. The Protestant gentry encapsulate for him all that is worst in British colonialism, as he attempts to explain to the sergeant:

> REILLY: It's an affront. That's what I call it. You'd think we were still a subject people. People didn't give their lives for children to go on beating peasants out of the bushes for our overlords!
> SERGEANT: <u>Pheasants</u>, I think.
> REILLY: Peasants or pheasants. There is little difference (*TRS*, 48).

The arrival of the gamekeeper in the Garda barracks to deliver some game to the sergeant confirms Reilly's worst suspicions:

> REILLY: 'With the compliments of Sir Cecil and Lady Stafford King-Harmon.' It seems that more than the people of the estate are on the Rockingham payroll (*TRS*, 49).

In school the following day, the pupils are subjected to a history lesson that covers seven centuries of British oppression. The memory of Paddy Moran, a real-life historical figure who fought

in Jacob's Factory during the 1916 rebellion, is evoked passion-
ately.[4] So too are many of the atrocities committed by the British
army in Ireland. Reilly bemoans how quickly people forget the
heroic deeds of the past: 'And after all that we have our own little
Britain with us yet behind the demesne wall' (*TRS*, 59). In another
document (P71/766) in the NUI Galway Archive outlining the
background to *The Rockingham Shoot*, McGahern pointed out the
situation that pertained in Ireland at the beginning of the last
century:

> When the British withdrew from the 26 counties an insular
> Church joined with an insecure state to create a society that
> was narrow and inward-looking … The history of the British
> presence in Ireland is no pretty picture and it left the new
> Free State with a convenient flogging boy for most of its ills.
> (P71/766)

Reilly is one of those who are quick to blame the British for
all of Ireland's woes, but he fails to see how unjust his own treatment of the students who miss school is. The severity of the
beating he administers to them causes a group of irate parents to
visit the school teacher at his home. Reilly is fortunate that his
brother Johnny is around to defuse the situation. Nevertheless a
warning is issued in no uncertain terms by one of the men:

> MULLOY: You haven't seen the end of this. You haven't seen
> the end of this by half. We'll fix you for this if it's the last thing
> we ever do. And if you so much as leave a finger, leave one
> frigging finger on any of those children from this day out,
> you'd better be able to get out of the country quick (*TRS*, 73).

Reilly realises after this incident that he went too far and that
there could be serious consequences for him. The following day
the sergeant visits the school to inform him that the estate manager from Rockingham has lodged a complaint about the children from the estate being beaten because of their absence during
the shoot. Reilly assures the sergeant that they were punished

---

4. Paddy Moran, after being released from an internment camp in England
in 1916, subsequently became a Captain in the IRA during the Irish War of
Independence before being captured and hanged. He was to assume myth-
ical stature in his native Roscommon after his execution.

for reasons of homework and discipline, and not for being absent. The cane he used to beat them was shredded at the time
and several of the children had to go to the doctor to have their
wounds treated. Reilly is reminded 'that the people who set up
this State were big people. They allowed room for everybody.'
Even though aware of the precariousness of his position, he
cannot resist a sarcastic retort to the sergeant:

> When I need a lesson on the foundation of the State, I'll cert-
> ainly not forget to consult you. Remember, I have work to do.
> Do you have any more profundities to contribute? (*TRS*, 78)

Reilly is fortunate to have a powerful ally in his school manager. The Canon is annoyed that the teacher's action has placed
him in an awkward position, especially delicate because the
estate is involved. He exhorts Reilly to approach things in a
more sedate manner: 'You'll have to learn that you can't bend
human nature to an idea, no matter how good that idea is' (*TRS*,
91). This is sound advice to offer a man who only ever sees one
side of any argument and is blind to any conflicting opinions. In
his notes, McGahern observed: 'The drama attempts to trace how
an intelligent and idealistic man, in the grip of narrow nationalism, could be so blinded as to spread his own hatred outwards,
even to the children he teaches' (P71/766). If a man like this
were to assume power, what hope would there be of compro-
mise and negotiation? The Canon may be in a position to contain the crisis his teacher caused on this occasion, but one is left
wondering what would happen if there were another similar
outburst, if Reilly's over-zealous nature once more wreaked
mayhem. He was lucky that all the workers on the estate were
Catholics, which meant the Canon could bring them to heel. The
Church's role as arbiter of disputes and guardian of the common good is evident in McGahern's drama.

Reilly saw teaching as a way to create a better Ireland. He
comments to his mother: 'It was our country. It was in our hands
for the first time. We'd make it the new Jerusalem. Now look
what it's come down to' (*TRS*, 84). He regrets not having chosen
a profession like law: 'I should have been a lawyer. A lawyer.
Not a doubt. Someone who lives off the natural stupidity and
greed of the people' (*TRS*, 84). Instead, his role is to educate

young children who seem eager to move with the times and to forget about the past. Reilly makes speeches outside the church that no one listens to. He sees himself as someone with a duty to make people aware of their republican inheritance, their Irish identity, their allegiance to the Catholic Church. In the end, he appears to be just talking to himself. In 'From a Glorious Dream to Wink and Nod', first published in *The Irish Times* on 3 April 1991, McGahern pointed out that the 1916 Rising was not considered to be of any great importance in the country he grew up in. Shortly after independence a new elite had emerged that was closely allied to the Church and State. They were responsible for promoting orthodoxy and ensuring that their own position was enhanced. By 1991, the fruits of this were clearly visible:

> In the increasingly diverse and fragmented Ireland we live in
> – healthily fragmented, for the most part, in my view – I think
> that we can best honour 1916 by restoring those rights and
> freedoms that were whittled away from the nation as a whole
> in favour of the dominant religion. We should put the spirit of
> the Proclamation into our laws. What we are likely to get,
> though, are more of the outward shows – maybe even a grant
> or two – while Wink goes out in search of Nod (*LW*, 127).

Subsequent events have revealed the full extent of the 'Nod and Wink' mentality in Ireland and the problems that resulted from a lack of adequate monitoring and regulation of our institutions. Religion was regularly viewed as a means of social advancement, because the Church appeared to be a strong influence on the political classes. The 'spirit' of the 1916 proclamation referred to by McGahern in the quote above was never properly implemented in our legal system. Reilly was clearly a fan of the men of 1916, but he does not possess the pragmatism to create a meaningful role for himself in an independent Ireland. McGahern's point is that Reilly fails to see that rebels often end up fighting the death of their revolution, its mutation into something that is often a sad charade of their bravery and the idealistic vision that inspired their actions. Republicanism, like religion, is used by people for their own purposes and enhancement. Thus, the purists are soon branded fanatics and find themselves marginalised by the ruling elite. That is the sad fate that befalls

Reilly, a fate that befell many other Irish people in post-independent Ireland. The situation evolved greatly during the decades of huge growth of the Celtic Tiger that were characterised by a desire to look forward and be progressive rather than dwelling on the past. Those who clung to tired ideologies found themselves being left behind, ostracised, treated like pariahs. It is significant that McGahern was commissioned by the BBC Northern Ireland to do this drama at what was a particularly grisly period of 'The Troubles'. The stand-offs between Reilly and the officials of the State and the remnants of the Protestant Ascendancy bring into focus many of the thorny aspects of Irish Republicanism, an issue that is also touched on in *That They May Face The Rising Sun* in the person of the local undertaker and IRA activist, Jimmy Joe McKiernan.

The *Power of Darkness* is an adaptation of the Tolstoy play of the same name. McGahern explained how the people who offered him the commission 'felt that the play could translate naturally into Irish country speech because of the strong religious presence there and the absence of a class system' (*PD*, vii). As we know, McGahern had been a fan of Tolstoy for some time and so it is not surprising that he was tempted by the opportunity to work on an adaptation of one of his works. His correspondence with Michael McLaverty reveals that he particularly admired *The Death of Ivan Ilyich*, a pessimistic novella that charts the life of a high-ranking Russian magistrate who discovers through illness that a life lived easily does not make for a comfortable death.[5] In his Introduction to the play, which appeared solely in his own name, McGahern explains the attraction it held for him:

> *The Power of Darkness* is uncannily close to the moral climate in which I grew up. The old fear of famine was confused with terror and damnation. The confusion and guilt and plain ignorance that surrounded sex turned men and women into exploiters and adversaries.
>
> Amid all this, the sad lusting after respectability, sugar-coated with sanctimoniousness and held together by a thin

---

5. On the 22 August 1959, he wrote the following lines to McLaverty: 'I had read all the stories you mentioned except *Ivan Ilyich*: It is the greatest of them all', *Dear Mr McLaverty*, p 18.

binding of religious doctrine and ceremony, combined to form a very dark and explosive force that, generally, went inwards and hid (*PD*, vii).

There is a lot of crime and violence in Tolstoy's play that dates from 1886. Murder, drunkenness, infanticide, adultery are all present, but the most salient ingredient is Tolstoy's obsession with death and dying. McGahern admitted a close identification with the subject matter of *The Power of Darkness*, pointing out that the 'moral climate' of Russia mirrored closely that of the West of Ireland during the 1940s and 50s, but also that of 1980s Ireland, when events like the Kerry Babies and the Ann Lovett tragedy struck a chord with him.[6] In spite of the cool critical response to his first foray into drama, McGahern came back again and again to the play in an attempt to reshape it into something more accomplished. Christopher Murray notes that between the 1972 radio play and a final version dated 15 July 2005, he re-wrote the play no fewer than thirty-nine times.[7] He also mentions that his preference for naturalism led McGahern to explore issues like human instinct and the impact of heredity and the environment on people's behaviour:

> If you said 'but this is realism, telling it as it is', you would be at least half right. But what you would be omitting is that naturalism says we are animals first and foremost and are destined to struggle and adapt as all animal life must. It says that God is dead and that we exist in a universe that is essentially tragic. But it says all this as art, and not as sociology.[8]

---

6. On the 31 January 1984 a fifteen year-old schoolgirl, Ann Lovett, died after giving birth to a stillborn son. She was not in hospital when she gave birth: no, she was alone in a grotto in Granard, Co Westmeath, under the watchful gaze of the statue of the Virgin Mary. The significance of this event was well captured by Rosita Boland: 'What happened in Granard twenty years ago was the shame of all Ireland: collectively, as a society, we were all responsible. We were forced to ask ourselves horrible questions about our society at a time when we were unused to asking ourselves such questions. The Kerry Babies, the X case, and the saga of Bishop Casey's son were all still to come'. 'Death in the Grotto', in *The Irish Times*, 31 January 2004. I will return to the Kerry Babies scandal later in the chapter.
7. Murray, 'The "fallen world",' p 82.
8. Murray, 'The "fallen world",' p 81.

Clearly, we are entering the realm of the great French novelist Emile Zola, the most renowned exponent of naturalism, when we apply such rhetoric to a literary form. Zola was the one who examined in detail the social and physical environment of his characters, their family background, religious beliefs, professions, with a view to presenting his readers with a forensic DNA that could explain their actions. In a sense, for Zola, people, like animals, behave in a predictable manner and have little say in the course that their lives take.

By attempting to adapt Tolstoy's play, however, McGahern was straying into the dangerous terrain of melodrama, held in some suspicion by the Irish public since the riots surrounding Synge's *Playboy of the Western World* in 1907. Bertrand Cardin points out that McGahern may have been influenced in his decision to experiment with theatre by the success his contemporaries Brian Friel, Thomas Kilroy, Frank McGuinness and Tom Murphy enjoyed with adaptations of work by foreign playwrights, most notably Chekhov.[9] However, unlike these established playwrights, McGahern had no previous experience of the theatre and soon found himself in uncharted waters. Cardin quotes the reservations expressed by Émile-Jean Dumay for whom the plot summary at the beginning of the play betrays the dependence of the artist on prose narrative: 'Providing a brief description of the past, present and future of the "personae" is tantamount to calling into question the validity and persuasive power of the dialogues which make up the play'.[10] Cardin goes on to state that the adaptation of Tolstoy's work by McGahern seriously changed a number of important aspects. Firstly he shortened the original play by about a half and the number of characters was reduced from twenty-five to seven. As a result, the dialogue is confined to describing the events that take place and thus there is not ample opportunity to dwell on the motivation and psychological dilemmas encountered by the characters. Everything therefore has the appearance of artificiality, of

9. Betrand Cardin, '*The Power of Darkness*: Tolstoï adapté par McGahern', in Thierry Dubost (ed), *L'adaptation théâtrale en Irlande de 1970 à 2007* (Caen: Presse Universitaires de Caen, 2010), pp 135-50.
10. Cited by Cardin, 'Tolstoï adapté par McGahern', p 138. The original review by Dumay appeared in *La Licorne*, no 32, 1995, p 168. (My translation.)

being contrived; the plot seems to lack depth and the characters are reduced to mere types.[11] McGahern may well have been attracted to the way in which Tolstoy suffered the humiliation of his work being censored in his native Russia. Written in 1886, *The Power of Darkness* found a powerful ally in the Tsar Alexander III, who admired the play but could not prevent its subsequent banning on the grounds that its author was a nihilist. The play was not performed in Russia until 1895, although a production took place in Paris in 1888. Tolstoy's treatment at the hands of the Russian authorities must have resonated with McGahern's own experience around the time of the banning of *The Dark*.

Given the huge success of *Amongst Women* when it was published in 1990, one might have reasonably expected *The Power of Darkness* to enjoy a more positive response than it did. McGahern was at the zenith of his powers at this point and Garry Hynes had assembled a formidable cast for the first performances of the play – the likes of Mick Lally, Sean McGinley, Marie Mullen and Bernadette Shortt were all involved. Murray quotes some of the reviews published to demonstrate the hostile reaction generated by the play. Gerry Colgan in *The Irish Times* called it a 'melodramatic morass' that often 'topples into unintentional, broad farce, generating that uneasy laughter among the audience that bespeaks the death of the play's serious intentions'. Des Rushe wrote the following critique in the *Irish Independent*: 'The play slides downhill, swinging from loud melodrama to unintentional farce …'[12]

McGahern explained that he was initially commissioned by BBC Radio 3 to write the play: 'They wanted a work which showed a peasant society where religion was a living presence. I felt that I had written it too colourfully, and I used to work on it when I was doing nothing else. Then, after *Amongst Women*, Pam Brighton found out that the play existed, and she sent it to the Abbey'.[13] As events unfolded, the transition from fiction to radio to live theatre was not a smooth one for McGahern. An ad-

11. Cardin, 'Tolstoï adapté par McGahern', p 147.
12. Cited in Murray, 'The "fallen world",' p 86.
13. Clíodhna Ní Anluain (ed), *Reading the Future: Irish Writers in Conversation with Mike Murphy* (Dublin: The Lilliput Press, 2000), pp 137-156, p. 152.

ditional problem was the transposition of Tolstoy's text into an Irish context. Where McGahern saw parallels, the audience detected distortion and this in part accounts for the discomfort experienced by audiences at what they perceived to be a negative and at times exaggerated representation of Irish life and mores. When he arrived into the Abbey the day after the first performance, McGahern was approached by the actor Mick Lally who announced: 'Andy O'Mahoney liked the play in preview and he wants you to do a radio show and there's a car waiting for you in half an hour. Will you go out to RTÉ and talk, especially about resurrection and salvation, to see if you can keep these swing doors open?'[14] Not surprisingly, Lally emphasised the religious aspects of the play (specifying 'resurrection and salvation') as being the elements that would be most likely to click with the Irish public, who obviously associated McGahern with issues pertaining to religion. In spite of the author's best efforts – the controversy did at least result in healthy bookings – *The Power of Darkness* was generally perceived to be something of a failure.

A brief discussion of the plot will hopefully cast light on why the play was so poorly received in 1991. There are six main characters: Peter King, a rich farmer; Eileen, his second wife; Maggie, Peter's daughter from a first marriage; Paul, a workman on the King farm, and his parents, Oliver and Baby. Then there is Paddy, a former soldier who suffers from alcoholism and who also works for Peter King. King is a good deal older than his second wife, who is very taken with Paul, something of a philanderer to all outward appearances. We learn at the beginning of the play that a girl working in the American bar, Rosie, has claimed she is pregnant with Paul's child. His parents visit the King farm with a view to discussing this issue. Baby, the mother, is a manipulative and street-wise woman who recognises that Eileen is attracted to her son. Seeing the advantages that could accrue if Peter passed away and Eileen and Paul were to marry, she sows a seed in the mind of the young woman: 'There was never much jizz left in poor Peter the best day ever he was' (*PD*, 7). Whereas Baby is pragmatic, even opportunistic, Oliver is the

---

14. Ní Anluain, *Reading the Future*, p 152.

religious conscience of the play. He tells his wife that Paul ought to do the right thing by Rosie: 'You can twist things in people's eyes but you can't twist them in God's eyes … the wrong done to the girl must be put right before God' (PD, 10). Baby tells him that the girl is known to be easy when it comes to offering her body to willing males, but Oliver insists: '… the wrong done to the girl must be put right before God' (PD, 10). Peter King and Oliver are of a similar religious disposition, which is obvious from the following observation made by Oliver:

> Often, Peter King, we twist things to favour ourselves and refuse to take God into account. And what we think to be best for ourselves turns out to be the worst because we left God out (PD, 10).

Paul, influenced by his mother, denies the claim made by Rosie and this marks the beginning of his slide into moral delinquency. Baby works on Eileen and encourages her to poison Peter before she is written out of his will – he has sent for his sister Martha in what is viewed as a suspicious move by the two women. As he keeps all his money in a safe upstairs, with the numbers to the combination on a slip in his wallet, they resolve to put a lethal dose of tablets in his tea and then to store the money in a safe place once he has passed away. Peter comes downstairs unexpectedly, just at the moment when Paul enters the kitchen. The old man apologises to Paul for how he has treated him:

> I may never have a chance to speak to you again. I feel I'm going. I want to ask your forgiveness for any wrong I've ever done you. I've said many a hard word to you in my time. Forgive me (PD, 21).

Slightly embarrassed by this entreaty, Paul assures Peter that there is nothing to forgive – the fact that he has been carrying on with Eileen would seem to indicate that it is he who should be seeking forgiveness and not the other way round. The old man is then given the fatal drink and dies almost instantly. Paul feels guilty for his betrayal of Peter's trust, but is harried by his mother into hiding the money they find in the safe before Maggie returns with Aunt Martha. Thus ends Act Two.

The remaining three Acts show the far from harmonious situation in the King household. Paul marries Eileen but spends a huge amount of time with Maggie, on whom he is frittering away his ill-gotten fortune. Eileen is beginning to wonder if her crime was worth the effort. She is determined to get Maggie out of the house and attempts to set up a match with a Mikey Coyne. She mentions the idea to Oliver: 'We'd like to see Maggie settled. There's never enough room for two women in any one house. There might be more peace if we were on our own' (PD, 31). The fact that Maggie is pregnant with Paul's child makes a quick match essential. Oliver is horrified at his son's heavy drinking and dissolute lifestyle. He witnesses him putting Eileen out of the house after she has an argument with Maggie and warns: 'I've never seen such conduct. God, you know, couldn't be in a house like this. God couldn't be in this house' (PD, 35). As far as Oliver is concerned, Paul's problems began when he refused to accept responsibility for Rosie's condition: 'A sin is always a sin until you go on your knees and beg forgiveness. You can hide sin from people but you can't hide it from God' (PD, 36). In his usual sanctimonious manner, he urges Paul to repent. In spite of his drunken state, his father's words stick with Paul and it begins to dawn on him that all bad deeds have a habit of coming back to haunt you.

Maggie's wedding brings everything to a head. As the wedding party returns to the King farm for the post-wedding celebration, Baby comes to tell her son that Maggie has had a miscarriage and that he will have to dispose of the bundle containing the foetus. Such events were topical in Ireland at the time McGahern was writing this play. He specifically mentions the Kerry Babies Tribunal of 1985 in his Introduction. This shocking occurrence revolved around a single woman, Joanne Hayes, who had been having an affair with a married man Jeremiah Locke, and was accused of stabbing her illegitimate baby and, with the help of her family, of disposing of the body in the sea at Dingle. The baby that was found initially with all the stab wounds was actually discovered in Caherciveen, which rendered the chances of its making the journey from Dingle highly unlikely. When the body of another baby was located on the Hayes farm near Castleisland, close to the spot where Joanne had claimed she

gave birth on her own, the police investigation came up with the
outlandish theory that Joanne had had sex with two different
men within 48 hours and conceived by both – this is referred to
as superfecundation, a process described by an expert witness
as being 'so exceedingly rare that one rules it out'.[15] In spite of
the highly implausible basis of their case against Joanne Hayes,
the investigating Gardaí nevertheless continued to argue that
she had given birth to two babies, one of whom she stabbed on
numerous occasions before disposing of it in the sea at Dingle.
They further argued that she had then given birth to the second
baby in a field near her house. Reflecting on the incident some
years later, Tom Inglis observed:

> The past may be a foreign country; things might have been
> done differently then. But to understand who we are today, to
> understand contemporary Irish society, we have to reflect crit-
> ically on how the past is embodied in us. For this is not just the
> story of one unfortunate woman. It is a story of Irish women,
> about honour and shame, about Ireland awakening from the
> Catholic Church's monopoly on sexual morality, about the
> state and what happens when people turn a blind eye to the
> way the police operate, of the way the legal field operates, and
> of the synergy between police, lawyers and judges.[16]

I make reference to the Kerry Babies incident because it
underlines the extent to which attitudes in Ireland towards sexuality were still rather Victorian up to the 1980s. The Hayes family were undoubtedly treated in an unjust manner. Nevertheless, a Tribunal concluded that the Gardaí had acted in good
faith and had not coerced witnesses into giving false statements.
There is another point that needs to be made here and it is that a
woman like Joanne Hayes came to represent a danger to the
hold the Catholic Church had over Irish society in matters pertaining to morality. Diarmuid Ferriter offers the following assessment: 'It [Kerry Babies saga] raised the question as to
whether the treatment of Hayes, who was accused of no crime,
was a paradigm for Irish male attitudes to women and to single

---

15. Cited in Tom Inglis, *Truth, Power and Lies: Irish Society and the Case of the
Kerry Babies* (Dublin: UCD Press, 2003), p 75.
16. Inglis, *Truth, Power and Lies*, p 3.

mothers, though in truth Hayes was not "the classic Irish single mother". She did not hide, or give up her baby, she was "a bold and transgressive figure": indeed, the case illustrates how "sexually transgressive women" became isolated, marginalised and oppressed'.[17]

Joanna Hayes did indeed fall in love with a married man, conceived at least two children by him (one of whom survived) and made no attempt to hide the affair: such behaviour was a flouting of the moral teaching Joanne and other women of her generation would have received at home and in school. But some of the religious instruction appeared to stay with her, as is evident in her attitude to artificial contraception. Because she was in love with Jeremiah Locke, having recourse to contraceptives never crossed her mind. Inglis concludes:

> There was not a contraceptive mentality. Love and sex were conflated. They were seen in the Catholic sense of the complete giving or surrender of the self to the other. To use contraception would be to reduce sex to an instrumental means of satisfying one's desires.[18]

Christopher Murray finds McGahern's comments about how Tolstoy's play mirrored the moral climate in which he grew up significant, especially as the prevailing morality tended to attach guilt to sexuality in an unhealthy manner. In mentioning the Kerry Babies incident specifically, which became a 'feminist *cause célèbre*', McGahern may have wanted to highlight how much repression persisted in Irish society up until quite recently. But, by presenting the main female characters in *The Power of Darkness* as dangerously manipulative and calculating, by showing the men to be the victims of the women's manic obsessions, McGahern's play 'flew in the face of this public awareness'.[19] Also, whatever 'redemption' is evident in the play is confined to the men. Paul remarks to his mother, 'I wish I had been dead before I was born' (*PD*, 45), and he marvels at how he could have so callously thrown Maggie's dead baby in a gripe. His mother cajoles him as best she can, insists that he will have

17. Ferriter, *Occasions of Sin*, p 527.
18. Inglis, *Truth, Power and Lies*, p 148.
19. Murray, 'The "fallen world",' p 88.

to address a few words to the wedding party before Maggie leaves with the groom, but the young man has no strength left to persist with all the lies and subterfuge. His attempt to hang himself is thwarted by the fact that the rope he uses is attached to the drunken ex-soldier Paddy. Then Oliver comes into the barn and offers a way out of the dilemma: 'You have to confess and God will forgive you. You don't have to fear anybody if you tell the truth before God' (*PD*, 51). In a symbolic gesture, Paul takes off his shoes and walks barefooted towards the house where he confesses all his sins to those gathered there. The consequences for him and for the women will be catastrophic and one has the sense that the biblical tone of the last scene is somewhat contrived. We know that Paul feels an acute need of forgiveness and redemption, but his final gesture is melodramatic to say the least. Bertrand Cardin notes the simplistic manner in which the characters in McGahern's play are divided between the generous and the calculating, the idealists and materialists, the good and evil. In Tolstoy's play, Nikita, on whom Paul is based, finds himself torn between his sexual needs and his thirst for truth, whereas Paul 'is merely a cowardly whiner who constantly expresses his regret at having been born'.[20] Likewise the other characters in McGahern's adaptation are mere caricatures who never assume any genuinely human dimensions. They fail to move us, to make us enter their world, to share their suffering.

McGahern maintained in his Introduction that the 'remote and dark age' to which *The Power of Darkness* apparently alluded was not very remote at all – the Kerry Babies Tribunal findings were testimony to this fact. He continued: 'It is in the nature of things that such a climate also creates the dramatic hope, or even necessity, of redemption' (*PD*, vii). For Christopher Murray, 'McGahern's "fallen world" … remains fallen'[21] and the play fails to captivate the reader in the same way as the novels and short stories do. The religious atmosphere of *The Power of Darkness*, while in some ways consistent with McGahern's memory of the 'moral climate' in which he grew up, feels foreign, fabricated, inauthentic. There is a lack of the type of social and moral insights which we associate with McGahern. One excep-

---

20. Cardin, 'Tolstoï adapté par McGahern', p 145. (My translation.)
21. Murray, 'The "fallen world",' p 90.

tion is the following gem by Paddy: 'You have the one small death and then you're with kings and county councillors' (*PD*, 52). Such nuggets are unfortunately all too rare in the play.

Taken together, *The Rockingham Shoot* and *The Power of Darkness* provide glimpses of several of McGahern's religious preoccupations, but without ever attaining the universal resonance with which his best work is always infused. You have fanaticism, moral blindness, repression, decadence, murder and lies in abundant supply, but they do not touch us with anything like the same force as in the fiction. This may well be because fanatical Catholicism was steadily losing its grip in Ireland during the second half of the twentieth century when change was to be seen everywhere. As Tom Inglis observes:

> The monopoly that the Catholic Church had developed over Irish morality began to fragment. Young men and women began to distance themselves from the rhetoric of piety, humility, purity and chastity developed by the Church and inculcated in the homes, schools, communities and everyday life in which they were brought up.[22]

Bertrand Cardin makes a very interesting observation at the end of his evaluation of *The Power of Darkness* when he points out how McGahern had to view the negative reaction to his play as an artistic failure on his part. It was ten years before his next publication, *That They May Face the Rising Sun*, a novel in which dialogue plays such a dominant role. This emphasis on dialogue is the result of the writer's experimentation with the theatrical form, in Cardin's view: 'In addition, in this text [*That They May Face*] which has the appearance of being both a novel and a play, the author demonstrates a preference for presenting the facts rather than narrating them, to the extent that the reader does not have the impression that the action of the novel is narrated so much as lived out in front of him on the stage'.[23] Sometimes artists learn more from the experiments that don't come off than from the successes. The next and final chapter of this book will discuss two of McGahern's crowning achievements, *Amongst Women* and *That They May Face the Rising Sun*.

---

22. Inglis, *Truth, Power and Lies*, p 221.
23. Cardin, 'Tolstoï adapté par McGahern', p 149. (My translation.)

CHAPTER FIVE

Grasping the 'Amazing Glory' we are part of:
Amongst Women *and*
That They May Face the Rising Sun

When it comes to assessing McGahern's literary legacy, his last two novels are an indispensable reference point. It is in these works that his painstaking commitment to style (to 'getting the words right'), his evocation of traditional Irish rural life with its beauty and brutality, its foibles and eccentricities, its superstition and religiosity, all come together in an intoxicating blend that attains a universal resonance.[1] The writer succeeds in making of one small place an everywhere and readers of his work who follow the trajectory from *The Barracks* through to *That They May Face The Rising Sun* gain a familiarisation with the settings, the characters, the rituals, the speech, the longings and the frustrations that the oeuvre as a whole encapsulates. It is really the one work of art from beginning to end and the writer becomes more accomplished as he chisels away at his material, striking the right note, conveying the image that is at the core of his literary quest, the rhythm that gives life to the image, the memory that fuels the imagination and nurtures the vision. *Amongst Women* and *That They May Face The Rising Sun* also helped to bring McGahern to the attention of a reading public who had previously been unaware of his writings. The nomination of *Amongst Women* for the Booker Prize, its highly successful adaptation into a TV drama (a collaboration between the BBC and RTÉ) with the late Tony Doyle brilliant in the role of Moran, undoubtedly played a significant role in copper-fastening McGahern's reputation and enhancing his profile. Another factor that intervened in ensuring a more positive reaction to his work was the manner in which Irish society had moved on in

1. I develop this aspect of his work in my monograph *John McGahern: From the Local to the Universal* (2003).

the interval between the 1960s, when his first novels were published, and the 1990s and 2000s, which saw his final novels and *Memoir* on the bookshelves. Kevin Whelan points out that McGahern 'was among the first to pinpoint the compromised complicity of a diseased version of Catholicism with this emerging Irish State'. He continues:

> In McGahern's sequence of powerful novels, from *The Barracks* to *Amongst Women*, we are presented with lives unlived as much as lived, restricted by harsh political and social circumstances, played out in the micro-world of family.[2]

While this is undoubtedly true of the fiction up to and including *Amongst Women*, the same cannot be said of *That They May Face the Rising Sun*, which is more celebratory of life and of people than any of the previous fiction. Dermot McCarthy puts forward a plausible explanation for this change of tone and emphasis. He claims that the 'Death of the Father' at the end of *Amongst Women* was 'the necessary condition for the resurrection of the mother. At the end of the memoir, when the reader comes to McGahern's comments on the father's death, there is an almost palpable sense of release … which may explain why *That They May Face the Rising Sun* … is tonally unlike anything McGahern had written before.' McCarthy's conclusion is particularly compelling:

> In terms of the mythopoeic structure of McGahern's total body of work, *That They May Face the Rising Sun* is the promised Mass he never said for his mother; it is a work that brings the rituals of confession, atonement, purification and communion intrinsic in his fiction to a transcendent closure.[3]

Such a reading allows one to fruitfully explore the two novels as representing an end and a new beginning, a death and a resurrection. It also allows for a more enlightened discussion of the portrayal of Roman Catholicism in the work as a whole and in these two novels in particular. This reading would not be at variance either with the thesis developed by Kevin Whelan who

---

2. Kevin Whelan, 'Time, Space and History', in John Kenny (ed), *The John McGahern Yearbook*, Vol 3 (Galway: NUI Galway, 2010), pp 14-23, pp 16-17.
3. McCarthy, *John McGahern and the Art of Memory*, p 20.

notes how McGahern's later prose uses words 'with a theological substrate' – 'blessed', 'dear presence', 'light' – which develops
'a secularised Christian vocabulary that signals an ethical way
of seeing and being in the world, a balance of gravity and grace,
in Simone Weil's terms'. He concludes:

> Like the late poetry of Patrick Kavanagh and Seamus
> Heaney, this is a post-Catholic ethic, a secular spirituality
> rooted in nature. There is a profound way in which
> McGahern has remained a spiritual writer, not just interested
> in morals (how we behave towards other people) but in spir-
> ituality – our relationship with the meaning of life and every-
> thing that surrounds our lives.[4]

In the discussion of the final novels, I will attempt to ascer-
tain whether we are dealing, in fact, with a 'post-Catholic ethic'
or whether it is merely an ethic that is typically Irish, one that
has not changed to any significant degree with the passing of
time. It is equally important to differentiate between a religious
and a spiritual disposition in order to determine which is the
better adjective to apply in McGahern's case. Many of his characters yearn for a transcendent vision that is sometimes provided
by nature, at other times by religious rituals, and which more
often than not proves inaccessible.

Amongst Women is a forceful evocation of a family's struggle
to survive against the ravages of emigration, poor communication between the family members, physical and verbal violence,
intolerance and the tides of change that are enveloping a country. At the heart of the family is one Michael Moran, the former
leader of an IRA flying column during the War of Independence. As the novel opens, we discover that his daughters and
their stepmother Rose are trying desperately to reinvigorate the
man who has been at the centre of their lives and who is now apparently stumbling towards death. They believe that by reviving
Moran's celebration of Monaghan Day, as the one-day February
fair in Mohill was called, they might bring him back from the
brink. For years, this day was the occasion when Moran was
reunited with his former comrade-in-arms, McQuaid. They got

---

4. Whelan, 'Time, Space and History', p 23.

together to discuss the war, relive the intensity that was attached to the armed struggle, eat a sumptuous meal (accompanied by copious amounts of whiskey on McQuaid's part) prepared by the daughters, before McQuaid repaired to bed. What the women fail to realise is that the last time McQuaid visited Great Meadow, as the Moran household is called, their father's compulsion to dominate at all costs caused a rift to develop that never healed.

McQuaid had first of all upset Moran by referring to incidents that his former superior officer considered inappropriate in front of his daughters. For example, he recounted how a member of their squadron, after a night standing in the cold, had terrorised a young woman who came out of her house in the morning to go to the toilet only to have the freezing barrel of a gun placed on her backside. McQuaid then brought up Moran's prowess with the ladies: 'The rest of us had to scrape and scrounge for the girls, Michael, but whatever you had they always fell into your hands like ripe plums' (*AW*, 19). Prior to this comment, they had differed on their view of the outcome of the struggle for independence. Moran felt that it had resulted merely in the emergence of 'a crowd of small-minded gangsters out for their own good', a view which McQuaid rejected: 'The country is ours now anyhow. Maybe the next crowd will be better than this mixture of druids and crooks that we're stuck with' (*AW*, 18). Moran then entreated him to 'leave the priests out of it', which his friend pointedly refused to do. McQuaid, a successful cattle dealer, has fared well in the new dispensation and has no time for a clergy that had been quick to condemn the activities of the IRA from the pulpit. He has chosen the secular path, espousing commerce and the material gains associated with it, whereas Moran, who distrusts change, sticks with a rather righteous and outdated notion of how people should conduct themselves. McQuaid then attacks the vulnerable point, Moran's religiosity, arguing there might be no next life, which would make refusing the army pension foolhardy:

'Man proposes ...', Moran said darkly.
'And God stays out of it', McQuaid twisted round the old saw (*AW*, 20).

The disagreement between Moran and McQuaid illustrates the differences between a person determined to maintain a certain order on life, at least within the walls of his own home, even though he realises that change is inevitable, and one whose pragmatism prompts him to avail of whatever opportunities come his way. Moran is obviously disillusioned with the Ireland that has emerged from his fight for freedom and he has difficulties with those whom he perceives to have benefited most from independence – the doctors and the priests. Nevertheless, he maintains the outward appearances of reverence when it comes to the clergy, because religion is the means by which he justifies his control over the family. The daily recitation of the Rosary, which follows a set pattern, with Moran saying the first decade and then handing on to Rose and the children according to age, reinforces the routine he seeks to inculcate at every turn. Prayer for him is little more than one of the many catchphrases that punctuate life at Great Meadow such as the following: 'Who cares? Who cares anyhow'; 'God, O God, O God'; 'The family that prays together, stays together'; 'Alone we might be nothing. Together we can do anything'.[5] Denis Sampson notes that 'Moran expresses himself through routines and rituals which are sometimes accompanied by bitter refrains …'[6] In Sampson's estimation, Moran's pious exterior masks a disdainful attitude towards any weakness he detects in others. This is especially apparent in relation to priests. For example, on two occasions he calls into question the priests' thoughts on death: 'Strange, to this day I have never met a priest who wasn't afraid to die. I could never make head or tail of that. It flew in the face of everything' (AW, 74). He draws attention to an important point here, the distance between the message preached by the clergy and their personal belief system and behaviour. If one truly believes in the tenets of the Catholic faith, one should not be frightened of death. As someone who for a number of years did not know if he would live to see the next dawn, but whose commitment to the cause meant that fear did not paralyse him, Moran is entitled to question why the priests of his acquaintance reacted in the manner they did when faced with their mortality.

5. No individual references given because they are too numerous.
6. Sampson, *Outstaring Nature's Eye*, p 225.

Priests do not feature to any large extent in *Amongst Women*, and yet religion is a strong theme in the book. On the occasion of his wedding to Rose and the meal that was held in her house afterwards, a precondition Moran had laid down if they were to get married – much to the dismay of her family who would have much preferred to go to a hotel – the priest made a short speech 'praising the families for the outstanding simplicity of the wedding feast'. According to him: 'There was too much emphasis nowadays on show, on Rolls-Royces and big hotels, wasteful, expensive display. It was pleasant seeing people returning to the old ways ...' (*AW*, 43-4). The priest's words mirror exactly what Moran had in mind, a lack of ostentation, a simple ceremony and meal, a return to 'the old ways'. The novel also makes clear that Moran is a miser and that he would resent seeing people for whom he had not a scintilla of respect being fed and watered at his or Rose's expense. At no time did he display any undue haste about getting married a second time and once he agreed to it, he immediately resented the decision. So, he was forthright in his determination to avoid any fuss.

When the newly marrieds arrive back at Great Meadow with the children, they engage in family prayer. The Rosary, for Moran, is primarily about maintaining order. There has been a long tradition of mariolatry in Ireland and, by seizing on this prayer, Moran is very much in tune with what was considered normal practice in rural Ireland for centuries. John Healy, writing about his youth in Ireland during the 1940s, notes the centrality of the Rosary:

> There was no need for words now. The clock would strike ten. Grandma would put her sewing aside. From a nail on the wall she'd take the big Rosary beads ... [W]e got up from our seats, knelt down with our backs to the fire and one another, leaned our elbows on the seat ... and made the responses. It was so in my mother's day and it would be so in my childhood days.[7]

Antoinette Quinn argues that *Amongst Women* 'reveals some of the forces that have shaped modern Ireland'. She justifies this claim in the following manner:

7. Cited by Louise Fuller, *Irish Catholicism Since 1950*, p 25.

In its characterisation of the ex-guerilla hero, Moran, it shows
the destructive legacy of political evolution: the channeling of
frustrated energies and ambitions into petty authoritarianism
and violence, the invocation of Catholicism to support a
domestic reign of terror, the maiming of a succeeding generation through denial of individuality and insistence on conformity.[8]

While it is undoubtedly used by Moran to bolster his 'domestic reign of terror', the Rosary does exert a calming influence
also. The mechanical droning of the responses gives the same
type of reassurance as a day spent saving the hay or doing any
of the other tasks that form the daily routine of life on a farm.
Moran is unquestionably the exemplar of a certain kind of Irish
father who in the past used religion to bolster their power in the
home. Denis Sampson sees the Rosary in *Amongst Women* 'not so
much as an expression of religious faith as it is a ritual with
powerful binding force within this miniature tribe'.[9] Eamonn
Wall, on the other hand, argues that Sampson underestimates
the religious aspects of the prayer whose very repetitiveness is
central to Catholic religious ritual and part of the timeless rituals
of rural life.[10] I think it is a bit of both, a 'binding force' within
the family and an integral part of lived Catholic experience. At
moments when he feels he is no longer the centre of attention,
Moran spills the rosary beads into his hands and gets the family
to kneel down in prayer. The prayer is offered for whatever intention is considered most pressing. For example, the evening
after Maggie departs for London, 'Moran said the Rosary early,
at the end of which he added a prayer for the girl's safekeeping
in the world she was about to enter' (*AW*, 62). Then he invokes
help for Sheila in making up her mind about studying medicine
in university or taking up a position in the Civil Service:

8. Antoinette Quinn, 'A Prayer for my Daughters: Patriarchy in *Amongst Women*', in *Canadian Journal of Irish Studies*, Vol 17, No 1, July 1991, pp 79-90, p 79.
9. Sampson, *Outstaring Nature's Eye*, p 219.
10. Eamonn Wall, '"The Living Stream": John McGahern's *Amongst Women* and Irish Writing in the 1990s', in *Studies: An Irish Quarterly*, 351 (88) (Autumn 1999), pp 305-24.

'Tonight we'll have to pray for her guidance ...' (*AW, 87*).[11] When both Sheila and Mona have left to take up their jobs in Dublin, Moran, sensing the depression that has taken hold of Rose and Michael, kneels down on the concrete floor and announces: 'We'd be better if we'd say our prayers.' However, this attempt at relieving the gloom does not have the desired effect: 'The prayers had done nothing to dispel the sense of night and stirring trees outside, the splattering of rain on the glass' (*AW,* 90). This bleak atmosphere will eventually prove too claustrophobic for young Michael, who will seek his diversion elsewhere.

Linden Peach, while acknowledging that *Amongst Women* is primarily concerned with the perpetuation of a system which allows fathers to become tyrants, maintains that 'it is also a critique of the damaging effects of Catholic discourse on families and on the lives of women in particular'.[12] He argues that the prayer from which the novel gets its title, the 'Hail Mary', declares one to be 'blessed amongst women', whereas Moran 'is haunted rather than blessed'.[13] Moran regularly invokes the Rosary priest, Fr Peyton's assertion that 'The family that prays together stays together', whereas his own family is totally fragmented. Likewise, he uses the prayer to occlude the outside world: 'This night Moran enunciated each repetitious word with a slow clarity and force as if the very dwelling on suffering, death and human supplication would scatter all flimsy vanities of a greater world ...' (*AW,* 79). The muted responses of the family members are a strong indication that they are not as fully engaged in this process as he is. Try as he might, Moran is incapable of keeping the family together, or of stemming the tides of change. The motivation for reciting the prayer is therefore a desire to preserve and legitimise the power of the patriarch.

11. Sheila is eventually broken down by her father's cantankerous attitude to medicine and opts for the Civil Service. At no stage did Moran ever intend to allow her take up a profession for which he had much disdain and which would take such a long time to complete, so his use of the Rosary is merely a hypocritical hiding behind the ritual here.
12. Linden Peach, *The Contemporary Irish Novel: Critical Readings* (London/ NY: Palgrave Macmillan, 2004), p 84.
13. Peach, *The Contemporary Irish Novel*, p 87.

However, to be successful, there is a need for female corrobora-
tion according to Siobhán Holland: 'The Rosary validates the
power of the father figure but it also places a special emphasis
on the benign intervention of a mother figure, so in order to
make the prayer cycle work in his favour, Moran has to reinforce its masculine associations over and above its Marian
links.'[14] He attempts to achieve this by emphasising the importance of the prayer in preserving the family unit and the indispensable role of the father within this unit. This is why the
Rosary is said at moments of his choosing and for the intentions
he singles out. But, as we have seen, his ambition enjoys nothing
like full success.

At Christmas, when all the family with the exception of Luke
return to Great Meadow, there is genuine excitement in the
preparation for the big day: 'All they had to do was observe the
happy rituals: help prepare the turkey, remove the curtains
from the front windows and light a single candle in each window' (AW, 96). Obviously the Rosary is a central part of the
evening in the run-up to midnight Mass. Moran, never one to
miss an opportunity for dramatic effect, begins: '"In the name of
the Father and of the Son and of the Holy Ghost, we offer up this
most holy Rosary for the one member of the family who is absent from the house tonight," and the dramatising of the exception drew uncomfortable attention to the disturbing bonds of
their togetherness' (AW, 96). Mention of Luke brings to mind the
reason for his refusal to return to Great Meadow. What exactly
happened between father and son to make the relationship so
bitter? Michael, talking to his lover Nell, a returned emigrant
from the United States, explains: 'Once he made Luke take off all
his clothes in the room. We heard the sound of the beating' (AW,
113). This beating mirrors many others recounted in the fiction
and in Memoir which are usually portrayed as inciting sexual
arousal in the person inflicting the punishment. There is no
overt reference to any sexual abuse in Amongst Women, even
though some unease is palpable in the scene when on the morn-

---

14. Siobhán Holland, 'Re-Citing the Rosary: Women, Catholicism and
Agency in Brian Moore's Cold Heaven and John McGahern's Amongst
Women', in Liam Harte and Michael Parker (eds), Contemporary Irish Fiction:
Themes, Tropes, Theories (London: Macmillan, 2000), pp 56-78, p 72.

ing he is to marry Rose, Moran comments on how this is the last
time that he and Michael will share a bed. The boy is not anxious
to dwell on such philosophical issues and manages to draw free
'from the kneading hand' (*AW*, 39), a description that might indicate at least a potential threat to the son had he not escaped so
quickly. Michael is never beaten as savagely as his older brother,
which could be a sign that Moran changed his behaviour after
Luke's departure. Equally, it could merely be a sign that his
physical strength is fading and that he is not capable of enforc-
ing his will with the same venom as heretofore. He does seek
forgiveness from his first born before he dies and is obsessed
with hearing news of him, but this could have to do with the
frustration Moran feels at Luke being the only child to remain
resolutely outside of his tight stranglehold on the family.

Prior to his death, Moran becomes acutely aware of the vivid
landscape that had escaped his attention throughout his life. He
becomes fascinated with the meadow at the back of the house:
'It was no longer empty but filling with a fresh growth, a faint
blue tinge in the rich green of the young grass' (*AW*, 179). Then
comes the startling revelation: 'He had never realised when he
was in the midst of confident life what an amazing glory he was
part of' (*AW*, 179). This is the most poignant moment in the
novel, as it portrays a frail old man stripped of the trappings of
power and faced with his imminent demise. Quinn observes
that at this moment 'Moran transcends egotism and arrives at a
metaphysical appreciation' of the 'glory' of nature.[15] That he
should 'see' for the first time the splendour that has surrounded
him all his life at this point makes his death all the more arduous
and prompts the remark: 'I never knew how hard it is to die'
(*AW*, 179). A priest comes to hear his Confession and then gives
him Communion and Extreme Unction. Once more he states his
bemusement at never having met a priest who wasn't afraid to
die. He himself 'slipped evenly out of life' (*AW*, 180), surrounded
by Rose and his daughters – Michael had gone to town with his
son – whom he had instructed to pray. The last words he uttered
were 'Shut up!' just as Maggie began her decade. This final
order, which is ignored, is an illustration of Moran's recognition
that the prayer to which he has shown such outward devotion

15. Quinn, 'A Prayer for my Daughters', p 89.

throughout his life was merely a means to an end, that end being the validation of his power. When he sees it is of no further use in this regard, he seeks to dispense with it. By now, however, the power has switched from the father to the daughters: '… it was as if each of them in their different ways had become Daddy' (*AW*, 183).

The description of the funeral takes up little more than three pages. Everything had been prepared for the moment of death. Rose had got her sister to buy the brown Franciscan habit some time previously. A local man, Woods, was called on to lay out the body, drink was bought and sandwiches made, the priest and doctor contacted. An expensive oak coffin was chosen by Rose and Moran was laid out with the Rosary beads placed between his fingers. Before the coffin was closed, a decade of the Rosary was recited and then a cry of grief reverberated around the house. The writing is economical, but no detail is omitted. The grief of the family is perfectly rendered without having recourse to long descriptions. Short sentences delineate the enactment of the various rituals: 'The front door was opened. The coffin was carried to the open door of the hearse. The hearse crawled out to the iron gate and turned right under the yew. All that night the coffin would lie before the high altar …' (*AW*, 182). A 'faded tricolour' covered the coffin, its tatty appearance an illustration of how Moran's efforts on behalf of his country had been largely forgotten, and then, before burial, a small man, 'old and stiff enough to have fought with Fionn and Oisin came out of the crowd' (*AW*, 183) and folded the flag. The local politicians watch the proceedings 'in undisguised contempt' (*AW*, 183). It is noticeable that there is more emphasis on politics than on religion in the final pages of the book.

One is left wondering to what extent Moran's lifelong commitment to religious rituals has had any real impact on him or his family. McCarthy argues that *Amongst Women* 'clearly depicts Moran and his influence as emblematic of the hypocritical, religiose, repressive, unimaginative, xenophobic, inward-turning, navel-worshipping national clerical society that McGahern recalls in his memoir'.[16] In a somewhat similar vein, Joe Cleary looks on McGahern as 'a detached philosophical existentialist'

---

16. McCarthy, *John McGahern and the Art of Memory*, p 245.

who ultimately produced 'a secular humanist version of the more religiously-inflected reconciliation with the quotidian that animates the late Kavanagh'.[17] These comments bring us back to Kevin Keogh's thesis quoted at the beginning of the chapter where he spoke of McGahern's 'secular spirituality rooted in nature'. Moran is not in any way the character who best voices the writer's personal views, but he does encapsulate some of McGahern's misgivings about the form of authoritarian Catholicism that he lived with as a child and for much of his adult life. I feel there is a strong 'existential' dimension to his writing and that the links to nature are prominently displayed, but I also believe that it is very difficult, if not impossible, to pronounce definitively on McGahern's stance in relation to Catholicism. As is clearly demonstrated by *Memoir*, there is more than a tinge of paganism in some of the customs one encounters throughout McGahern's fiction – we will see this, in particular, from several descriptions in *That They May Face the Rising Sun*. Working in such close proximity to nature marks the characters' outlook on life and impacts on their behaviour. At times, it introduces a certain earthiness, especially when it comes to the sexual vocabulary employed. Witness the catcalls directed at Rose as she makes her way to the post office where she hopes to meet Moran: 'Sink log! All find their way to the dirty hollow ...' (*AW*, 25).

In *Amongst Women*, McGahern does assume some of the characteristics of 'a detached philosophical humanist', to use Cleary's phrase, but, as is always the case in his treatment of Catholicism, his position is nuanced. While the influence of nature is definitely of great importance and while religious rituals are sometimes devoid of any real spiritual dimension, there is also an appreciation of those who display a genuine attachment to their religious faith. There is plenty of pragmatism in evidence also as can be seen in Sheila's decision to get married in Dublin, which is what her father demands in return for his presence at the ceremony, rather than in the local church:

Sheila cried a little when she discovered that she would not

---

17. Joe Cleary, *Outrageous Fortune: Capital and Culture in Modern Ireland* (Dublin: Field Day, 2007), p 165.

be making vows at the same altar rail at which she had received her Confirmation and First Communion, would not be coming out of the church into the shade of those great evergreens that had guarded her childhood (*AW*, 150).

At the wedding, the grief of Sean's mother at seeing her son married rather than ordained is acute: 'He was her special one. One day she would kneel and watch him raise the Host in the local church' (*AW*, 154). Instead, she has to watch him commit his life to another woman and lose all hope of his ever becoming a priest, a desire shared by many mothers in McGahern's fiction. Moran's own hope of effecting a reconciliation with Luke is similarly dashed when the son announces he is travelling back to London that evening. Moran dismisses this excuse with a 'God help you' and dejectedly leaves the hotel. On the journey home the family recites the Rosary and the prayer has a reassuring impact on the car passengers: 'the murmur of "Glory Be to the Father" following "Hail Mary" and "Hail Mary" and "Our Father" was as smooth and even as the purr of the engine passing Dromod, Drumsna and Jamestown' (*AW*, 156-7). Like the towns and villages they pass through, the prayers are familiar to them and have a poetry and rhythm that pacify the spirit.

After Sheila's wedding, Moran remains bothered by the enmity between himself and Luke and resolves to write and ask his forgiveness: 'Let me say I had no wish to harm you in the past and I have no wish to harm you in the future and if I have done so in thought, word or deed I am sorry' (*AW*, 176). On receiving the letter, Luke senses immediately that his father must be dying. He writes back to say that there was nothing to forgive and that he too was sorry if he had caused any hurt to Moran. This exchange, while it does not have the benefit of grace imputed to Confession, nevertheless has a strong Catholic flavour in terms of the vocabulary used – Moran speaks of harm brought about 'in thought, word or deed', a formula used in a typical examination of conscience. It brings about a healing of sorts of the rift between the two men before Moran departs this earth.

When considering the role Catholicism plays in *Amongst Women*, one needs to be aware of the symbolic capital that was associated with being perceived to be a good Catholic in the

Ireland of mid-twentieth century. Children were brought up to
bless themselves when going past a church, to kneel before the
tabernacle, to kiss a bishop's ring, to attend Mass every Sunday,
to receive the sacraments on a regular basis. It was extremely
difficult to completely ignore Catholic teaching, even after faith
was replaced by disbelief. Moran's children do not share their
father's preoccupation with religion and live far more liberal
lives than their parents did. Michael has a full-blown sexual relationship with Nell Morahan at only fifteen years of age and
when he subsequently goes to live in London, he gets another
older woman pregnant. He talks to Luke about it, explaining
how, as an English Catholic, she would not agree to their living
together – she was far more strict than many Irish Catholics of
his acquaintance. Luke's dry comment to this is: 'She can't be all
that strict' (*AW*, 170). What is significant about Michael's revelation is how little it shocks his family. Even Moran accepts the
woman and child into his home after Michael marries the mother.
It's almost as if religious principles are cast aside when
pragmatism dictates a change of attitude is necessary. Moran
might appear immutable and unshakeable in his beliefs, but he
knows that he cannot control his children once they are outside
the walls of Great Meadow. In addition, shortly after he has the
revelation of beauty in the meadow, he is quick to question why
priests should be afraid of dying. Stanley van der Ziel notes
that the positioning of these two scenes (the 'epiphany' in the
meadow and the calling into question of the priests' attitude to
death) at the end of the novel, 'suggests a direct juxtaposition
between two very different forms of religious experience. This
juxtaposition functions as an indication of how the traditional
role of Catholicism in McGahern's work is gradually being
taken over by a new pagan-sensation spirituality – what I propose to call an *aesthetic of redemption*, based on a celebration of
the ordinary that is made possible by the discovery of the simple
act of *seeing*.'[18] This 'pagan-sensation religion' is most prevalent
in *That They May Face the Rising Sun* but one has glimpses of it

18. Stanley van der Ziel, 'Fionn and Oisín in the Land of Wink and Nod:
Heroes, History and the Creative Imagination in John McGahern's *Amongst
Women*', in *Canadian Journal of Irish Studies* 31.2 (Autumn 2005), pp 10-18,
p 15. (Italics in original).

also in *The Barracks* and *Amongst Women*. Nature acts as a kind of trigger for moments of heightened perception that could be confused with religious insights were it not for the fact that they have no apparent transcendent dimension. Martin Ryle provides a useful bridge between *Amongst Women* and *That They May Face the Rising Sun* when he writes:

> McGahern's notations of place, light, weather, and season are never rhetorical or effusive, but their aim goes beyond the rendering of material detail: as in the high tradition of romanticism, contemplation of nature evokes Wordsworth's 'sense of something far more deeply interfus'd'. The writer's concern is not only with a particular landscape, but with the power of nature to provoke reflection on mutability and to offer aesthetic pleasure and a sense of cyclical renewal ...[19]

This 'power of nature to provoke reflection' is prominent in McGahern's final novel, as we shall now see. If we accept that the 'Death of the Father' at the end of *Amongst Women* has allowed the gentleness of the beloved mother to re-emerge, it will not come as a surprise that McGahern's last offering to long fiction, a paean to the woman he associated with kindness, an appreciation of natural beauty and of the goodness in people, should be completely different to anything the writer had produced heretofore. The absence of a central father figure and the enmity such a presence causes in all the fiction has the effect of lessening the tension, with the result that the book has more of a pastoral than a literary feel to it.[20] Seamus Deane saw in it 'a mixture of various genres of writing' with similarities to memoir and anthropology being especially evident. He also viewed it as a 'therapeutic reprise of the author's own career, a celebration of an Ireland that had formerly been the object of chill analysis as well as loving evocation'.[21] There is definitely a

---

19. Martin Ryle, 'Place, Time and Perspective in John McGahern's Fiction', in Britta Olinder and Werner Huber (eds), *Place and Memory in the New Ireland,* Irish Studies in Europe, Vol 2 (Trier: Wissenschaftlicher Verlag, 2009), pp 127-136, p 128.
20. This is a quality that is reflected in the title of Eileen Battersby's review of the novel, 'A superb earthly pastoral', in *The Irish Times,* 8 December, 2001.
21. Seamus Deane, 'A New Dawn', Review of *That They May Face the Rising Sun,* in *The Guardian,* 12 January 2002.

warmer feel to this book and I remember when I had finished reading it thinking that McGahern would not write another novel. Already he seemed to have slipped into the memoir genre with the childless couple, Ruttledge and Kate, a barely fictionalised version of the writer and his wife Madeline, to whom the novel is dedicated. The returned emigrants come to live in a house and a few acres located around a lake in a setting that was too closely modelled on the McGaherns' abode in Foxfield, County Leitrim for it to be purely coincidental. The Ruttledges are the focal point of the community and receive daily visits from people like their neighbours Jamesie and Mary, and the former 'homeboy' Bill Evans, who still performs tasks like drawing water from the well for a local farmer who treats him poorly. Every Sunday Ruttledge's uncle, 'The Shah', comes round the lake from the town where he runs a thriving business to eat with the couple. Other lakeside inhabitants like the handyman Patrick Ryan and the sexual deviant widower John Quinn are more infrequent visitors.

Ruttledge, like McGahern, is an unbeliever and he and Kate are almost the only residents from the area who never attend Mass or religious services. This is a source of playful banter between Jamesie and the Ruttledges. When Jamesie asks the reason for their non-attendance, Ruttledge says that he misses going but that he doesn't believe, which prompts the following riposte: '"I don't believe", he mimicked. None of us believes and we go. That's no bar' (*RS*, 2). When asked in his turn why he goes if he doesn't believe, Jamesie says: 'To look at the girls. To see the whole performance ... We go to see all the other hypocrites' (*RS,* 2). A former seminarian, Ruttledge seeks answers to the existential questions that confront him outside of any allegiance to organised religion. He retains affection for the ceremonies of the Catholic Church but would feel a real hypocrite were he to attend religious services in the knowledge that he no longer believed. His quest leads him to ponder on the meaning of life, its mysteries, the beauty of nature, the goodness and evil in human beings, death and eternity, but he does all this with a serenity that is starkly different to what one encounters in most of McGahern's other characters. When Jamesie tells of how his brother Johnny ruined his life by moving to England in pursuit of the great love of his life, Anna Mulvey, who ended up marry-ing a policeman who converted to Catholicism, Ruttledge ob-serves to Kate that he would have turned for her had she asked him to. Quick as a light, Jamesie pipes up: 'Spoken like a true heathen. They'll all turn, Kate. If they have to pick between their religion and the boggy hollow, they'll all turn!' (RS, 7). (Note the use of almost the identical phrase – 'the boggy hollow' – as that employed by the locals in their catcalls to Rose as she makes her way to the post office in *Amongst Women*). Although the inhabit-ants of the lakeside community are middle-aged or older, they all retain a keen interest in sex. We will see later how the exploits of John Quinn are followed with avid curiosity and, although his treatment of women is brutal, he is more admired than reviled by the community.

Bill Evans is a fascinating figure in light of the revelations of what happened to Irish children like him who were institution-alised from a very young age. Aged 14, he was sent from the religious institution to work on his first farm. His whole life was spent toiling away for farmers from whom he received barely enough to live on. Shortly after they came to live in the area, the Ruttledges received a visit from Bill who had been locked out of the house by his employers during an absence of a few days. Starving, he had been left with no option other than to ask his neighbours for some food. His story mirrors that of so many children from poor backgrounds who found themselves aban-doned by Church and State:

> He would have known neither father nor mother. As a baby he would have been given into the care of nuns. When these boys reached seven, the age of reason, they were transferred to places run by priests or Brothers.
> ... They were also sent as skivvies to the colleges; they scrubbed and polished floors, emptied garbage and waited at tables ... (RS, 10).

Ruttledge recalls how a Dean in the school he attended in-flicted a vicious beating on one of these boys because his soutane was splashed when some plates were dropped on the floor. In some ways, witnessing such an event was as bad as being beaten: 'Many who had sat mutely at the tables during the beating were to feel all their lives that they had taken part in the beating through their self-protective silence' (*RS*, 11). The accuracy of McGahern's description is borne out by the first hand evidence of those who spent time in industrial schools and other such institutions. While it is undeniable that corporal punishment was prominent in almost every home and school in Ireland a few decades ago, the degree to which children placed in care were beaten and abused must be a source of shame and horror for everyone. Those who ended up in these institutions, most often for the simple reason that they came from poor homes, were illegitimate or found guilty of some petty crime, tended to be viewed by the priests, brothers and nuns as lowlifes, the spawn of criminals and whores. Essentially, prison camps were created in Ireland where horrific and illegal crimes were perpetrated on innocent young children. The male and female religious were aided in their barbarity by the State and its agents, who knew what was going on, but did nothing to stop it. The case of Peter Tyrrell, who spent 6 years in Letterfrack industrial school in Connemara during the 1920s, illustrates just how appalling the regime was. He and others were constantly beaten with sticks or straps cut from a rubber tyre, or horsewhips. A Dr Lavelle visited Letterfrack regularly during Tyrrell's time there, but did little or nothing to protect the inmates from further exposure to this torture. One cannot reasonably claim that people were ignorant of what was happening in the industrial schools, orphanages and Magdalene laundries. Members of the local community where these institutions were located were aware of the goings on but, as was the case of allegations of clerical sex abuse, the reactions ranged from inaction to cover-up or complicit silence. Tyrrell's memoir, *Founded on Fear*, is a shocking account of the reality of how his experiences in Letterfrack completely transformed his life. One description in particular demonstrates the validity of Ruttledge's memory of the boy being beaten in the refectory by the Dean. It relates how a particularly violent Brother named Vale used to flog the children with a rubber hose after placing them on his knee and pinching them, playfully at first, and then with more force until the boys would cry out. Tyrrell notes:

Having experienced this kind of beating it's even more horri-
fying to watch, than the actual beating. In other words the
victim in this case is better off than the onlooker.[22]

It is not coincidental that a character like Bill Evans features
in *That They May Face the Rising Sun*. Bill represents yet another
aspect of the hidden Ireland that McGahern sought to expose
throughout his career. We are told that 'his kind was now almost as extinct as the corn-crake' (*RS*, 9). In spite of the cruel
treatment they meted out to him, 'his instinct to protect his
keepers and his place was primal' (*RS*, 8). He reacts badly to
Ruttledge's attempts to elicit information from him with the
exclamation, 'Stop torturing me' (*RS*, 12). After a time, Ruttledge
comes to the realisation that he is dealing with a man who
chooses to live in the present rather than delving into the horrors of the past. Writing about *The Report of the Commission to
Inquire into Child Abuse* (the Ryan Report), Diarmuid Ferriter offers the following explanation as to why children were allowed
to suffer humiliation and abuse in industrial schools, orphanages and other State-run institutions:

> Souls, not bodies, were the intense preoccupation and this
> became overwhelming in a small Catholic country with little
> tradition of Church opposition and an exaggerated deference
> towards those deemed to be pillars of the community. There
> was a casual indifference to everyday violence that would
> not have been tolerated in other countries. The children en-
> during the thrashings were mostly poor and held in con-
> tempt, victims of an invidious snobbery in a country that
> liked to pretend it was classless.[23]

Bill Evans, a victim of this callous indifference, finds a place
in the hearts of those living around the lake. He seems happy as
long as he is supplied with food and cigarettes, and in general is
well accepted by everyone: 'Bill Evans could no more look forward than he could look back. He existed in a small closed circle

---

22. Peter Tyrrell, *Founded on Fear: Letterfrack Industrial School, War and Exile*,
edited and introduced by Diarmuid Whelan (Dublin: Transworld Ireland,
2008), p 162.
23. Ferriter, *Occasions of Sin*, p 333.

of the present' (*RS*, 167). His presence in the novel serves to prod
our memories about injustices that were allowed to go
unchecked up to a few short decades ago in Ireland. Towards
the end of the novel, through the combined efforts of Ruttledge
and Fr Conroy, Bill is given a place in an affordable housing
scheme in the town known as *Tráthnóna*, the Irish word for
'afternoon'. As he enters his twilight years, Bill continues to live
in the present, never daring to take a backwards glance at his
life. Fr Conroy is a little concerned that this token gesture towards Bill's welfare might simply disorientate the poor man:
'Sometimes I think it may be better to let these mistakes run
their course. Attempting to rectify them at a late stage may bring
in more trouble than leaving them alone' (*RS*, 254-5).

Fr Conroy is the most sympathetic portrayal of a priest in
McGahern's work. He is a pleasant and unobtrusive man, a
force for good within the community. He is not someone who
delivers dramatic sermons or lays down the law to his parishioners. That said, he has an obvious liking for and empathy with
the people. Patrick Ryan sums up the views of many when he
states: 'Fr Conroy is plain. The priests had this country abulling
with religion once. It's a good job it's easing off' (*RS*, 82). He is
embarrassed when his bishop instructs him to call on the
Ruttledges: 'I'm not here on my own account. I believe in living
and letting live. The man up in Longford [the bishop] is very interested in you and why you left the Church and has me persec-
uted about you every time he comes' (*RS*, 66). A good rapport
develops between the priest and the agnostic, who show respect
for one another and collaborate on a number of projects, such as
the housing of Bill Evans. Fr Conroy does a bit of farming and is
often seen at the local marts, where he blends in well with the
other farmers. His ministry is one that is admirably suited to his
tact and understated demeanour. He is capable on occasions,
however, of offering a harsh critique of some of the ills of Irish
society. An example of this can be seen in the sermon he gives at
Johnny's funeral, where he evokes the economic necessity that
forced so many Irish people to emigrate to England: 'While
there were some who prospered and did well, there were others
who experienced great hardship and there were many that fell
by the wayside' (*RS*, 295). In addition, these emigrants were

often looked down on by those who remained at home. Jamesie is deeply appreciative of all the priest did around the time of Johnny's death: 'He was in the house less than an hour after we found him slumped in the chair, gave him the last sacraments, received him in the church, said the funeral Mass and preached a most beautiful – most beautiful sermon' (*RS*, 294-5).

Johnny's death is a focal point in the novel. After a day spent in the company of Ruttledge, where his skill at throwing darts earned him the respect of those who witnessed the masterful performance, he heads off to Jamesie's house, where he dies peacefully. Johnny came home every year from England and his arrival was marked by a massive clean-up operation by his sister-in-law Mary: 'The house couldn't have been prepared better for a god coming home to his old place on earth' (*RS*, 5). He was a mild-mannered, gentle sort of man, prone to few pronouncements apart from declaring everything to be 'alphabetical', his word for 'great'. The summer visits put a strain on Mary, but when Johnny was considering a permanent return to Ireland, she and Jamesie went into a tailspin: 'They could not live with him and they could not be seen – in their own eyes or in the eyes of others – to refuse him shelter or turn him away' (*RS*, 186). The crisis is averted when Johnny decides to finish his days in England, much to the relief of his brother and sister-in-law. His death occurs without warning and, as is normal for traditional Irish families described by McGahern, there are certain things that have to be attended to as a matter of urgency. Thus it comes to pass that, in the absence of Patrick Ryan who cannot be located, Ruttledge is asked by Jamesie if he will lay out the body. This scene constitutes a key moment in McGahern's writing, as Ruttledge is awestruck at what a fine physical specimen Johnny had been: 'The innate sacredness of each single life stood out more starkly in death than in the whole of its natural life' (*RS*, 273). McCarthy views this as a 'spiritual' moment, only 'in the sense of McGahern's non-transcendental spirituality, his reverence for the sanctity of the human, and his "religious" sense of the bonds that bind us all in the acts and experiences of our coming and going'.[24] When questioned by Kate about how he felt

---

24. McCarthy, *John McGahern and the Art of Memory*, p 303.

when performing the task, Ruttledge replies: 'It made death and the fear of death more natural' (RS, 279). The title of the novel can be traced to Johnny's burial scene, when Patrick Ryan explains to Ruttledge that the head of the dead man must be facing west: 'He sleeps with his head in the west ... so that when he wakes he may face the rising sun ... We look to the resurrection of the dead' (RS, 282). There is a nice blend of Christianity and paganism in this pronouncement. The pagan worship of the sun is counterbalanced by the Christian belief in the resurrection of the dead. Seamus Deane comments that this is 'a religious belief that is not confined to believers in religion'. According to his reading: 'Ryan's histrionics are perfectly in place here; this is a sober truth and it is a dramatic gesture ... These dead and their traditions no longer weigh like a nightmare on the brain of the living. They have been incorporated into consciousness.'[25] There is a certain liberation produced from how death is approached in the novel. This may have had something to do with McGahern's own health problems around the time of its composition and his increased awareness of his mortality – having said that, from the very start of his literary career he was fascinated with the notion of mortality.

His brother's death prompts Jamesie to ask Ruttledge if he believes in an after life. The latter replies: 'I don't know from what source life comes, other than out of nature, or for what purpose. I suppose it's not unreasonable to think that we go back into whatever meaning we came from' (RS, 294). McCarthy argues that, 'This is McGahern's 'last word' on the question of life, death and the afterlife, a final, resounding rejection of the faith of his childhood.'[26] I am not sure that it is as clear cut as McCarthy claims, but it is certainly a moving away from the Catholic dogma that Ruttledge and McGahern would have learned in school. In the absence of religious faith, Ruttledge attempts to conjure up a secular or philosophical vision of existence. Returning to 'whatever meaning we came from' is an intriguing image of life beyond the grave. In many ways, Ruttledge does not completely dismiss theological notions like

---

25. Deane, 'A New Dawn'.
26. McCarthy, *John McGahern and the Art of Memory*, p 308.

'heaven' and 'hell': 'I suspect hell and heaven and purgatory – even eternity – all come from our experience of life and may have nothing to do with anything else once we cross to the other side' (*RS*, 294). The emphasis on our earthly lives in the earlier quote suggests a glimpsing of the divine through the contemplation of nature and it is in this regard that McGahern's last novel offers a unique understanding of how the writer positioned himself in relation to the cosmos. The landscape is a character in its own right in *That They May Face the Rising Sun*, perhaps the most important character in the novel. Just after leaving Jamesie and Mary, as he and Kate head back to their house, the natural scene imposes itself on Ruttledge's consciousness:

> The night and the lake had not the bright metallic beauty of the night Johnny had died: the shapes of the great trees were softer and brooded even deeper in their mysteries. The water was silent, except for the chattering of the wildfowl, the night air sweet with the scent of the ripening meadows, thyme and clover and meadowsweet, wild woodbine high in the whitethorns mixed with the scent of the wild mint crawling along the gravel on the edge of the water (*RS*, 296).

The pantheistic dimension of this description captures the mood of a man who was profoundly in love with the natural environment. There is no mention of God in these lines; the awe that is evinced is inspired by the lake, the trees, the wildfowl, the meadows, the smells. But the process of 'naming' the foliage and the animals is an important element of the commemoration or celebration that forms an integral part of the novel. It also completes the circle that began with the opening lines: 'The morning was clear. There was no wind on the lake. There was also a great stillness. When the bells rang for Mass, the strokes trembling on the water, they had the entire world to themselves' (*RS*, 1). *Memoir* takes up where *That They May Face the Rising Sun* left off, with an intricate account of the soil, fields, hedges and lakes of Leitrim: 'The soil in Leitrim is poor, in places no more than an inch deep. Underneath is daub, a blue-grey modelling clay, or channel, a compacted gravel' (*M*, 1). When I questioned him in an interview about the extent to which the tenderness with which he evoked the Leitrim landscape may have had a 'spiritual' dimension, McGahern replied: 'No. Not that I'm aware of. We are part of nature, like the animals and the trees, and we are all part of that passing world we learn to love and to leave. Naturally, it is described with care or attention, as everything else should be, and it is also seen through a certain vision, maybe fallible and flawed, but mine, or those of my characters.'[27] I am still inclined to believe that the incantatory quality of 'naming' evokes a similar sensation to what others achieve through prayer. Note how, as Jamesie is being driven to the station, he 'named every house they passed, not with his usual fierce interest but as if it were a recitation of prayer' (RS, 196). Van der Ziel's remarks are apposite in this context:

> McGahern's prose, in short, and in his own words, 'comes into its own *like song or prayer or superstition*', and although the novel seems, like its main character, to reject any formal religious doctrine and embrace a vibrant paganism – as suggested by the title, which refers to a Celtic burial ritual – it seems to take on through its rhythms the ritual, as well as the spiritual quality of prayer.[28]

Denis Sampson adopts a slightly different stance: 'These passages function not as a description or backdrop; they are the dynamic force within the fiction to which all life is assimilated and given a sense of transcendent purpose.'[29] We have moved some distance from the spirituality of Elizabeth Reegan who, while she was undoubtedly moved by her contemplation of nature, was still nevertheless attached to the prayers and ceremonies of the Church, the superstitious faith of Mahoney, or the religiosity of Moran. Traditional Catholic belief has been replaced by a more hybrid form of spiritual experience. In this respect, the exchange between Ruttledge and Patrick Ryan, as they work on the shed that has been left unfinished for years, is significant.

---

27. Maher, *From the Local to the Universal*, p 159.
28. Stanley van der Ziel, 'The Aesthetics of Redemption: John McGahern's *That They May Face the Rising Sun*', in *Studies: An Irish Quarterly*, vol 93, No 372 (Winter 2004), pp 473-485, p 481. (Emphasis in original.)
29. Denis Sampson, '"Open to the World": A Reading of John McGahern's *That They May Face the Rising Sun*', in *Irish University Review*, Spring/Summer 2005, Vol 35, No 1, pp 136-146, pp 142-3.

Ryan asks his friend what he is looking at and is told: 'At how the rafters frame the sky. How the squares of light are more interesting than the open sky. They make it look more human by reducing the sky, and then the whole sky grows out from that small space.' Not used to this type of deep reflection, Ryan replies: 'As long as they hold the iron, lad, they'll do' (*RS*, 68). Ryan, like the majority of the inhabitants of Shruhaun, accepts the world and its foibles without too much soul-searching. The Church's teaching is not questioned in any serious way, but nor is it followed in a scrupulous manner. It is noticeable that the day after the burial of his close friend Johnny, Ryan arrives at the Ruttledges' determined to finish that 'cathedral of a shed' (*RS*, 297). He says they'll make a start, 'in the name of the Lord', one of the many religious refrains encountered in the novel. Denis Sampson rightly points out how the comparison of the shed to a cathedral evokes the oft-cited phrase of Proust by McGahern in relation to how the French Gothic cathedrals raised the people's eyes from the avaricious earth. He concludes: 'Although McGahern's world is a decidedly secular one, and the Church has a very limited place in it, the structure has a suggestive presence in the text.'[30] This is undoubtedly the case. Catholicism as a repressive, powerful force may well be on the wane, but it is unlikely it will disappear altogether. Ruttledge is struck by how few people are wearing ashes on Ash Wednesday, whereas when he was young even those who hadn't been to church would have thumbed the sign of the cross in a visible manner on their foreheads. At Christmas, nevertheless, it is hard to resist the lit crib on the steps of the church just before midnight Mass: 'For this night anyhow, its modern ugliness had disappeared and it resembled a great lighted ship set to sail out of the solid middle of the town into all that surrounds our life' (*RS*, 198). The church momentarily takes on the mantle of hope as its light spreads from the town out into the lives of the people.

The negative side of religion is not absent either. Reference is made to the bombing of Enniskillen and the carnage it wreaked on so many innocent people and their families. Many of the

30. Sampson, 'Open to the World', p 143.

atrocities committed by groups like the IRA were carried out in the name of religion. Then there is the case of John Quinn, who, through the sacrament of marriage, is given access to the coveted fields of his wife Margaret's family. Immediately after the church ceremony, he brings his bride out to the side of the hill, where in full view of the wedding guests, he claims his marital rights: 'He lifted the blue dress up over her head and put her down on the blanket. The screech she let out would put your heart crossways' (RS, 28). Quinn was laying down a marker for his wife and her family. Margaret's father never recovered from that ugly hillside coupling and died shortly afterwards. Quinn knew that once he had attained the status of husband he was in an unassailable position in the eyes of the Church and the local community: 'It was said he didn't let Margaret wear knickers in the house so that he could do her there and then whenever he wanted …' (RS, 29). His children all demonstrated a high regard for their father, however, especially after he intervened with their national school teacher to ensure they were not beaten in class. They achieved great success in life and came back to visit him at regular intervals. After the premature death of his wife and when his children had grown up, Quinn acquired a succession of women to satisfy his sexual longings. He took pleasure in bringing them all to church, where he would boldly plonk himself in the front seat for Mass and light candles with his lady friend afterwards. Naturally, the priests could not do anything to prevent this charade without provoking a scene.

There is great excitement when the news goes round that Quinn is about to be married again. All the neighbours are invited to the ceremony. When they arrive back at the hotel, the groom brings his new bride upstairs, which triggers bawdy innuendo among the guests:

'Maybe she's just dying for the hog', Patrick Ryan said provocatively, coarsely. …
'It's better for herself if she wants it', Jamesie said quietly.
'Whether she likes it or not she'll have to open the door.'
'She'll get the rod', Bill Evans said suddenly (RS, 168).

According to Eamonn Hughes, 'That They May Face the Rising Sun does not have any time for that cliché about the repressed sexuality of Irish rural communities; rather 'the text deals with sex as something natural and animal which does not abash its characters.'[31] The characters discuss sex openly, even 'coarsely' at times, and they are fascinated with the antics of John Quinn, for whom they display a certain admiration. In another McGahern novel, Quinn would have had a central role and would have assumed more menacing traits. The big change in this final novel is that the patriarch is adored by his children and accepted by the other members of the community in spite of his insatiable sexual appetite and devious business dealings. When his new bride leaves him shortly after the wedding (his second and third wives both abandon him), he remorsefully describes to Jamesie what a wonderful woman she was: 'She was as ripe as a good plum picked when it was about to fall off the tree.' And sex with her was sublime: 'It was like going in and out of a most happy future' (*RS*, 175). Eamonn Hughes argues that Quinn 'fits into the sexual economy of the text'[32] because his children have all left the lake, like those of the other inhabitants, and also because he counterbalances the sexlessness of someone like Patrick Ryan: 'I don't have to even countenance that job … John Quinn has agreed to do my share' (*RS*, 202). Sex is something that people talk about more than perform in this novel. The atmosphere of guilty repression has been replaced by a much more accepting approach of sex and the joys it can bring.

Happiness is also a theme that is broached, albeit obliquely. The life of Ruttledge and Kate appears fulfilling. They have a harmonious relationship. Patrick Ryan observes: 'They never seem to go against one another. There are times when they'd make you wonder whether they are man and woman at all' (*RS*, 77). Similarly, they enjoy the company of their friends, and the contemplation of what is by any standards a beautiful natural environment. Unlike Moran, they can 'see' the beauty that spreads itself before their eyes. After a day spent working in the fields, Ruttledge observes:

When all the meadows were cut they looked wonderfully

31. Eamonn Hughes, '"All that Surrounds Our Lives": Time, Sex and Death in *That They May Face the Rising Sun*', in *Irish University Review*, Spring/Summer 2005, Vol 35, No 1, pp 147-163, p 159.
32. Hughes, "All that Sourrounds Our Life", p 159.

empty and clean, the big oak and ash trees in the hedges towering over the rows of cut grass, with the crows and the gulls descending in a shrieking rabble to hunt frogs and snails and worms (*RS*, 106).

There are several depictions like this one throughout the novel which convey the impression of people who are in harmony with nature, conscious of the changing seasons, the energy of spring, the wholesomeness of summer, the vivid colours of autumn and the dark cold of winter. Eileen Battersby's review of the novel noted that, 'More than ever McGahern is determinedly observing the natural world: the lakeside landscape assumes a powerful presence with the lake changing as often as the sky or a human face'. In Battersby's estimation, 'This time nature for him [McGahern] is not a backdrop, it is both stage and a major character in its own right'.[33] As well as enjoying the resuscitating goodness of nature, the Ruttledges take strength also from the support of Jamesie and Mary, Patrick Ryan, 'The Shah', Bill Evans and all those whose friendship and visits enrich their lives. Toiling on the land with Jamesie makes the work much more pleasant for Ruttledge and these two regularly help each other with the hay and other jobs. Jamesie keeps a watchful eye on Ruttledge's Shorthorn when she is calving, for which he earns the grateful comment: 'You're an angel of the Lord' (*RS*, 53). Cups of tea, glasses of whiskey, comical conversations, meals shared and gossip exchanged, the comings and goings between the two couples take on an almost sacred dimension. Thus, after sharing a particularly pleasant few hours with his friends, Ruttledge reflects:

> … he felt this must be happiness. As soon as the thought came to him, he fought it back, blaming the whiskey. The very idea was as dangerous as presumptive speech: happiness could not be sought or worried into being, or even fully grasped; it should be allowed its own slow pace so that it passes unnoticed, if it ever comes at all (*RS*, 183).

Where, in any of the rest of McGahern's fiction, would you come across a passage like this? It has a calm assurance that only

---

33. Eileen Battersby, 'A superb earthly pastoral'.

comes through familiarity with the sentiments expressed and it displays an acceptance of the world as it is, with its pitfalls and transience, its joys and sorrows, its deep mysteries. Like memory, you cannot will happiness into being; you just allow it to work at its own slow pace and to weave its magical web. In an interview with Robert McCrum, McGahern stated: 'I think that complete happiness isn't possible in life and when it happens it's not noticed. I think that people forget that complete unhappiness is as equally unachievable as complete happiness.'[34] Things have definitely moved on from the persistently gloomy atmosphere of *The Barracks* and *The Dark*: the writer appeared much more carefree in his philosophy of life at the beginning of the third millennium. The serenity that underpins *That They May Face the Rising Sun* was acquired only after McGahern had exorcised through his art the demons of his early life. Gone are the resentment of the strict, abusive father, the uncertainty of embarking on a literary quest that would force him to re-enact the trauma of childhood, the struggle to be accepted by the Irish public who initially viewed his writings as unsavoury and discomfiting. By 2002, McGahern was viewed as a writer who encapsulated most successfully a way of life that appeared to be disappearing fast. Many of the issues he had courageously tackled were shown to have been accurate and he who was once reviled had now come to be revered. The catharsis experienced by writer and readers alike generates a type of mystical rebirth which is tangible in the mood and tone of the novel. Declan Kiberd comments on the 'stoic philosophy' of Ruttledge who refuses to pronounce definitively on whether there is an afterlife or not. This is deemed 'appropriate in a book which itself offers no comfortable certainties about religion' and 'which expresses beautifully, even if it can never solve, the human mystery'.[35]

That They May Face the Rising Sun has a timeless quality. The characters described in the novel seem to belong to a world that is on its last legs – they are all in their twilight years and the next generation has moved away from the lake – but which achieves

---

34. 'The whole world in a community'. Interview between Robert McCrum and John McGahern, in *The Observer*, 6 January, 2002.
35. Declan Kiberd, 'Fallen Nobility: the World of John McGahern', in *Irish University Review*, Spring/Summer 2005, Vol 35, No 1, pp 164-174, p 173.

a wonderful articulation before its final demise. The Church and its ceremonies are still an important part of the life of the community but, as McGahern himself remarked: 'The people in the novel are from a more pagan and practical world in which the Christianity is just a veneer.'[36] The tenderness with which the novelist describes the customs and sayings of these people, their immutability, is what marks the novel as being different from anything that came before. It prepared the way beautifully for McGahern's final take on his life in the beloved County Leitrim, *Memoir*. As I have already stated, there are places where one can see a merging of the two, such as in the following descriptions:

> A pair of herons moved sluggishly through the air between the trees of the island and Gloria Bog. A light breeze was passing over the sea of pale sedge like a hand. The blue of the mountain was deeper and darker than the blue of the lake or the sky. Along the high banks at the edge of the water there were many little private lawns speckled with fish bones and blue crayfish shells where the otters fed and trained their young (*RS*, 42)
> The sun was now high above the lake. There wasn't a wisp of cloud. Everywhere the water sparkled. A child could easily believe that the whole of heaven was dancing (*RS*, 247).

Passages like these cannot be faked. They require an experienced eye, as well as an empathy with the workings of nature. In his reverential attention to detail, his obsession with being utterly truthful to the world in which he lived and the people who populated it, McGahern demonstrated the religious nature of his calling. Writing was his way of giving homage; it was his form of prayer. At the end of *Amongst Women* something changed as the writer buried the father and, with him, the painful past, which allowed the celebration of life that is so evident in *That They May Face the Rising Sun*. Repressive Catholicism gave way to a spiritual espousal of the dignity of human life. One can learn all there is to be learned about existence by staying put and looking around you, as Jamesie so memorably points out: 'I may not have travelled far but I know the whole world' (*RS*, 296). All

---

36. 'The whole world in a community.'

of life is contained in McGahern's novels, drama and short stories, which at times have the enigmatic wisdom of parables.

Throughout the final phase of McGahern's work, there is a type of reappraisal of his relationship with the external world. Institutional religion, stripped of its previous repressive and domineering nature, no longer exerts such a negative impact on his characters' lives. This leads to a more serene atmosphere, an accommodation with the landscape and inhabitants that had done so much to shape the writer's vision of the world, a world he was now able to appreciate and celebrate in a fitting manner. By concentrating on the lives of ordinary people struggling with the mysteries of existence, McGahern manages to focus the reader's attention on the extraordinary beauty in which we are all participant, believers and non-believers alike, because for the writer, such distinctions were meaningless.

Conclusion

Writing in *The Tablet* in 2006, Mark Lawson noted that with the death of the Scottish writer Muriel Spark (1918-2006) and John McGahern (1934-2006), it was questionable whether fiction inspired and underpinned by the Catholic faith had a future. In Lawson's view, any author who has been a Catholic for a serious length of time carries 'an almost inescapable tribal and psychological imprint'.[1] This was definitely the case with McGahern to an extent that that it could never be said of the vast majority of contemporary novelists such as Anne Enright, Roddy Doyle, Dermot Bolger, Colm Tóibín, Emma Donoghue, Joseph O'Connor and Colm McCann. Poets like Patrick Kavanagh and Seamus Heaney, or playwrights like Tom Murphy and Brian Friel, in a similar way to McGahern, found it well nigh impossible to escape from the vocabulary associated with Catholicism. Fintan O'Toole maintains that while most Irish writers don't have any close connection to religion in a formal sense, being for the most part atheists, agnostics or, at best, unorthodox believers, the residual impact of Catholicism nevertheless seeps into their work. In O'Toole's view, 'the world in which Catholic beliefs and institutions played so central a part is too imaginatively rich to be dispensed with without deep regret'.[2] These sentiments capture the type of thesis I have been attempting to assemble throughout this book.

John McGahern was an unbeliever, a man who left the Catholic Church at a point in his life when he found, like Ruttledge, that he no longer believed in the dogma, all the para-

---

1. Mark Lawson, 'Catholicism's Indelible Mark on the Page', in *The Tablet* (29 April, 2006), pp 16-17.
2. Fintan O'Toole, 'Why artists can't quite give up on Catholicism', in *The Irish Times*, 5 December 2009, p 5.

phernalia, the triumphalist aspects of organised religion. But affection remained, an affection that was nurtured by his memory of his mother's deep faith and by the theatre he detected in church ceremonies, the colourful vestments worn by the priests, the smell of incense, the stories of the gospel. Towards the end of *Memoir*, he acknowledged this debt:

> I have affection still and gratitude for my upbringing in the Church: it was the sacred weather of my early life, and I could no more turn against it than I could turn on any deep part of myself (*M*, 222).

This attachment did not blind McGahern to the many faults he detected in what he considered to be a caricature of Catholicism – the hypocrisy of people who went to Mass regularly without having any real commitment to the message of the gospel, those who made a point of placing themselves in the most prominent seats in the church and were corrupt in their dealings with others, or who beat their children savagely, treated their wives or husbands with disdainful arrogance. He is also articulating a complex nostalgia that has to be understood in relation to the specific features of his childhood and adolescence where the Church and its calendar of rituals drew him out of what he experienced as an unhappy home life. Thus we read in 'The Church and its Spire': 'The movement of focus from the home and school to the church brought with it a certain lightness, a lifting of oppression, a going outwards, even a joy ...' (*LW*, 137). All these positive aspects of religion he associated with his mother, whose love of flowers, books and God left a deep impression on her son: 'When we left the church, we always felt uplifted' (*M*, 75); 'Behind her practicality and quiet cheerfulness, and the unusual gift of making people feel better about themselves, was deep religious belief' (*M*, 47); 'She never really left us. In the worst years I believe we would have been broken but for the different life we had known with her and the love she gave that was there like hidden strength' (*M*, 271). Likewise, the father represented a different side of Catholicism: 'He was religious too, but his religion was of outward show, of pomp and power, edicts and strictures, enforcements and observances and all the exactions they demanded. In his shining uniform he always walked with slow steps to the head of the church to kneel in the front seat' (*M*, 47). (His mother, on the other hand, would always seek an inconspicuous place at the back of the church.) This was the same man who failed to visit his wife during the last weeks of her life. Instead, he wrote let-ters in which he often called her faith into question, knowing full well how such comments would cause her anxiety:

> My mother's faith must have been a strength, but even this was used against her when my father accused her of losing her faith in God. No matter how strong that faith was, it could hardly alleviate the human pain of losing everyone who depended on her whom she loved and held dear. She had no one to communicate this to after forty-two years in a world where many loved her (*M*, 117).

As he grew older and had to face the prospect of his own death, McGahern returned more and more to the idyllic moments he shared with his mother. This may explain why he never jumped on the bandwagon and excoriated the Church when rev-elations of clerical child abuse made the headlines in the 1990s, or when it was discovered that two high-profile clerics, Bishop Eamonn Casey and Fr Michael Cleary, had fathered children while still involved in active ministry. Peter Guy remarks that the Church in Ireland did not operate outside the public sphere in some hermetic space: 'In some ways, the absolute power of the Church is no different than the absolute power allotted to bankers after the sudden collapse of clerical authority in the early nineties. So long as people are willing to tolerate absol-utism, absolutism will thrive and whether you are handing out indulgences or crippling forty-year mortgages, the difference in levels of abuse is scant'.[3] Guy is expressing something that one does not hear too often in public discourse, the idea that the Church in its own way is merely one in a long line of human in-stitutions which are prone to the same sort of weaknesses and failures. Guy bases this argument on the prescient comments

---

3. Peter Guy, 'Earth Crammed with Heaven and every Common Bush Afire with God: Religion in the Fiction of John McGahern', in Eamon Maher and Eugene O'Brien (eds), *Breaking the Mould: Literary Representations of Irish Catholicism* (Oxford: Peter Lang, 2011), pp 141-156, p 155.

made by McGahern in an essay, 'God and Me', which was published shortly before his death:

> When a long abuse of power is corrected, it is generally replaced by an opposite violence. In the new dispensations, all that was good in what went before is tarred indiscriminately with the bad. That is, to some extent, what is happening in Ireland today. The most dramatic change in my lifetime has been the collapse of the Church's absolute power. This has brought freedom and sanity in certain areas of human behaviour after a long suppression – as well as a new intolerance (*LW*, 150-1).

While welcoming the 'freedom' that came in the wake of a more liberal Ireland, a freedom that can be seen in relation to sexuality, the role of women in society, the greater access to education, increased mobility, no adequate replacement has been found for what McGahern terms 'the religious instinct', which he differentiates from simple morality by quoting E. R. Dodds' view expressed so eloquently in *The Greeks and the Irrational*: 'religion grows out of man's relationship to his total environment, morals out of his relation to his fellow-men' (*LW*, 151). In the case of McGahern, the cult religiosity of his childhood was gradually displaced by a type of spirituality that comes more and more to the fore as his career evolves. Quoting John Worthen's description of D. H. Lawrence as being 'religious without religion', Peter Guy finds that this is a very apt description of McGahern's trajectory also: 'he [McGahern] never satisfactorily attempted to explain himself save that he was grateful for his spiritual upbringing, but that the faith was gone.'[4] When questioned by James Whyte about his description of literature as 'a religious activity', the writer was quick to differentiate between religious and spiritual: 'I think that literature of any good is spiritual. Nothing survives that hasn't a spiritual quality. What is style but the reflection of personality in language, and that surely is the spirit of that person.' Whyte rightly pushed McGahern on that point stating that 'religion is essentially a private thing and that, at the same time, formal religion is a socialising activity', which elicited the response:

4. Guy, "Earth Cammed with Heaven", p.148.

Reading, like prayer, I see as essentially private, but there is also the theatrical experience which is the equivalent of church ceremonies. Here the private and the public come together in a great shared communion.[5]

All of which, though very interesting, does not supply any concrete explanation as to what exactly McGahern's views on Catholicism were. We know what he disliked about the institutional Church and what he found appealing about its ceremonies. He recognised the positive effects the ceremonies of the dead and the rituals of life had on the inhabitants of Leitrim. The 'theatrical' element was particularly appealing for them given the fact that the countryside could be a dull place from harvest until spring and the Church brought a splash of colour and provided a venue that brought people together. McGahern's own repeated insistence that he did not believe in a transcendent being has to be respected. It also begs the question as to the extent to which a Catholicism gutted of belief and practice is still Catholicism. It is my contention that McGahern cannot be considered a Catholic in the traditional sense of that term, and I have no wish to turn him into one after his death. My desire, rather, is to foreground the role this religion played in his life and work.

Now that the Catholic Church in Ireland seems to be on its knees, shaken by more and more revelations of abuse and cover-up, perhaps the moment is ripe for a re-evaluation of some of the positive aspects associated with its doctrines – love of neighbour, truth, justice for all, virtuousness, moderation. It is possible too that its apparent weakness and vulnerability at the moment will hold an added attraction for our writers. This is certainly what Fintan O'Toole seems to believe when he writes that, 'any declining thing is an irresistible magnet for the writer's nib'.[6] The decline of something as important as Catholicism in Ireland cannot take place without at least the occasional nostalgic glance backwards. What have we found with which to replace religion? At the moment, the God of Mammon has proved even less effectual than the divine Being reputedly located in heaven. In O'Toole's

5. Whyte, History, *Myth and Ritual*, p 230.
6. O'Toole, 'Why artists can't quite give up on Catholicism', p 9.

estimation, it is likely that only our creative writers have the capacity to apply balm to the wounds of a badly beaten up nation:

> We need to live in a richly textured universe and as the layers
> of Catholic imagery and ritual are stripped away for many
> by the corrosive effects of corruption, they need to be re-
> placed. The paradox is, of course, that it is the accursed breed
> so despised by the Church – the writers – who best appreci-
> ate the need and come closest to meeting it.[7]

Maybe this explains the huge outpouring of grief that
emerged after McGahern passed away in March 2006. His work
had assumed a particular resonance for Irish readers, many of
whom experienced the slightly eerie sensation that he was in
some way telling their story, recounting their lives, laying bare
their innermost secrets. Many of the comments in the national
and international press spoke of someone with a unique understanding of the Irish psyche, someone to whom the population
looked for direction, stability, wisdom. His obituary in *The Irish
Times* on the 31 March 2006 acclaimed him 'as the foremost
existential writer in English of his generation' and underlined
his attachment to Catholicism: 'A non-believer, he nevertheless
acknowledged Catholicism as the most important influence on
his life'. Numerous commentators spoke of his contribution to
making people aware of the problems that lurked under the sur-
face of so-called 'respectable' Catholic Ireland. Eileen Battersby
remarked: 'It was he who encouraged a reluctant country which
has never enjoyed looking at itself to shed the old sentimentali-
ties and complacencies and admit the hypocrisies.'[8] Fintan
O'Toole described him as 'the man who revealed our world to
us and forced us to recognise it. He changed Ireland, not by arguing about it, but by describing it.'[9] Colm Tóibín saw him as
the role model against whom a whole generation of Irish writers
benchmarked themselves: 'He had been deeply wounded by his
early experiences of censorship, but instead of arguing with the

---

7. O'Toole, 'Why artists can't quite give up on Catholicism', p 9.
8. Eileen Battersby, 'A student of the ordinary and teller of truths', in *The
Irish Times*, 31 March, 2006.
9. Fintan O'Toole, 'Picking the locks of family secrets', in *The Irish Times*, 1
April, 2006. O'Toole captures the essence of McGahern's art in these lines.

Church or the State, instead of bitterness or shrillness, he worked on his sentences.'[10] In assessing his legacy, *The Irish Times* editorial of 1 April 2006 quoted President Mary McAleese's allusion to his 'enormous contribution to our self-understanding as a people' before remarking: 'His was an intuitive and deeply insightful understanding of the society that emerged, with all its faults and failings, in the first decades of the new State – the same society which, with its certainties and dogmatic outlook, banned his work and drove him from his position as a national school teacher.' There is a definite impression from these comments of people mourning the loss of an icon, a comforting presence, a man they could relate to, a writer who had left an indelible mark. Such accolades are usually reserved for figures from the sporting world, or exceptional politicians, or saintly figures like Mother Teresa. With writers, it is more normal to wait for the judgement of posterity before a pronouncement is made as to their legacy. But McGahern had the unique ability to convince readers that his fictional world was a real world, a familiar world populated with familiar characters. It is this intimacy, this close identification with his subject matter, that draws one back again and again to his work. John Scally offers this assessment of his legacy:

> The secret of life is that only in love for the living is the spirit praised forever. His [McGahern's] legacy is to remind us that our challenge is to allow this love to be a lamp for our steps and a light for our eyes and to remember our call to bear witness to a faith which has a vital, personal quality rather than being something worn ostentatiously like a religious emblem and a spirituality that is deep, mysterious and beautiful, a religion that gives sympathy to our hearts and understanding to our minds.[11]

It would be impossible to do McGahern's work justice without remarking on the central place the Catholic religion plays in it. It is omnipresent in the language his characters use, their regular invocation of God, the Virgin Mary and the saints, the

---

10. Colm Tóbín, 'Amongst shadows', in *The Irish Times*, 1 April, 2006.
11. John Scally, 'The Spiritual Legacy of John McGahern', in *Doctrine and Life* 60, 10 (December 2010), pp 17-27, p 26.

recitation of prayers, the customs and practices that govern their lives. It is a world that is currently under siege from the forces of globalisation and secularisation. The declining number of people working the land and inhabiting the countryside shows that McGahern's fictional universe is gently fading away. It is precisely because it is no longer normal practice to spill out the Rosary beads in the evening to recite one's prayers, or to attend Mass and receive the sacraments on a regular basis, or to think deeply about issues like sin and grace, good and evil, that McGahern's world has become so precious. His literary vocation was closely linked to a religious quest, a quest that required a painful dredging up of past traumas, that demanded a cold look at the society that shaped him and a complete commitment to render in a truthful manner the people and society that made him into the writer he would subsequently become. Such a retrospective brought deception at times, especially in relation to what he viewed as the wanton abandonment of the ideals of 1916:

> When Britain placed the Catholic Church on an equal footing with the Church of Ireland, they did so because they saw it as a tool of social order. The country I grew up in was a theocracy in all but name, but I had naïvely thought that in the early days of the State lip service at least would have to be paid to the Proclamation of the Republic in 1916 which guaranteed equal rights to all citizens irrespective of class or creed; but here it was, without a miss of a beat, still in charge, even as the old dispensation gave way to the new (*M*, 48-49).

While this failure to live up to the ideals of the founders of the State was a disappointment to McGahern, the determination of the Church to cling on to power at all costs led him to wonder to what extent this could have been the sort of institution the founder of Christianity envisaged. Nevertheless, for all its faults, McGahern would have acknowledged the excellent work the Church did in areas such as health care and education. He also recognised how priests in small parishes continue to serve their parishioners with commitment, tact and humanity, cognisant of the importance their role has for the people to whom they minister. The memories of the religious ceremonies stayed with the writer throughout his life:

Corpus Christi was summer. Rhododendron and lilac branches were taken by cart and small tractors from the Oakport woods and used to decorate the grass margins of the triangular field around the village. Coloured streamers and banners were strung across the road from poles ... The Host was taken from the tabernacle and carried by the priests beneath a gold canopy all the way round the village, pausing for ceremonies at each wayside altar. Benediction was always at the post office (*LW*, 138).

The colour and spectacle, the theatrical aspect of the vestments worn by the priests, all this appealed to McGahern's artistic temperament and he regretted not being able to participate in their magic when he ceased to believe. The Benedictine monk and writer Mark Patrick Hederman sees in artists the one great hope for religion in Ireland. He is of the belief that they are constructing an 'underground cathedral where the true God might be worshipped'. McGahern is an important signpost in this regard. While in no way a recruiting agent for the Catholic Church (how could he be, when he did not adhere to any of its doctrines?), his work, based as it is on truth and the dignity of the human person, performs a similar function to the church spire: it raises our eyes upwards to contemplate the mysteries of the world. Hederman notes:

Art has the imagination to sketch out the possible. When this happens something entirely new comes into the world. Often it is not recognised for what it is and is rejected or vilified by those who are comfortable with what is already there and afraid of whatever might unsettle the *status quo*.[12]

Catholicism is something that cannot be discounted in any discussion of the Ireland in which McGahern lived and which he depicts in his writings. For historical reasons and as a result of its geographical position on the periphery of Europe, Ireland 'was insulated from social, educational and economic developments which took place in continental Europe in the aftermath of the Second World War', according to the historian Louise Fuller. She continues:

12. Mark Patrick Hederman, *Underground Cathedrals* (Dublin: The Columba Press, 2010), p 13.

From the perspective of the Irish bishops, the 'isolation' which was 'enjoyed' by Ireland was something for which to be grateful. They did not perceive that Ireland was cut off from the long-established intellectual and cultural tradition of Catholic Europe and that this might have left Irish Catholicism somewhat impoverished. They simply concent-rated on the negative aspects of that culture, and both bishops and politicians had an exalted, somewhat superior idea of the uniqueness of Irish Catholicism.[13]

The bishops may not have been conscious of the impoverish-ment resulting from Ireland's isolation from Europe, but a writer like McGahern certainly was, being someone who had suffered at the hands of the narrow, moralistic brand of Catholicism to which he was exposed. At the beginning of his literary career, especially after the publication of *The Dark* in 1965, he did not enjoy anything like unconditional support from the Irish public, largely as a result of the unflattering portrait he sketched of Catholic rural Ireland. But he stuck to his task, knowing that the job of the artist is to describe, to express reality as it actually is and not as people would like it to be. Similarly, at no stage did he seek to curry favour with those who could advance his career and he refused to present a false picture of the world. Courageous at all times, he was prepared to suffer re-jection and vilification for the sake of a higher ideal. This is why he reneged on his promise to his mother that he would one day become a priest. He had a grander scheme, one which allowed him to shape and mould his own imaginative world, a world in which Catholicism was omnipresent (albeit not always in a pos-itive sense) and where the face of his mother shone through the detritus of modern society. Towards the end of *Memoir*, he ex-presses his ultimate respect for Susan McGahern's faith and her constant presence at his side throughout his life:

> Without the promise that one day I'd say Mass for her I doubt if I would have been able to resist my father when he wanted to take me out of school. I did, in the end, answer to a different call than the one she wished for me, and followed it the whole of my life. When I reflect on those rare moments

13. Louise Fuller, *Irish Catholicism Since 1950*, p 231.

when I stumble without warning into that extraordinary
sense of security, that deep peace, I know that consciously
and unconsciously she has been with me all my life (*M*, 272).

As for his father, whom he never fully understood, he chose
to leave him 'with God, or whatever truth or illusion or longing
for meaning or comfort that word may represent' (*M*, 271). The
resentment of the father never fully abated, even in these part-
ing comments, and one can only surmise the poisonous nature
of their relationship which would seem to date back to childhood and the manner in which Francis McGahern treated his
wife and children – in fairness to the father, we only have the
writer-son's account of what exactly went on between them. The
mother was the great influence of his life and he regularly acknowledged her deep trust in God. The Church mattered greatly
to her:

> Through the violent history of Catholicism run the two di-
> viding movements: the fortress churches with their edicts,
> threats and punishments; and the churches of the spires and
> brilliant windows that go towards love and life … (*M*, 271).

There is no doubt in the writer's mind as to which camp
Susan McGahern belonged. Similarly, McGahern himself had
no time for institutions whose sole motivation was the manipulation of power and the laying down of laws that had to be
obeyed. On the other hand, those Churches who fostered love
and enriched life were cherished above all else. Reunited in the
lovely cemetery of Aughawillan, I like to imagine the spirit of
mother and son soaring above the Leitrim landscape, with its
lakes and hedges, its wild flowers, animals, intriguing inhabitants, houses and lanes. From this vantage point they have a perspective akin to that of the idyllic churches and their noble
spires that are so lovingly evoked in McGahern's work. They
now know the answers to the secrets that await beyond the
threshold of death. I like to think they are happy with whatever
revelations they have had.

APPENDIX

Catholicism and National Identity in the works of John McGahern[1]

Interview between Eamon Maher and John McGahern

EM: John McGahem, it is a great privilege to welcome you here today. I won't embarrass you by enumerating your many achievements as a writer, the prizes awarded you, the reputation you enjoy at home and abroad. Rather, I'd like to focus our discussion on the theme of Catholicism and national identity in your works, a theme which is, in my view, central to everything you write. We might start by discussing the environment in which you were brought up. Was yours a typically Irish Catholic upbringing?

JMG: Yes. I mean it was the only upbringing I knew and in that sense you can't consider it typical. The Church dominated everything.

EM: Your parents would have been religious?

JMG: I think my mother was very spiritual. My father was very outwardly religious.

EM: Rituals like you describe in many of your novels were commonplace?

JMG: The Rosary was said every evening. I always liked that sentence about the medieval Churches, that they were the Bibles of the poor. The Church was my first book and I would think it is still my most important book. At that time, there were very few books in the house. The only pictures we could see were religious pictures, the Stations of the Cross. The only music we would hear was religious hymns; and it's [the Church] all I came to know of ceremony, even of luxury – the tulips that used to come in the flat boxes when I was an altar boy, the candles, the incense.

---

1. Tapescript of an interview between Eamon Maher and John McGahern that took place at the Institute of Technology Tallaght on 8 December 2000. Reproduced with the kind permission of *Studies: An Irish Quarterly*, where it was published in Spring 2001.

EM: These memories stay with you.

JMG: Yes, but also one of the problems for a novelist in Ireland is the fact that there are no formal manners. I mean some people have beautiful manners but there's no kind of agreed form of manners. For a novelist there has almost to be an agreed notion of society. In that sense, I often think that you could never find Jane Austen writing poems or short stories. And it's through the Church that I first came to know all I'd know of manners, of ceremony, of sacrament, of grace.

EM: Some people might be surprised that you paint such a positive picture of your relations with the Church.

JMG: I would think it is neither positive or negative – it's just a fact. I remember when *The Dark* was banned I went on *The Late Late Show* from, of all places, The King's Hall in Belfast. I was expected to attack the Catholic Church and I said that I could no more attack the Catholic Church than I could my own life. I remember there was a Unionist in the audience and he got up and said: 'There's a man, whose book has been banned by the southern government, who has been sacked out of his school by the Archbishop of Dublin and he comes down here to Belfast and gets up on his hind legs and praises the Catholic Church.' He says: 'Could Moscow do a better job of brain-washing than that?'

EM: Speaking about Archbishop John Charles McQuaid, you were in Scoil Eoin Baiste in Clontarf at the time. He actually intervened with the parish priest, the Manager of the School, didn't he?

JMG: Actually, the Manager was a charming man. He was a Fr Carton and I don't think he had any interest in Catholicism or spirituality. He came from the rich family that supplied all the potatoes to the Dublin market and he loved whiskey and food. He complained to me constantly about 'them bowsies of doctors'. I was, I suppose, spiritual at the time and I equated spirituality with a priest. I was a bit shocked when he said to me one day in the school yard: 'If you listened to those bowsies of doctors, life wouldn't be worth living!' I thought that a priest was supposed to have a more elevated view of life.

EM: I just wonder, John, if the religious instruction you received as a child had a detrimental impact on your spirituality?

JMG: No, I mean I have nothing but gratitude to the Church. I would think that if there was one thing injurious about the Church, it would be its attitude to sexuality. I see sexuality as just a part of life. Either all of life is sacred or none of it is sacred. I'm inclined to think that all of life is sacred and that sexuality is a very important part of that sacredness. And I think that it made a difficult enough relationship – which is between people, between men and women – even more difficult by imparting an unhealthy attitude to sexuality. By making sexuality abnormal and by giving it more importance in a way than it has – by exaggerating it.

EM: It was always the way in this country that religion and sexuality were entwined and that practising Catholics were expected to obey the rules handed down from on high.

JMG: Yes. When I was in my 20s it did occur to me that there was something perverted about an attitude that thought that killing somebody was a minor offence compared to kissing somebody.

EM: And then of course the Papal encyclical *Humanae Vitae* came along and it caused a lot of pain for many sincere Catholic couples who were trying to avoid having children.

JMG: In a way, I had left Catholicism at that time, but the debt remained. And of course it was a very simple form of Catholicism and to a certain extent I always thought that as well as being my most important book the Church was also my first fiction. I think fiction is a very serious thing, that while it is fiction, it is also a revelation of truth, or facts. We absolutely believed in Heaven and Hell,

Purgatory, and even Limbo. I mean, they were actually closer to us than Australia or Canada, that they were real places.

EM: A physical state?

JMG: I remember writing once that there was an orchard beside the barracks, Lenehans' orchard, and somehow in my imaginings of Heaven, Lenehans' orchard was some place around the entrance.

EM: It may have had something to do with the Garden of Eden.

JMG: I don't know, maybe it had.

EM: Elisabeth Reegan, the main character in your first novel, *The Barracks*, suffers much and yet is receptive to the beauty of nature and the cycle of life. Her exclamation before her death of 'Jesus Christ!' as she looks out one morning at the spectacular countryside seems to me to be something of an epiphany. What is the role and meaning of revelation in your novels?

JMG: I don't think that the writer can say that. That belongs to the reader. I mean all the writer tries to do is get his words right and in order to do that you have to think clearly and feel deeply. I like a thing that Chekhov said: 'When a writer takes a pen into his hand he accuses himself of unanswerable egotism and all he can do with decency after that is to bow!' I also think that the only difference between the writer and the reader is that each of us has a private world which others cannot see and that it's with that private world that we all read. It's a spiritual, private world. And the only difference between the writer and the reader is that he (the writer) has the knack or talent to be able to dramatise that private world and turn it into words. But it's the same private world that each of us possesses. Joyce once described the piano as a coffin of music and I see the book as a coffin of words. A book, in fact, doesn't live again until it finds a reader and you get as many versions of the book as the number of readers it finds.

EM: Speaking as a reader, I find that passage particularly moving where Elizabeth looks out on that splendid Roscommon vista which up until then she had never fully taken in. Now, when she is close to death, the beauty strikes her with poignant force.

JMG: That's a dramatic problem. When you're in danger of losing a thing it becomes precious and when it's around us, it's in tedious abundance and we take it for granted as if we're going to live forever, which we're not. I think there's a great difference in consciousness in that same way in that when we're young we read books for the story, for the excitement of the story – and there comes a time when you realise that all stories are more or less the same story. I think it's linked to the realisation that we're not going to live forever and that the way of saying and the language become more important than the story.

EM: In an interview you did once with Julia Carlson, you remarked how amazing it was that a Catholic country like Ireland should have produced so many writers who were lapsed Catholics. But is this fact all that surprising? Maybe the writers would have been more Catholic if the country had been less so.

JMG: That was a very hurried interview and it was never revised or corrected. I mean I think that's a fact and I think that we had a very peculiar type of Catholic Church here in that it was a fortress Church. Very much like an army, it demanded unquestioned allegiance. I remember reading in Proust's letters where they were trying to throw the curé off the school committee and Proust says that he should remain if for nothing but the spire of his church which lifts men's eyes from the avaricious earth. Elsewhere in that same letter he describes the 18th-century Church in France as 'the refuge of ignoramuses'. I would think that the Church, the personnel of the Church I grew up in – which I separate from the sacraments, the prayer, the liturgy – I would suspect might even have been a refuge of ignoramuses also. Proust said also that he agreed with Tolstoy that one would never have thought when looking back at the 18th-century Church that one would see the revival of spirituality that was seen in the 19th century. Proust stated as well that Baudelaire was intimately connected with the Church, if only through sacrilege.

EM: Yes, that's an interesting comment with regard to Baudelaire, who was the quintessential *poète maudit* and yet was also very spiritual.

JMG: But you can't commit sacrilege if you believe in spirituality.

EM: No, indeed, that is true. In the same interview with Julia Carlson you pointed out that Irish identity was very confining. To be Irish was to be against sexuality, against the English. How do you think our national identity has evolved since the 1960s?

JMG: I think I was remarking on something that I would see as childish. Trying to define yourself as being against something is poor, I think. The way I see it is that all the ol' guff about being Irish is a kind of nonsense. I mean, I couldn't be anything else no matter how hard I tried to be. I couldn't be Chinese or Japanese.

EM: Strangely enough, it's almost becoming 'sexy' to be Irish, which certainly wasn't the case a few decades ago.

JMG: Well, that's just another version of the same thing. What's interesting is to be human, to be decent or moral or whatever. Everything that we inherit, the rain, the skies, the speech – and anybody who works in the English language in Ireland knows that there's the dead ghost of Gaelic in the language we use and listen to and that those things will reflect our Irish identity. And I actually see it as being very childish for anyone to have to beat their breast and say 'I'm Irish!' I mean, isn't it obvious?

EM: You present a very different picture of Ireland from some of your contemporaries like Brian Moore, John Broderick (who was a cousin of yours, I believe), Edna O'Brien and Frank McCourt. What is your opinion of their depiction of Irish mores?

JMG: Well, I can't speak for them.[2] I would think that I write out of my own private or spiritual world. I would see my business as to get my words right and I think that if you get your words right you will reflect everything that the particular form you're writing in is capable of reflecting. And, in fact, I think that if you actually set out to give a picture of Ireland that it would be unlikely to be interesting, that it would be closer to propaganda or journalism. Because when an author starts a book, he has no idea where it's going. It's a voyage or a work of discovery. And I have a suspicion that if the tension wasn't there for the writer that it wouldn't be there either for the reader. Art is a mysterious thing, the fingerprints of the writer are all over it and you can't fake anything from the reader. If the tension's not there, the reader will sense that it's actually not dramatised, not thought out, not felt. There's a very interesting analogy that Auden made where he said that while the scientist knows his work, the work doesn't know him. Whereas the work always knows the writer.

EM: But even as a reader – you would read fiction – there must be Irish writers whom you admire.

JMG: Oh yes, many. When I was young both Beckett and Kavanagh were writing and publishing and they were for me the most exciting writers at the time. They weren't the most fashionable – O'Faoláin and O'Connor were the most fashionable. And I would think that Kate O'Brien is a most important writer and she was considered nobody then. I like strange people: I like Ernie O'Malley, I like Tomás O'Crohan's *The Islandman*. I like Michael Mc

2. In some written notes that McGahern submitted to me, he supplied the following answer to a similar question that is worth reproducing here: *I read a few of Moore's novels. The craft and care are obvious, and have to be respected. But I never found in Moore what I look for in writing.* Angela's Ashes *interested me much more. I found it a very strange book, a mixture of farce and clearly honed American evocative writing and literary pretention. The pretention was its weakest part. A work it reminded me of was Synge's* Playboy of the Western World, *also a farce. It was farce as a great kick at misery and passive suffering. If it's not a farce then the concluding chapter is in serious bad taste and the whole book a sort of porridge.*

Laverty, some of Corkery's short stories. I mean the obvious ones are Joyce and Yeats.

EM: Joyce and Yeats cast a shadow over Irish writers who came after them. You inherit a certain literary tradition – before you become a writer, you're a reader – which has to influence you.

JMG: Yeah, sure. But I don't consider them shadows. In fact, I would think that they're an enormous source of sustenance and pride. In a sense Yeats was a terribly important figure because he made it difficult for the mediocre to get a footing. Not only was he a brilliant poet but he almost single handedly established a tradition that wasn't there before. In fact, he paved the way for Joyce and Synge and you could say even Beckett. I see some of Beckett's works as full of Yeats. I think the play *Purgatory* is very close to *Waiting for Godot*. I edited for a French publisher John Butler Yeats' letters and there's a charming letter where John is very upset that Willie has rejected his play for the Abbey because he said it had no system. John Butler Yeats was drawing a portrait of Synge at the time and he was complaining to the latter about Willie's rejection of his play. Synge said: 'You should go back and ask him if his plays have a system!'

EM: You often portray characters who are veterans of the War of Independence. Men like Reegan (*The Barracks*) and Moran (*Amongst Women*) are disenchanted with the Irish Free State, which is ultimately the fruit of their struggles. In Moran's words, it has resulted merely in 'a few of our own johnnies in the top jobs instead of a few Englishmen'. Is he echoing your own view of the situation here?

JMG: No, not really my view, but my father fought in the War of Independence and one of my uncles. He (the uncle) was expelled out of the IRA. He won a King's scholarship, he was a very intelligent man, a pedant. He got expelled out of the IRA for insisting that they all learn Irish after the war was over. He joined the Blueshirts then. To a certain extent, Moran is an imaginary figure but he is also

based on a number of people. That was, in a way, a prevalent reaction – in that the dream didn't become the reality.
A lot of it was confused with their youth which would
end anyhow. It was also the most exciting and dramatic
time of their lives. I think they had a kind of dream – you
see it in O'Malley's *Another Man's Wound* too – that they
were bound together by something bigger than themselves. And then normal life restored itself and the
Church and the medical profession got power. And, if
anything, the country got poorer.

EM: Yes, as often happens after a conflict like that, it was a
minority that benefited.

JMG: And it was a very unattractive minority, I think, that did
well out of the State, in that they were the shopkeepers,
the medical profession, the Church. People were looked
down on that had to go to England to earn a living as if
they had committed sin in some way, as if it was any
virtue to have the luck to remain on in Ireland.

EM: In the modem context, we have a 'new' type of country
now with the Celtic Tiger, which is also benefiting a
minority.

JMG: Ah, I think a lot more people are better off now. I think it's
a wonderful thing and that they don't have to go unless
they want to go abroad.

EM: Because emigration, as far as you'd be concerned, was a
major problem. And then you had to emigrate yourself.

JMG: I thought that romantic notion of the writer having to go
abroad was foolishness, even when I was young. It
looked like a nonsense to me that someone like Larkin or
Evelyn Waugh – I think Larkin is a great poet – or Thomas
Hardy would have to go abroad to be an English writer. I
remember saying once that I thought a person could write
badly in Ireland as well as anywhere else – you didn't
have to go abroad to write badly!

EM: I suppose once more, because Joyce did it, it became fashionable.

JMG: It's a sign of an inferiority complex. It is our country now and we don't have to apologise to anybody. In fact, I remember when *The Dark* was banned I was friendly with the very distinguished editor of *The Listener*, Joe Ackerley, and he said that it was marvellous about the scandal surrounding the book, that it would boost sales. I actually didn't think that at all: I was quite ashamed. You know, it was our own country and we were making bloody fools out of ourselves. When I was young in Dublin we thought the Censorship Board was a joke and that most of the books banned were like most of the books published: they weren't worth reading anyway, and those that were could be easily found and quickly passed around. There's no fruit that tastes so good as the forbidden fruit. And then I was actually a bit ashamed to be mixed up in it and I would refuse to make any protest about it. In fact, it's well known that the people in Paris wanted to make a protest and that Beckett was approached. He said that first of all he would have to read the book and then to ask McGahern if he wanted a protest. And only for Beckett I would never have been asked that. When they asked me, I said that I didn't want a protest, that I was enormously grateful to them and to thank them and Mr Beckett, but that I thought that by protesting one gave it too much importance.

EM: You were amazingly low-key. I mean you were a *cause célèbre* at the time and you did nothing to highlight the wrong that was done to you.

JMG: Ah, I don't think it was a virtue: it was pride more than anything. I wouldn't like to claim too much credit for it.

EM: Does the writer of fiction have a role to play in forging a national consciousness in your opinion?

JMG: Not deliberately. The only role a writer has is to get his words right and to do that, as Flaubert said, you have to feel deeply and think clearly ...

EM: And write coldly.

JMG: ... in order to find the right words. But think clearly means coldly. I think that if you do that, you will reflect everything that is worth reflecting. Whereas when you set out to reflect something you end up reflecting nothing. There's a very interesting thing that Scott Fitzgerald said: 'If you start with a person, you end up with a type, but if you start with a type, you wind up with nothing.' You set out to discover something in your writing and it is through the attempt to discover that you reflect. If you have your mind made up about something, you'll reflect nothing.

EM: So really you are a wordsmith and what emerges is there for the reader to interpret, accept or reject.

JMG: I think that if it is good work – and that's for the reader to decide – it actually does become the history of our consciousness.

EM: Anthony Cronin has suggested that you, in common with Edna O'Brien, persist in misrepresenting Ireland – which Cronin sees as urban, open and secular – by portraying characters who are dominated by rural values, taboos and religious repressions. What is your reaction to this critique?

JMG: Well he's (Cronin) a reader and he's attacked my work from the beginning, as he has every right to – in fact, I'd defend his right to do that – but I would see in that the vulgarity of making subject matter more important than the writing. In fact, a writer doesn't really have much choice over his subject matter in that the subject matter claims him/her and that all that matters is what he does with the subject matter. The quality of the language, the quality of seeing and thinking are the important things, not whether it's rural Ireland, or whether it's in Foxrock or in bohemian Dublin. I think that all good writing is local, and by local I don't differentiate between Ballyfermot and north Roscommon. If the writer gets his words right, he'll make that local scene universal. The great Portuguese writer, Miguel Torga, said the local is the universal, but without walls.

EM: In his *Irish Journal*, Heinrich Böll wrote that for someone who is Irish and a writer, there is probably much to provoke him in this country. Has this been your experience?

JMG: I would think that to be a writer anywhere is always a difficult thing because you have the same problem of finding the right words. I read Böll's book and liked it, but I thought it was a love affair with Ireland, and it was a fantasy world. It was very charming because of that, but it was a dream world – and every world is to a certain extent a dream world.

EM: The strange thing about Böll, as I see it, is that when he's actually writing about Germany he's extremely cutting and his observation is very acute. Whereas he seems to have glossed over completely the more unsavoury aspects of Ireland, the poverty, emigration – he has this notion of emigration as being almost a romantic thing for the Irish.

JMG: Well, of course, he knows more about Germany, almost certainly. That's why family rows are the worst, because everyone knows too much about one another and can inflict wounds that an outsider wouldn't be able to inflict.

EM: Do you think that the Peace Process will succeed?

JMG: I've been asked that many times and I think that Northern Ireland is fashionable because of the violence. When I was growing up, there were two sectarian states, one here and one in the North. Despite public claims and utterances, they were very happy with one another: one could point the other out in self-justification. I know people from both sides of the divide in the North and I don't actually understand the Northern situation because I think that it's an emotional situation. It's sectarian and you need to be brought up in it to understand it. It just seems strange and foreign to me. It doesn't engage me personally. I don't think it's right that people should be killing one another. From my point of view, life is more sacred than any idea.

EM: You speak about two sectarian states. Do you feel that the Irish Republic was in its own way sectarian?

JMG: When I was growing up it was completely Catholic, sectarian. It was almost like a theocracy.

EM: You were accused on a number of occasions of portraying Protestants in a sympathetic manner.

JMG: Yes, that's right. I grew up very close to the Rockingham estate and there were many Protestants there. They dwindled: I think that the marriage laws had a big impact on them. They were a very attractive people to me. Everybody had good manners, they were better off and, of course, some of them did convert to Catholicism in order to get married. I write about that in 'The Conversion of William Kirkwood.'[3] I remember saying on French television once about the North of Ireland that it was a very mysterious place to me, that it seemed to me that the Catholics hated the British and they looked down on the people in the South as degenerate and the Protestants hated the people in the South and they looked on the British as being degenerate. They conducted their warfare in Washington, London and Dublin and the one place where they wouldn't talk to one another was in the North of Ireland. I didn't think that anything would happen in the North of Ireland until they were actually kept up there and talked to one another, which seems to be what is happening now, whether it will endure or not. I live beside the border and I have a cousin who was a diocesan examiner and he tells me that to examine religious doctrine in the schools when you go six to seven miles across the border, Catholicism is 40-50 years behind the times in the North of Ireland. He was talking about 15 years ago.

EM: I'd say the situation isn't dramatically different today.

JMG: When you grow up in the South, you have a different experience altogether. There's a very nice statement of David Hume's: 'I never discuss religion', he says, 'Because its basis is faith, not reason.' I would apply the same thing to the North of Ireland.

3. This short story appeared in *The Collected Stories* (London: Faber & Faber, 1992), pp 331-350.

EM: A final question to you, John. We've just come to the end
      of the first year of the new millennium. What sort of Irish
      identity do you see emerging in the coming decades?

JMG: I don't know. It'd be a wise man that would try to predict
      that. It doesn't really interest me because I believe that the
      real adventure is a spiritual adventure and that that's a
      human adventure. One's Irish experience is given and it's
      what one does with it that counts. That's just the accidental
      place (Ireland) that life happens and it's the only place
      and it's the place we love and it's passing. We will have
      an identity, but I think we wouldn't have it long if we
      started worrying about it.

EM: John McGahern, thank you very much for your time and
      patience.

Select Bibliography

NOVELS, SHORT STORIES AND OTHER WRITINGS BY JOHN MCGAHERN

(a) Novels
The Barracks (London: Faber & Faber, 1963).
The Dark (London: Faber & Faber, 1965).
The Leavetaking (London: Faber & Faber, 1974) Revised edition (London: Faber & Faber, 1984).
The Pornographer (London: Faber & Faber, 1979).
Amongst Women (London: Faber & Faber, 1990).
That They May Face the Rising Sun (London: Faber & Faber, 2002).

(b) Short Story Collections
Nightlines (London: Faber & Faber, 1970).
Getting Through (London: Faber & Faber, 1978).
High Ground (London: Faber & Faber, 1985).
The Collected Stories (London: Faber & Faber, 1992). (Includes 2 new stories, 'The Creamery Manager' and 'The Country Funeral'. Several of the original stories were also adapted).
Creatures of the Earth: New and Selected Stories (London: Faber & Faber, 2006). (Includes 2 new stories, 'Creatures of the Earth' and 'Love of the World', and amended versions of many others).

(c) Drama (Radio, TV, Film, Stage)
Sinclair, radio adaptation of his own short story, 'Why We're Here', produced by Ronald Mason and broadcast on BBC Radio 3, 16 November 1971. Published in *The Listener*, 18 November 1971, pp 690-2.
The Sisters, television adaptation of James Joyce's short story of the same title, directed by Stephen Frears, produced by Gavin Millar and Melvyn Bragg; first broadcast as part of *Full House* on BBC 2, 17 February, 1973.
Swallows, television adaptation of McGahern short story of the same title, directed by Robert Kidd. First broadcast as part of *Second City First* series on BBC 2, 27 March 1975.
Wheels, film adaptation of short story of the same title. Directed by Cathal Black (Cathal Black Films and The Arts Council, 1976).
The Rockingham Shoot, original television drama, directed by Kieran Hickey (BBC Northern Ireland). First broadcast as part of

Screenplay: Next series on BBC 2, 10 September 1987.

Korea, film adaptation of the short story of the same title. Screenplay by Joe O'Bryne, directed by Cathal Black (ZDF, RTÉ, NOS and Bord Scannán na hÉireann/The Irish Film Board, 1995).

Amongst Women, television adaptation of the novel of that title. Screenplay by Adrian Hodges, directed by Tom Cairns, 4 episodes (BBB Northern Ireland, RTÉ, and Bord Scannán na hÉireann/The Irish Film Board). First broadcast on RTÉ 1, 17 May-7 June 1998.

(d) Documentary

Pat Colins (dir.), *John McGahern: A Private World* (RTÉ/Hummingbird production, 2005).

(e) Selected non-fiction by John McGahern

Dear Mr McLaverty – The Literary Correspondence of John McGahern and Michael McLaverty 1959-1980. Edited by John Killen (Belfast: The Linen Hall Library, 2006).

Stanley Van der Ziel (ed), with an Introduction by Declan Kiberd, *Love of the World Essays: John McGahern* (London: Faber & Faber, 2009). This book brings together in one tome a large number of essays and articles – approximately 100 in total – by John McGahern.

SELECTED INTERVIEWS AND PROFILES

Anon, 'McGahern's Legacy', *The Irish Times* editorial, 1 April 2006.

Battersby, Eileen, 'A Student of the Ordinary and Teller of Truths', *The Irish Times*, 31 March 2006.

Carlson, Julia, *Banned in Ireland: Censorship and the Irish Writer* (London: Routledge, 1990), pp 53-67.

Carty, Ciaran, 'John McGahern: "It would be an insult to be called an Irish Writer"' (Interview), *Sunday Independent*, 11 June, 1978.

Carty, Ciaran, 'Sex, Ignorance and the Irish' (Interview), *The Sunday Tribune*, 29 September 1991, p 27.

Downey, Mary, 'Unbearable Darkness of Being', *Sunday Independent*, 6 May 1991, pp 25-6.

González, Rosa, 'An Interview with John McGahern', *European English Messenger* 4.1 (Spring 1995), pp 17-23.

Jackson, Joe, 'Tales from the Dark Side', *Hot Press*, 14 November, 1991, pp 18-20.

Johnston, Fred, 'John McGahern at 50', *The Irish Times*, 13 August 1985, p 10.

Kennedy, Eileen, 'Q & A with John McGahern', *Irish Literary Supplement*, 3 (Spring 1984), p 40.

Lavery, Brian, 'From Rural Ireland, Prose Carved with Precise Simplicity', *New York Times*, 1 May 2003.

Louvel, Liliane, Giles Ménégaldo and Claude Verley, 'Entretien avec John McGahern', *La Licorne* (Poitiers: UFR Langues Littératures, 17 November 1994), pp 19-30.

Luby, Tom, 'In from The Dark', *The Irish Times*, 14 June 1979.

Lynch, Audrey, 'An Interview with John McGahern', *Books Ireland*, 88, 1984, p 213.

Maher, Eamon, 'Catholicism and National Identity in the Works of John McGahern' (Interview), *Studies: An Irish Quarterly*, 90 (357), Spring 2001, pp 70-83.

Maher, Eamon, 'An Interview with John McGahern', Appendix 1, *John McGahern: From the Local to the Universal* (Dublin: The Liffey Press, 2003), pp 143-161.

Maher, Eamon, 'Drawing from a Life of Fugitive Days' (Interview), *The Irish Book Review*, Vol 1, No 2, Autumn 2005, pp 12-3.

McCrum, Robert, 'The whole world in a community' (Interview), *The Guardian*, 6 January 2002.

McGarry, Patsy, 'McGahern Emerges from the Dark', *Irish Press*, 7 May 1991, p 20.

McGarry, Patsy, 'Writer's funeral was a triumph of Compassion', *The Irish Times*, 28 March 2007.

Murphy, Mike, 'John McGahern', *Reading the Future: Irish Writers in Conversation with Mike Murphy*, Ed. Clíodhna Ní Anluain (Dublin: The Lilliput Press, 2001), pp 137-155.

Ollier, Nicole, 'Entretien de John McGahern avec Nicole Ollier', *La Licorne* (Poitiers: UFR Langues Littératures, 1995), pp 55-86.

O'Toole, Fintan, 'The Family as Independent Republic', *The Irish Times Weekend Supplement*, 13 October 1990, p 2.

O'Toole, Fintan, 'Picking the locks of family secrets', *The Irish Times*, 1 April 2006.

Sampson, Denis, 'A Conversation with John McGahern', *Canadian Journal of Irish Studies*, 17, July 1991, pp 13-18.

Tóibín, Colm, 'Amongst shadows', *The Irish Times*, 1 April 2006.

Wallace, Arminta, 'Out of the Dark' (Interview), *The Irish Times*, 28 April 1990.

Walsh, John, 'Throwing Light on our Dark Side', *Irish Independent*, 4 May 1990, p 6.

Whyte, James, 'An Interview with John McGahern', Appendix to *History, Myth and ritual in the Fiction of John McGahern: Strategies of Transcendence* (Lewiston, Queenstown, Lampeter: The Edwin Mellen Press, 2002), pp 227-35.

Wroe, Nicholas, 'Ireland's Rural Elegist' (Profile), *The Guardian*, 5 January 2002.

CRITICISM OF MCGAHERN'S WORK

a. Books
Goarzin, Anne, *John McGahern: Reflets d'Irlande* (Rennes: Presses Universitaires de Rennes, 2002).
Maher, Eamon, *John McGahern: From the Local to the Universal* (Dublin: The Liffey Press, 2003).
Malcolm, David, *Understanding John McGahern* (Columbia: University of Carolina Press, 2007).
McCarthy, Dermot, *John McGahern and the Art of Memory* (Oxford: Peter Lang, 2010).
Rogers, Lori, *Feminine Nation: Performance, Gender and Resistance in the Works of John McGahern and Neil Jordan* (Lanham: University Press of North America, 1998).
Sampson, Denis, *Outstaring Nature's Eye: the Fiction of John McGahern* (Washington: The Catholic University of America Press, 1993).
Whyte, James, *History, Myth and Ritual in the Fiction of John McGahern* (Lewiston, Queenstown, Lampeter: The Edwin Mellen Press, 2002).

b. Special Journal Issues on McGahern's Work
The Canadian Journal of Irish Studies, 17.1 (July 1991), edited by Denis Sampson.
Études Britanniques Contemporaines 6 (January 1995).
Études Irlandaises (Automne 1995), edited by Claude Fierobe and Danielle Jacquin.
Journal of the Short Story in English/ Les Cahiers de la Nouvelle 4 (Spring 2000).
La Licorne 32 (1995): *John McGahern*, edited by Jean Brihault and Liliane Louvel.
Irish University Review, Vol 35, No.1 (Spring/Summer 2005), *Special Issue John McGahern*, edited by John Brannigan.
The John McGahern Yearbook, Volume 1 (2008), edited by John Kenny.
The John McGahern Yearbook, Volume 2 (2009), edited by John Kenny.
The John McGahern Yearbook, Volume 3 (2010), edited by John Kenny.

c. Selected Reviews and Criticism on McGahern's Work
Banville, John, 'In Violent Times' (review of *Amongst Women*), *New York Review of Books*, 6 December 1990, pp 22-3.
Banville, John, 'To Have and to Hold' (review of *Amongst Women*), in *The Observer*, 6 May 1990.
Battersby, Eileen, 'A Superb Earthly Pastoral' (review of *That They May Face The Rising Sun*), *The Irish Times*, 8 December 2001.
Brannigan, John, 'Introduction: The 'Whole World' of John McGahern', in *Irish University Review*, 35.1 (Spring/Summer 2005), pp vii-x.
Brennan, Frank, 'The Precision of the Local', in *The John McGahern Yearbook*, Vol 2 (2009), pp 114-23.
Browne, Terence, 'Redeeming the Time: The Novels of John McGahern

and John Banville', in *The British and Irish Novel Since 1960*, edited by James Achesan (New York: St Martin's, 1991), pp 159-73.

Cahalan, James, 'The Conscience of the Midlands: John McGahern', in *The Irish Novel: A Critical History* (Dublin: Gill and Macmillan, 1988), pp 271-5.

Cahalan, James, 'Female and Male Perspectives on Growing Up Irish in Edna O'Brien, John McGahern and Brian Moore', in *Double Visions: Women and Men in Modern and Contemporary Irish Literature* (Syracuse: Syracuse University Press, 1999), pp 105-34.

Cardin, Bertrand, 'L'incommunicabilité dans *The Barracks*', in *Études Irlandaises* (Automne 1994), pp 65-74.

Cardin, Bernard, '*The Power of Darkness*: Tolstoï adapté par McGahern', in Thierry Dubost (ed), *L'adaptation théâtrale en Irlande de 1970 à 2007* (Caen: Presse Universitaires de Caen, 2010), pp.135-50.

Cleary, Joe, 'Modernization and Aesthetic Ideology in Contemporary Irish Culture', in Ray Ryan (ed), *Writing in the Irish Republic: Literature, Culture, Politics 1949-1999* (London: Macmillan, 2000), pp.105-29.

Coad, David, 'Religious References in *The Barracks*', in *Études Irlandaises* (Automne 1994), pp 131-8.

Coad, David, 'One God, One Disciple: The Case of John McGahern', in *Études Britanniques Contemporaines* 6 (Janvier 1995), pp 57-62.

Colgan, Gerry, 'Sadly Risible Drama Debut for McGahern' (review of *The Power of Darkness*), in *The Irish Times*, 18 October 1991.

Cronin, John, '"The Dark" is not Light Enough: The Fiction of John McGahern', in *Studies: An Irish Quarterly*, 58 (Winter 1969), pp 427-32.

Cronin, John, 'Art and the Failure of Love: The Fiction of John McGahern', in *Studies: An Irish Quarterly*, 77 (Summer 1988), pp 201-217.

Cronin, John, 'John McGahern's *Amongst Women*: Retrenchment and Renewal', in *Irish University Review*, 22 (Spring/Summer 1992), pp 168-76.

Cronin, Mike, 'McGahern and the GAA', in *The John McGahern Yearbook*, Vol 3 (2010), pp 84-93.

Crotty, Patrick, '"All Toppers": Children in the Fiction of John McGahern', in *Irish University Review*, 35.1 (Spring/Summer 2005), pp 42-57.

Crowley, Cornelius, 'Leavetaking and Homecoming in the Writing of John McGahern', in *Études Britanniques Contemporaines* 6 (Janvier 1995), pp 63-75.

Deane, Seamus, 'A Millimetre Away from Perfection' (review of *Amongst Women*), in *The Sunday Tribune*, 6 May 1990.

Deane, Seamus, 'A New Dawn' (review of *That They May Face the Rising Sun*), in *The Guardian*, 12 January 2002.

Deevy, Patricia, 'A Light in the Darkness', in *Irish Independent*, 30 December 2001.

DiBattista, Maria, 'Joyce's Ghost: The Bogey of Realism in John McGahern's *Amongst Women*', in Karen Lawrence (ed), *Transcultural Joyce* (Cambridge: Cambridge University Press, 1998), pp 21-36.

Dockery, Jamie, 'Writing out of Love: McGahern and the Influence of the Mother', in *Studies: An Irish Quarterly*, Vol 99, No 394 (Summer 2010), pp 205-18.

Foley, Michael, 'The Novels of John McGahern', in *The Honest Ulsterman* 5 (September 1968), pp.34-7.

Fournier, Suzanne, 'Structure and Theme in John McGahern's *The Pornographer*', in *Éire-Ireland* 22.1 (Spring 1987), pp 130-50.

Gambolini, Gerardo, 'Translating John McGahern', in *The John McGahern Yearbook*, Vol 2 (2009), pp 66-75.

Ganteau, Jean-Michel, 'John McGahern's *The Barracks*: An Interpenetrative Catholic Novel', in *Études Britanniques Contemporaines* 6 (Janvier 1995), pp.25-40.

Garfitt, Roger, 'Constants in Contemporary Irish Fiction', in Douglas Dunn (ed), *Two Decades of Irish Writing: A Critical Survey* (Cheadle: Carcanet Press, 1975), pp 207-43.

Garratt, Robert F., 'John McGahern's *Amongst Women*: Representation, Memory and Trauma', in *Irish University Review*, 35.1 (Spring/Summer 2005), pp 121-135.

Gilligan, Patrick, 'Volunteer Frank McGahern', in *The John McGahern Yearbook*, Vol 3 (2010), pp 58-73.

Gitzen, Julian, 'Wheels Along the Shannon: The Fiction of John McGahern', in *The Journal of Irish Literature*, 20.3 (September 1991), pp 36-49.

Goarzin, Anne, 'Mouvements de l'image dans les romans de John McGahern', in *La Licorne* 29 (1999), pp 13-27.

Goarzin, Anne, ''A Crack in the Concrete': Objects in the Works of John McGahern', in *Irish University Review*, 35.1 (Spring/Summer 2005), pp 28-41.

Grennan, Eamon, ''Only What Happens': Mulling Over McGahern', in *Irish University Review*, 35.1 (Spring/Summer 2005), pp 13-27.

Guy, Peter, 'In the Name of the Father: Lacan's *nom-du-père* and the Modern Irish Novel', in Maher, Eamon, Grace Neville and Eugene O'Brien (eds), *Modernity and Postmodernity in a Franco-Irish Context* (Frankfurt am Main: Peter Lang, 2008), pp 65-77.

Guy, Peter, 'McGahern, Proust and the Universality of Memory', in Bévant, Yann, Eamon Maher, Grace Neville and Eugene O'Brien (eds), *Issues of Globalisation and Secularisation in France and Ireland* (Frankfurt am Main: Peter Lang, 2009), pp 63-77.

Guy, Peter, 'Facing the High Windows', in *The John McGahern Yearbook*, Vol 3 (2010), pp 112-19.

Guy, Peter, 'Reading John McGahern in the Light of the Murphy Report', in *Studies: An Irish Quarterly*, 99.383 (Spring 2010), pp 91-101.

Guy, Peter, '"Earth Crammed with Heaven and Every Common Bush Afire with God": Religion in the Fiction of John McGahern', in Maher, Eamon and Eugene O'Brien (eds), *Breaking the Mould: Literary Representations of Irish Catholicism* (Oxford: Peter Lang, 2011), pp 141-56.

Harmon, Maurice, 'Generations Apart: 1925-1975', in *The Irish Novel in Our Time*, edited by Maurice Harmon and Patrick Rafroidi (Villeneuve-d'Ascq: Publications de l'Université de Lille, 1976), pp 49-65.

Holland, Siobhán, 'Re-citing the Rosary: Women, Catholicism and Agency in John McGahern's *Amongst Women* and Brian Moore's *Cold Heaven*', in Harte, Liam and Michael Parker (eds), *Contemporary Irish Fiction: Themes, Tropes, theories* (London: Macmillan, 2000), pp 56-78.

Holland, Siobhán, 'Marvellous Fathers in the Fiction of John McGahern', in *The Yearbook of English Studies*, 35 (2005), edited by Ronan McDonald, pp 186-98.

Hughes, Eamonn, '"All That Surrounds Our Life": Time, Sex, and Death in *That They May Face the Rising Sun*', in *Irish University Review*, 35.1 (Spring/Summer 2005), pp 147-63.

Imhof, Rüdiger, 'John McGahern', in the *Modern Irish Novel: Irish Novelists After 1945* (Dublin: Wolfhound Press, 2002), pp 213-36.

Kamm, Jürgen, 'John McGahern', in Rüdger Imhof (ed), *Contemporary Irish Novelists* (Tübingen: Gunter Narr Verlag, 1990), pp 175-91.

Kelly, Liam, 'The Local and the Ordinary', in *The John McGahern Yearbook*, Vol 1 (2008), pp 100-7.

Kennedy, Eileen, 'The Novels of John McGahern: The Road Away Becomes the Road Back', in Brophy, James D. and Raymond J. Porter (eds), *Contemporary Irish Writing* (Boston: Iona College/ Twayne, 1983), pp 115-26.

Kiberd, Declan, 'John McGahern's *Amongst Women*', in Maria Tymoczko and Colin Ireland (eds), *Language and Tradition in Ireland: Continuities and Displacements* (Amherst and Boston: University of Massachusetts Press, 2003), pp 195-213.

Kiberd, Declan, 'Fallen Nobility: The Whole World of John McGahern', in *Irish University Review*, 35.1 (Spring/Summer 2005), pp 164-174.

Kiberd, Declan, 'Forms of Life', in *The John McGahern Yearbook*, Vol 1 (2008), pp. 20-9.

Killeen, Terence, 'Versions of Exile: A Reading of *The Leavetaking*', in *The Canadian Journal of Irish Studies* 17.1 (July 1991), pp 69-78.

Kilroy, Thomas, 'The Autobiographical Novel', in Augustine Martin (ed), *The Genius of Irish Prose* (Cork: Mercier, 1985), pp 67-75.

Ledwidge, Grace Tighe, 'Death in Marriage: The Tragedy of Elizabeth Reegan on *The Barracks*', in *Irish University Review*, 35.1 (Spring/ Summer 2005), pp 90-103.

Liddy, Brian, 'State and Church: Darkness in the Fiction of John McGahern', in *New Hibernia Review* 3.2 (Summer 1999), pp 106-121.

Lloyd, Richard Burr, 'The Symbolic Mass: Thematic Resolution in the Irish Novels of John McGahern', in *Emporia State Research Studies* 36 (Autumn 1987), pp 5-23.

Louvel, Liliane, 'A Handful of Images', in *The John McGahern Yearbook*, Vol 3 (2010), pp 46-57.

Maher, Eamon, 'John McGahern: A Writer in Tune with His Time', in *Crosscurrents and Confluences: Echoes of Religion in Twentieth-Century Fiction* (Dublin: Veritas, 2000), pp 139-44.

Maher, Eamon, 'Disintegration and Despair in the early Fiction of John McGahern', in *Studies: An Irish Quarterly*, 90.357 (Spring 2001), pp 84-91.

Maher, Eamon, 'A Glimpse at Irish Catholicism in John McGahern's *Amongst Women*', in *Doctrine & Life*, 51.6 (July/August 2001), pp 346-55.

Maher, Eamon and Kiberd, Declan, 'John McGahern: Writer, Stylist, Seeker of a Lost World', in *Doctrine & Life* 52.2 (February 2002), pp 82-97.

Maher, Eamon, 'Catholicism in the Writings of John McGahern', in Böss, Michael and Eamon Maher (eds), *Engaging Modernity: Readings of Irish politics, Culture and Literature at the Turn of the Century* (Dublin: Veritas, 2003), pp 85-96.

Maher, Eamon, 'Death in the Country: An Intertextual Analysis of Jean Sulivan's *Anticipate Every Goodbye* and John McGahern's *The Leavetaking*', in Maher, Eamon and Grace Neville (eds), *France and Ireland: Anatomy of a Relationship*, (Frankfurt: Peter Lang, 2004), pp 111-21.

Maher, Eamon, 'Circles and Circularity in the Writings of John McGahern', in *Nordic Irish Studies*, 4 (2004), pp 156-66.

Maher, Eamon, 'The Irish Novel in Crisis? The Example of John McGahern', in *Irish University Review*, 35.1 (Spring/Summer 2005), pp 58-71.

Maher, Eamon, 'Shifting environments of Reception of the Work of John McGahern (1934-)', in *New Hibernia Review*, 9. 2 (Summer 2005), pp 125-36.

Maher, Eamon, 'John McGahern's Fictions – A Chronicle of Four Decades of Change in Ireland', in *Doctrine & Life* 55.4 (April 2005), pp 22-30.

Maher, Eamon, 'McGahern's Light Shining more brightly than ever before', in *The Irish Times*, November 6, 2006.

Maher, Eamon, 'John McGahern and the Commemoration of Traditional Rural Ireland', in *Studies: An Irish Quarterly*, Vol 95, No 379 (Autumn 2006), pp 279-290.

Maher, Eamon, 'John McGahern', in David Scott Kastan (Editor in Chief), *The Oxford Encyclopedia of British Literature*, Vol 3 (Oxford: Oxford University Press, 2006), pp 440-2.

Maher, Eamon, 'Religion and Art', in *The John McGahern Yearbook*, Vol. 1 (2008), pp 116-25.

Maher, Eamon, 'Pondering Eternity in a Stifling Rural Setting: François Mauriac's *Thérèse Desqueyroux* and John McGahern's *The Barracks*', in Jean-Christophe Penet (ed), *JOFIS*, E-journal in Franco-Irish Studies (2008), pp 76-89.

Maher, Eamon, 'McGahern's Appreciation for the Rituals of Death lives on', in *The Irish Times*, 24 March 2009.

Maher, Eamon, '"The Local is the Universal Without Walls": John McGahern and the Global Project', in Eamon Maher (ed), *Global Perspectives on Globalisation and Ireland* (Oxford: Peter Lang, 2009), pp 211-31.

Maher, Eamon, 'Irish Catholicism as seen Through the Lens of Kate O'Brien and John McGahern', in Bévant, Yann and Anne Goarzin (eds), *Bretagne et Irlande: Pérégrinations* (Rennes: TIR, 2009), pp 95-112.

Maher, Eamon, '"Ma paroisse est dévorée par l'ennui": Secularisation in Georges Bernanos' *Journal d'un curé de campagne* and John McGahern's *That They May Face the Rising Sun*', in Bévant, Maher, Neville and O'Brien (eds), *Issues of Globalisation and Secularisation in France and Ireland* (Frankfurt am Main: Peter Lang, 2009), pp 15-29.

Maher, Eamon, 'An Irish Catholic Novel? The Example of Brian Moore and John McGahern', in Mary Reichardt (ed), *Between Human and Divine: The Catholic Vision in Contemporary Literature* (Washington DC: The Catholic University of America Press, 2010), pp 69-85.

Maher, Eamon, 'Holding a Mirror Up to a Society in Evolution: John McGahern', in Julia Wright (ed), *A Companion to Irish Literature*, Volume 2 (Oxford: Wiley-Blackwell, 2010), pp 248-62.

Malcolm, David, 'A View from Europe', in *The John McGahern Yearbook*, Vol 2 (2009), pp 52-61.

Mays, Marianne Koenig, '"Ravished and Exasperated": The Evolution of John McGahern's Plain Style', in *The Canadian Journal of Irish Studies* 17.1 (July 1991), pp 38-52.

McCabe, Eugene, 'The Prophesy of The Dark', in *The John McGahern Yearbook*, Vol 3 (2010), pp 36-9.

McKeon, Belinda, '"Robins Feeding With the Sparrows": The Protestant Big House in the Fiction of John McGahern', in *Irish University Review*, 35.1 (Spring/Summer 2005), pp 72-89.

Mikowski, Sylvie, '*The Barracks* de John McGahern et Flaubert', in Maher, Eamon, Grace Neville and Eugene O'Brien (eds), *Reinventing Ireland Through a French Prism* (Frankfurt am Main: Peter Lang, 2007), pp.211-25.

Mikowski, Sylvie, 'A French Perspective', in *The John McGahern Yearbook*, Vol 1 (2008), pp 74-85.

Molloy, F. C., 'The Novels of John McGahern', in *Critique: Studies on Modern Fiction* 19.1 (Spring 1977), pp 5-27.

Mullen, Raymond, '"The Womb and the Grave": Living, Loving and Dying in John McGahern's *The Pornographer* and Albert Camus' *L'Étranger*', in Maher, Eamon, Grace Neville and Eugene O'Brien (eds), *Reinventing Ireland Through a French Prism* (Frankurt am Main: Peter Lang, 2007), pp 229-243.

Murray, Christopher, 'The "fallen world" of *The Power of Darkness*', in *The John McGahern Yearbook*, Vol 2 (2009), pp 78-91.

O'Brien, Kate, 'John McGahern, *The Barracks*' (review), in *University Review* 3.4 (1963), p 59.

Ó Ceallaigh, Philip, 'A half-rebellion', in *The John McGahern Yearbook*, Vol 3 (2010), pp 42-3.

O'Donnell, Shaun, 'Door into the Light: John McGahern's Ireland', in *Massachusetts Review* 25 (Summer 1984), pp 255-68.

O'Dwyer, Riana, 'Gender Roles in *The Barracks*', in *Études Irlandaises* (Octobre 1994), pp 147-64.

O'Toole, Fintan, 'Both Completely Irish and Universal' (review of *Amongst Women*), in *The Irish Times*, 15 September 1990.

Ó Tuathaigh, Gearóid, 'McGahern's Irelands', in *The John McGahern Yearbook*, Vol 2 (2009), pp 14-27.

Peach, Linden, 'Mimicry, Authority and Subversion: Brian Moore's *The Magician's Wife* (1997), Emma Donoghue's *Slammerkin* (2000) and John McGahern's *Amongst Women* (1990)', in *The Contemporary Irish Novel: Readings* (Basingstoke: Palgrave Macmillan, 2004), pp 68-96.

Pierre, DBC, 'Where Light Happens', in *The John McGahern Yearbook*, Vol 3 (2010), pp 40-1.

Quinn, Antoinette, 'A Prayer for my Daughters: Patriarchy in *Amongst Women*', in *Canadian Journal of Irish Studies* 17.1 (July 1991), pp 79-90.

Reynolds, Kevin, 'A Radioman's McGahern', in *The John McGahern Yearbook*, Vol 2 (2009), pp 98-101.

Ross, Ciaran, 'Some Painful Thoughts about *The Barracks*', in *Études Irlandaises* (October 1994), pp 119-30.

Ryle, Martin, 'Place, time and Perspective in John McGahern's Fiction', in Olinder, Britta and Werner Huber (eds), *Place and Memory in the New Ireland* (Trier: Wissenschaftlicher Verlag, 2009), pp 127-36.

Sampson, Denis, 'A Note on John McGahern's *The Leavetaking*', in *Canadian Journal of Irish Studies* 2.2 (December 1976), pp 61-5.

Sampson Denis, 'Introducing John McGahern', in *Canadian Journal of Irish Studies* 17.1 (July 1991), pp 1-11.

Sampson, Denis, 'The Lost Image: Some Notes on John McGahern and Proust', in *Canadian Journal of Irish Studies* 17.1 (July 1991), pp 57-68.

Sampson, Denis, '"Open to the World": A Reading of John McGahern's *That They May Face the Rising Sun*', in *Irish University Review*, 35.1 (Spring/Summer 2005), pp 136-46.

Sampson, Denis, '"The Day Set Alight in the Mind": Notes on John McGahern's Late Style', in *Irish University Review* 39.1 (Spring-Summer 2009), pp 122-8.

Sampson, Denis, 'Reading a Life', in *The John McGahern Yearbook*, Vol 2 (2009), pp 92-7.

Scally, John, 'The Spiritual Legacy of John McGahern', in *Doctrine and Life* 60.10 (December 2010), pp 17-27.

Schwartz, Karlheinz, 'John McGahern's Point of View', in *Éire-Ireland* 19.3 (Autumn 1984), pp 92-110.

Sheehy Skeffington, Owen, 'McGahern Affair', in *Censorship* 2 (Spring 1966), pp 27-30.

Shovlin, Frank, 'The Ghost of WB Yeats', in *The John McGahern Yearbook*, Vol 2 (2009), pp 42-51.

Toolan, Michael J., 'John McGahern: The Historian and the Pornographer', in *The Canadian Journal of Irish Studies* 7.2 (December 1981), pp 39-55.

Updike, John, 'An Oldfashioned Novel' (review of *The Pornographer*), in *The New Yorker*, 24 December 1979, pp 95-8.

van der Ziel, Stanley, 'The Aesthetics of Redemption: John McGahern's *That They May Face the Rising Sun*', in *Studies: An Irish Quarterly*, vol 93, no 372 (Winter 2004), pp 473-85.

van der Ziel, Stanley, '"All This Talk and Struggle": John McGahern's *The Dark*', in *Irish University Review*, 35.1 (Spring/Summer 2005), pp 104-120.

van der Ziel, Stanley, 'John McGahern: An Annotated Bibliography', in *Irish University Review*, 35.1 (Spring/Summer 2005), pp 175-202.

van der Ziel, Stanley, 'Fionn and Oisín in the Land of Wink and Nod: Heroes, History and the Creative Imagination in John McGahern's *Amongst Women*', in *Canadian Journal of Irish Studies* 31.2 (Autumn 2005), pp 10-18.

van der Ziel, Stanley, 'John McGahern: Nightlines', in Alexander, Cheryl and David Malcolm (eds), *A Companion to the British and Irish Short Story* (Oxford: Wiley-Blackwell, 2008), pp 488-497.

Wall, Eamonn, '"The Living Stream": John McGahern's *Amongst Women* and Irish Writing in the 1990s', in *Studies: An Irish Quarterly*, 351 (88), (Autumn 1991), pp 305-24.

Whelan, Kevin, 'Time, Space and History', in *The John McGahern Yearbook*, Vol 3 (2010), pp 14-23.

Whyte, James, 'The Nature of Imaginative Sympathy', in *The John McGahern Yearbook*, Vol 1 (2008), pp 34-45.

OTHER WORKS CONSULTED

Boland, Rosita, 'Death in the Grotto', in *The Irish Times*, 31 January 2004.

Booth, Wayne, *The Rhetoric of Fiction* (Chicago: University of Chicago Press, 1961).

Brown, Terence, *Ireland: A Social and Cultural History 1922-79* (London: Fontana, 1981; 3rd ed. Harper Perennial, 2004).

Camus, Albert, *The Outsider*, trs Joseph Laredo (London/New York: Penguin Modern Classics, 1983).

Cleary, Joe, and Claire Connolly (eds), *The Cambridge Companion to Modern Irish Culture* (Cambridge: CUP, 2005).

Cleary, Joe, *Outrageous Fortune: Capital and Culture in Modern Ireland* (Dublin: Field Day Publication, 2007).

Ferriter, Diarmuid, *The Transformation of Ireland 1900-2000* (London: Profile Books, 2004).

Ferriter, Diarmuid, *Occasions of Sin: Sex and Society in Modern Ireland* (London: Profile Books, 2009).

Fuller, Louise, *Irish Catholicism Since 1950: The Undoing of a Culture* (Dublin: Gill and Macmillan, 2002).

Fuller, Louise, 'New Ireland and the Undoing of the Catholic Legacy: Looking Back to the Future', in Fuller, Louise, John Littleton and Eamon Maher (eds), *Irish and Catholic? Towards an Understanding of Identity* (Dublin: The Columba Press, 2006), pp 68-89.

Fuller, Louise, 'The French Catholic Experience: Irish Connection and Disconnections', in Maher, Eamon, Grace Neville and Eugene O'Brien (eds), *Reinventing Ireland Through a French Prism* (Frankfurt am Main: Peter Lang, 2007), pp.97-112.

Hederman, Mark Patrick, *Kissing the Dark: Connecting with the Unconscious* (Dublin: Veritas, 1999).

Hederman, Mark Patrick, *Underground Cathedrals* (Dublin: The Columba Press, 2010).

Hoban, Brendan, *Change or Decay: Irish Catholicism in Crisis* (Kilglass: Banley House, 2004).

Inglis, Tom, *Moral Monopoly: The Catholic Church in Modern Irish Society* (Dublin: Gill and Macmillan, 1987).

Inglis, Tom, *Truth, Power and Lies: Irish Society and the Case of the Kerry Babies* (Dublin: University College Dublin Press, 2003).

Inglis, Tom, 'Something Rotten in the Barrel itself', in *The Irish Times*, 3 November 2005.

Inglis, Tom, *Global Ireland: Same Difference* (London: Routledge, 2008).

Joyce, James, *Portrait of the Artist as a Young Man* (London: Penguin Classics, 1996).

Joyce, James, *Dubliners* (London: Penguin Popular Classics, 1996).

Kenny, Colum, *Moments That Changed Us* (Dublin: Gill and Macmillan, 2005).

Kenny, Mary, *Goodbye to Catholic Ireland* (Dublin: New Island, 2000).

Keogh, Dermot, *Twentieth Century Ireland: Nation and State* (Dublin: Gill & Macmillan, 1994).

Kiberd, Declan, *Inventing Ireland: The Literature of the Modern Nation* (London: Vintage, 1996).

Kiberd, Declan, *Irish Classics* (London: Granta Books, 2000).

Lawson, Mark, 'Catholicism's Indelible Mark on the Page', in *The Tablet* (29 April, 2006), pp.16-7.

Lee, J. J., *Ireland 1912-1985: Politics and Society* (Cambridge: CUP, 1989).

Maher, Eamon, 'Representations of Catholicism in the Twentieth-Century Irish Novel', in Fuller, Louise, John Littleton and Eamon Maher (eds), *Irish and Catholic? Towards an Understanding of Identity* (Dublin: The Columba Press, 2006), pp 103-19.

Martin, Augustine, 'Inherited Dissent: The Dilemma of the Irish Writer', in *Studies: An Irish Quarterly* (Spring 1965), pp 1-20.

McGarry, Patsy, 'The Rise and Fall of Roman Catholicism in Ireland', in Fuller, Louise, John Littleton and Eamon Maher (eds), *Irish and Catholic? Towards an Understanding of Identity* (Dublin: The Columba Press, 2006), pp 31-46.

McGarry, Patsy, 'An Irish Catholic Agnostic', in Littleton, John and Eamon Maher (eds), *What Being Catholic Means to Me* (Dublin: The Columba Press, 2009), pp 13-24.

O'Brien, Carl, 'Report's findings are shocking – but all too familiar', in *The Irish Times*, 28 October 2010.

O'Brien, Kate, *The Ante-Room* (London: Virago, 1989).

O'Crohan, Tomás, *The Islandman*, trs Robin Flower (Oxford: Oxford University Press, 1978).

Ó Faoláin, Seán, 'The Modern Novel: A Catholic Point of View', in *Virginia Quarterly Review*, Vol II (1935), pp 339-51.

O'Flaherty, Liam, *Skerrett* (Dublin: Wolfhound Press, 1977).

O'Malley, Ernie, *On Another Man's Wound* (Dublin: Anvil, 1979).

O'Toole, Fintan, *The Ex-Isle of Erin* (Dublin: New Ireland, 1997).

O'Toole, Fintan, 'Why artists can't quite give up on Catholicism', in *The Irish Times*, 5 December 2009.

Pierce, David, *Light, Freedom and Song: A Cultural History of Modern Irish Writing* (New Haven and London: Yale University Press, 2005).

Reichardt, Mary (ed), *Between Human and Divine: The Catholic Vision in Contemporary Literature* (Washington DC: The Catholic University of America Press, 2010).

Sartre, Jean-Paul, *L'existentialisme est un humanisme* (Paris: Les Éditions Nagel, 1967).

Sonnenfeld, Albert, *Crossroads: Essays on the Catholic Novelists* (York, South Carolina: French Literature Publishing Company, 1980).

Sulivan, Jean, *Morning Light: The Spiritual Journal of Jean Sulivan*, trs Joseph Cunneen and Patrick Gormally (NY: Paulist Press, 1988).

Sulivan, Jean, *Anticipate Every Goodbye*, trs Eamon Maher (Dublin: Veritas, 2000).

Tolstoy, Leo, *The Death of Ivan Ilyich and Other Stories*, trs Ronald Wilks, Anthony Briggs and David McDuff, with an Introduction by Anthony Briggs (London: Penguin Classics, 2008).

Twomey, Vincent D., *The End of Irish Catholicism?* (Dublin: Veritas, 2003).

Tyrrell, Peter, *Founded on Fear: Letterfrack Industrial School, War and Exile*, edited and introduced by Diarmuid Whelan (London: Transworld Ireland, 2008).

Whitehouse, John, *Catholics on Literature* (Dublin: Four Courts Press, 1997).

Index